# Nancy Shavick's

# TAROT UNIVERSE

SANTA
MONICA
PRESS

Published by:
Santa Monica Press LLC
P.O. Box 1076
Santa Monica, CA 90406-1076
1-800-784-9553
www.santamonicapress.com

Printed in the United States

S A N T A

M O N I C A

P R E S S

Cover designed by Irina Averkieff
Book Interior designed by Susan Landesmann,
Susan Landesmann Design
Cover Photo ©1999 by Nancy Shavick.

ISBN 1-891661-08-6
Library of Congress Cataloging-in-Publication Data

Shavick, Nancy.
        Nancy Shavick's tarot universe/ by Nancy Shavick.
            p.    cm.
        ISBN 1-891661-08-6
            1. Tarot. I. Title. II. Title: Tarot universe.
    BF 1879, T2S5377   1999                99-36560
      133.3'2424--dc21                     CIP

This book is dedicated to all my treasured readers and clients from the past 15 years who have always gotten the point and have taught me more than they could ever imagine...

Love and gratitude go out to Gabrielle Audrey Shavick, the only mother I could have chosen in this lifetime!

Unfathomable thanks to Debra Rodman, who is so much a part of this book and the best friend a girl could have on any planet!

I am especially grateful to John Bryan Murphy for providing me with the conscious technology required to produce this book and to Roberta Hanley, a partner in higher crime for the past 23 years, for her unwavering support during the creation of this guide. Thank you Rosanna Arquette for all your help!

This book would not exist without the amazing timing of my old friend ed young, and my publisher Jeffrey Goldman, who made *Nancy Shavick's Tarot Universe* a reality literally overnight. Thanks to Minju Pak for her editing and everyone else at Santa Monica Press who assisted with this book.

# Table of Contents

# Author's Note

From the time I bought my first Tarot deck at the age of 14 in New York City, the objective of my Tarot odyssey has always been to demystify the meaning and purpose of the deck for the first time in its half-a-millennium history. With the

✳✳✳✳✳✳✳✳✳✳✳✳

AS SOCIETY TURNS MORE AND MORE TO SPIRITUAL BELIEFS FOR ANSWERS AND INSIGHT INTO MATTERS OF PERSONAL GROWTH, THE TAROT IS THE PERFECT NONDOGMATIC, UNIVERSAL GUIDANCE SYSTEM TO FULFILL THIS NEED.

✳✳✳✳✳✳✳✳✳✳✳✳

publication of *Nancy Shavick's Tarot Universe*, I have definitely completed my epic mission!

This book has been written in response to the requests of my many readers for the material I have been compiling since the appearance of my last Tarot book, *The Tarot Guide to Love and Relationships*. This new, comprehensive how-to guide is based on Tarot readings I have given to thousands of people who I have been lucky enough to counsel over the years; no other Tarot book provides so much detailed information on using the cards to analyze romantic, financial, and spiritual issues.

The Tarot gives me a way to classify everything in the world of reality and the higher senses and is a language that I helped create to teach others moral lessons about the inescapable spiritual laws that govern all creation. This Tarot book is my bible, my kabbalah, my scripture, my spiritual philosophy, and a result of my social observations and processing of my own healing issues. My goal with this new book is to teach you how to use the Tarot to help improve your life in every way and give you hope when you have none. As society turns more and more to spiritual beliefs for answers and insight into matters of personal growth, the Tarot is the perfect nondogmatic, universal guidance system to fulfill this need.

*Nancy Shavick's Tarot Universe* contains detailed instructions for giving insightful and accurate Tarot readings using any standard 78-card deck. The card definition section of this book provides lengthy descriptions of each Tarot card in a fantastic array of real-life correspondences to your love life, career, and spiritual development.

This book emphasizes that learning how to read the cards is a process without shortcuts and requires practice. The best way to study the Tarot is to read the cards whenever you wish to consult them about a particular matter. It is important to reinforce memorization of the abstract meanings of the cards and meditate on their arrangement in the spread patterns. With the nearly endless combinations of the 78 cards that are possible in a reading, it is a random harvest of the deck that defines the drama of the spread.

When you sit down to read, ask the deck specific questions and focus on receiving wisdom and guidance during the shuffling process so the brain to hand connection between the nervous system and the palms of the hands will be strong, and you will pull in cards whose interpretations are crystal clear. Do not be intimidated by the pictures on the faces of the cards. This book is a reference guide designed to lead you every step of the way through a reading. The cards are not meant to be incomprehensible or confusing; they are a user-friendly divination tool that help you initiate discovery and increase awareness.

The more you use the Tarot cards, the greater their associative meaning becomes for you. It is necessary to exercise your intuition when you read, internalizing or simply stating whatever images and examples occur naturally in your mind. Touch upon all the feelings that the cards evoke and their significance will expand with each reading. Gaining confidence in your Tarot-reading ability takes time, and it is best to begin reading for yourself and then close friends with the help of this book. When you are ready to take responsibility for your interpretations of the cards, it is time to give readings for other people. Utilizing this exchange will help you learn more about the cards and allow you to give insight to others.

You should never become totally dependent on the cards. Tarot readings should in no way rule your existence; they can only give you a second unbiased, thought-provoking opinion with a universal perspective. The act of reading the cards forces you to sit down and think an issue over quietly in total concentration to arrive at an independent, enlightened solution to your problem. This is perhaps the most enriching aspect of the Tarot. To run your life by the words of the cards is crazy, because eventually you become too attached to reading them. People who are obsessed with the Tarot are usually obsessive about everything. Those who overidentify with the cards are often lacking in other areas of their

✢✢✢✢✢✢✢✢✢✢✢

TAROT READINGS SHOULD IN NO WAY RULE YOUR EXISTENCE; THEY CAN ONLY GIVE YOU A SECOND UNBIASED, THOUGHT-PROVOKING OPINION WITH A UNIVERSAL PERSPECTIVE.

✢✢✢✢✢✢✢✢✢✢✢

lives. Too much fantasy, psychiatry, or self-analysis is unbalancing to the body, mind, and spirit, and as always, the best approach is moderation.

If you become too serious about the cards, you should lighten up and have more fun with them. The deck is not meant to be grabbed in desperation, but should be used either daily, as a passive exercise in gaining insight, or occasionally, when you need more information on a specific subject. And a reading always helps you think things over, sort out your options, arrive at potential solutions, and glimpse what is ahead on your horizon.

✳✳✳✳✳✳✳✳✳✳✳

THE TAROT FORMS A BIBLE OF
AGELESS WISDOM BY USING CARDS
BEARING ANCIENT AND MYSTERIOUS
SYMBOLS AND ARCHETYPES TO
CREATE A VAST KNOWLEDGE SYSTEM
THAT CLASSIFIES AND DESCRIBES EVERY-
THING IN THE UNIVERSE.

✳✳✳✳✳✳✳✳✳✳✳

# CHAPTER ONE
## THE TAROT: AN OVERVIEW

## What Is the Tarot?

The Tarot forms a bible of ageless wisdom by using cards bearing ancient and mysterious symbols and archetypes to create a vast knowledge system that classifies and describes everything in the universe.

✻✻✻✻✻✻✻✻✻✻✻

THE TAROT IS A PHILOSOPHICAL CODE OF SPIRITUAL LAW THAT EXPLAINS HOW OUR PERSONAL KARMA CONTROLS CYCLES OF ACTIVITY AND CHANGE AS WE FULFILL OUR PREORDAINED DESTINIES.

✻✻✻✻✻✻✻✻✻✻✻

The Tarot is a philosophical code of spiritual law that explains how our personal karma controls cycles of activity and change as we fulfill our preordained destinies.

The cards are personifications of lessons taught by natural metaphysical and psychological principles whose meaning is understood as you gain awareness of how the drama of your conscious reality connects to your ever-evolving subconscious intelligence, which depicts the greater picture of the purpose of your soul.

The Tarot cards are considered the sum total of enlightenment available to us, as the Tarot system defines all levels of physical, emotional, intellectual, and creative states as represented by the definitions of the 78 cards in the deck. They identify every type of feeling, incident, characteristic of humanity, and cosmic truth eternally found within the repetitive cycles of creation and destruction in the universe.

The Tarot reflects all your romantic, creative, professional, and spiritual urges, both harmonious and chaotic, as you work to attune your life to inescapable heavenly law. It can help you purify your unconscious and destructive tendencies and show you a higher path away from unhappiness and confusion as you improve every aspect of your existence.

The Tarot cards are a textbook for raising your consciousness by discovering the will of divine guidance, urging you to evolve and make positive choices in your journey toward individual freedom. The Tarot can reveal your true spirit and relay important information concerning the past, present, or future to determine obstacles and opportunities and gain greater independence and joy in the present.

Today, the Tarot is used as a tool for intuitive development and self-transformation. A reading becomes a form of therapy similar to a psychoanalytic talking cure that promotes healing through increased self-awareness of your own emotional process and instinctual behavioral patterns.

The Tarot is probably most utilized to make personal predictions about faith, money, and romance. Tarot card readings can also help you gain clarity about your career direction, expand the boundaries of your earning potential, and discover inborn talents and creative abilities.

In the best sense, a reading should be a private method of deliberation where you form your own opinion independently and make important decisions for yourself. The reading is a tool for thinking things over and working out your problems in a self-reliant manner. The very act of reading the cards forces you to sit down and center your attention, enabling you to find viable, successful solutions to your own problems.

The reading is never the final word on what will happen; it merely illustrates the options you have concerning a particular matter and what sort of behavior you can expect from everyone involved. A Tarot reading only reflects the current schedule of destiny that can be altered in the future and shows what is likely to happen later on. Therefore, you can know what will probably occur, which enables you to influence the outcome of your fate by fortifying your attitude and initiative toward a preferred result.

The Tarot can assist you in re-creating events from long ago through the cards that land in the past placements of the spread, enabling you to learn from previous experience as it relates to your present drama.

The Tarot is a science of observation that requires a memory of what the 78 cards mean and the utilization of your intuition to piece together the story inherent in the reading through the interpretation of the Tarot spread.

Through the analysis of the reading, your conscious and subconscious minds glean information mirrored in the Tarot spread. In this way, the cards help you view particular actions in relation to the moral and philosophical framework of the universe and not as isolated, incomprehensible events that are only one piece of the puzzle depicting your current sojourn on Earth.

The Tarot is a force of evolution for the good of the world as a source of comfort when inner guidance is needed to analyze your psychological and spiritual development. The Tarot can ease pain and anxiety when you are lost and feel stuck in a life that is not working. The cards can push you forward and help you make positive decisions for your future growth. In a time when our sense of connection to each other is at an all-time low, the Tarot can be the best friend you have in the world. The intimacy of allowing the Tarot into your life is an incredible force. As you sit with your deck, throwing the cards and quietly sifting through a book searching for the truth, you can glimpse the future and find hope when you have none.

Unlike clairvoyant psychic readings, where information is

invented in a void or channeled through an imaginary being, the Tarot cards are tangible, concrete objects. You can see and touch a Tarot card and look its meaning up in a book because you do not need telepathy to read the cards.

The Tarot enlightens you intellectually, ethically, ideologically, psychologically, and spiritually through profound and powerful readings that serve as points of clarification to propel you into action and steer your heart, mind, soul, and body toward achieving your goals for this current incarnation.

## The History of the Tarot

The Tarot is an imaginary world depicted through the artwork of a deck of cards based on centuries-old symbolism. As the oldest interpretable collection of ancient wisdom that the world has ever known, it is historically connected to the mythology and iconography of many diverse cultures. The earliest-known source of our modern Tarot deck is a series of cards from late-fourteenth century France. Although the Tarot probably predates this time, its true origin is unknown. Nobody can really say where or when the Tarot was created, thus adding to its mystique.

It is equally unclear whether the Tarot originated as a card game or a method of divination. Sometimes outlawed and often in vogue, from its first remnant in France, hundreds of different Tarot decks and derivative games—playing cards,

*❊❊❊❊❊❊❊❊❊❊*

THE TAROT CARDS ARE CONSIDERED THE SUM TOTAL OF ENLIGHTENMENT AVAILABLE TO US, AS THE TAROT SYSTEM DEFINES ALL LEVELS OF PHYSICAL, EMOTIONAL, INTELLECTUAL, AND CREATIVE STATES.

*❊❊❊❊❊❊❊❊❊❊*

chess, and mahjong—have become internationally popular. The Tarot has been used for gaming but is also a universal custom for seeking divine guidance during a Tarot reading, where questions are posed to the deck and the meaning behind the layout of the cards is interpreted in response to the inquiry.

The 78-card Tarot deck accentuates principles common to the symbolic dogma of numerous belief systems throughout the record of humanity and highlights archetypical circumstances that are shared by all civilizations at all times. The Tarot cards are allegorical pictorial representations rooted in ancient Greek and Egyptian legends and Gnostic, Hebrew, Christian, and Muslim belief systems. Alchemy, astrology, numerology, the Grail legends, the Kabbalah, the Bible, Hermeticism, Freemasonry, and the royal and Gypsy cultures of southern Europe have also been cited as theoretical points of origin for the Tarot.

The cards comprise an eccentric and often obscure metaphysical system that classifies the behavior of the cosmos as it influences people, events, and circumstances here on Earth. The imagery of the traditional Tarot deck glorifies moral and spiritual wisdom through the depiction of occupational figures from different hierarchical stratum of society dressed in costumes from the Middle Ages and the heraldic emblems and enigmatic characters that grace the trump cards.

There are Tarot cards that portray marriage, creation, death, and resurrection. Cards are named after planetary entities (Sun, Moon, Star, and Universe or World cards); courtly medieval personalities (Juggler, Fool, Hermit, Emperor, Empress, King, Queen, Knight, and Page); ancient virtues (Strength, Justice, Temperance); Greek and Egyptian mythological references (Juno or High Priestess, Jupiter or Priest or Hierophant, Magus or Magician, Osiris [Emperor], Isis [Empress], Sun, Chariot, Hanged Man); and biblical concepts (Devil, Last

Judgement [Judgement], Pope [Jupiter or Hierophant], Female Pope [Juno or High Priestess], Marriage [Lovers], and Tower of Babel [Tower]).

During the half of the millennium the Tarot cards have been in evidence, many different spiritual traditions have been cited as possible sources of its arcane symbolic system, and much has been written in an effort to understand its strange historical value and its mystical significance. Even the origin of the word "Tarot" and its correct English pronunciation are unknown. The deck is called the tare-oh' or tare'-oh or tare'-ut or tah-row', depending on the individual voice of choice.

✾✾✾✾✾✾✾✾✾✾✾

THE 78 CARDS IN THE DECK IDENTIFY EVERY TYPE OF FEELING, INCIDENT, CHARACTERISTIC OF HUMANITY, AND COSMIC TRUTH ETERNALLY FOUND WITHIN THE REPETITIVE CYCLES OF CREATION AND DESTRUCTION IN THE UNIVERSE.

✾✾✾✾✾✾✾✾✾✾✾

The word "Tarot," as we understand it today, is a French term describing the 78-card deck used for intuitive-based divinatory readings. After the 1500s in Italy, the deck was called "Tarocco," "Tarocchi," or "Tarocchini," though previously it was known as *cartes da trionfi* (cards with trumps) in that country. In other areas of Europe, the Tarot has been referred to as "Taro," "Taroc," "Tarok," and "Tarock" at different places and times.

A multitude of languages and cultures contain words that could be the basis of the word Tarot. Some scholars feel it is derived from the French term, *tarotee*, that refers to the plain or diagonal lines found on the reverse side of the cards. Another word, *tares*, is the name for the small dotted border around the cards. The River Taro in northern Italy is considered an area where the traditional deck was introduced to

# The Tarot: An Overview

******************

THE TAROT CARDS ARE A TEXTBOOK
FOR RAISING YOUR CONSCIOUSNESS BY
DISCOVERING THE WILL OF DIVINE
GUIDANCE, URGING YOU TO EVOLVE AND
MAKE POSITIVE CHOICES IN YOUR JOUR-
NEY TOWARD INDIVIDUAL FREEDOM.

******************

Europe. Tarot could also be derived from: the Hindu figure *Tara*, mother of Buddha, and *Tara*, the Tibetan goddess; *terra*, the Roman word for "earth"; *taru*, the Hindu term for "cards"; *rota*, the Sanskrit word for "wheel" or "wheel of life"; *ta-rosh*, an Egyptian name for "the royal way"; *Ator*, a name for the goddess Hathor, one of the most ancient Egyptian deities; *tariqa*, Arabic for "the Way"; *tao*, Chinese for "the Way"; *Torah*, the Hebrew word for the first five books of the Old Testament; and the Hills of Tara, the ancient seat of Irish kings.

The cards are generally believed to be a relic of the ancient Egyptian worship of Thoth and the early Italian veneration of Mercury as well as the Greek tradition of honoring Hermes. All these gods were considered messengers who ruled communication and had a sacred and divinatory purpose. In this time period, the Tarot was used as a means for discovering the intentions of the gods through the guidance of a reading. Another theory suggests that the Tarot was created in the eleventh century after the burning of the libraries in Alexandria to symbolically contain all the arcane knowledge of the Greek, Roman, and Egyptian texts lost forever in the fires.

The British Museum in London is the largest repository of historical Tarot decks and books in the world. The earliest Tarot cards in their collection are from the late 1300s and were painted for Charles VI of France by the artist Jacquemin Gringonneur. The first most complete remaining Tarot deck is from the 1400s and was created to commemorate a marriage between two ruling aristocratic families in Italy: the Visconti and Sforza families.

The museum also houses many of the earliest texts on the subject and has copies of books published in Venice in 1550, Antwerpen in 1666, Rome in 1747, Cremona in 1774, London (dedicated to the Duke of Wellington) in 1814, Amsterdam in 1828, Macerata in 1832, Paris in 1847, and Bologna in 1872, just to name a few. Many of the authors of these books remained anonymous due to the eternal public controversy surrounding the often illegal Tarot.

For five hundred years, the traditional Tarot deck remained virtually unchanged until the beginning of the twentieth century. The British Museum has a collection of decks that cover this entire era from every corner of Europe. The only real variations of the classic imagery associated with the cards are found on an early nineteenth-century deck from Milan that calls the Tower trump, "Thunder" or "the Hospital," and has a dancing couple on the Sun card. An eighteenth-century deck from Brussels has astronomers on both the Sun and Moon cards; the Tower shows lightning striking a tree; the Sun has a victorious soldier riding on a horse; the Chariot is a woman in a carriage pulled by a horse; the Hierophant card is called Bacchus; and to read the title of the Hanged Man you have to turn the card upside down.

Two interesting decks from Bologna are important: one from 1810 shows the Pope (the Hierophant or Jupiter) no longer surrounded by a group of wealthy merchants, but simply extending one empty hand for begging; and one from 1750 has the couple on the Lovers card looking directly at the inquirer, the Page of wands has dropped his wand, and the Page of cups has his cap off.

A Tarot deck produced in Milan in 1820 has a wreath of fruits and flowers as the only imagery for the Universe card and Justice has wings yet is still seated. An unusual Swiss deck from the eighteenth century shows Jupiter (the Hierophant) grabbing a handful of lightning out of the sky. With many of the early Tarot decks, the Fool card is slightly longer than the other 77 cards.

France is a major player in the history of the Tarot. The Tarot had become popular by the end of the fifteenth century, when the Tarot de Marseilles became widely available. It is still used today to play a game similar to bridge. Count de Gebelin (1723-1787) was the first person to connect the Tarot with the Egyptian mysteries. Two characters named Etteilla, a hairdresser who published books from 1770-1791, and Madame Lenormand (1772-1843), a self-promoting soothsayer, created their own Tarot decks that are still in print. Their decks and books were extremely popular during the French Revolution and the Napoleonic wars when people turned to fortunetelling for answers during chaotic and uncertain political times. Eliphas Levi (1810-1875), the first Tarot person to associate the Tarot with the Kabbalah, and Papus (1865-1916), continued to expand upon de Gebelin's theory of the Egyptian origin of the Tarot.

After the turn of the century, there was a renaissance of

✻✻✻✻✻✻✻✻✻✻✻✻

THE TAROT CAN REVEAL YOUR TRUE SPIRIT AND RELAY IMPORTANT INFORMATION CONCERNING THE PAST, PRESENT, OR FUTURE TO DETERMINE OBSTACLES AND OPPORTUNITIES AND GAIN GREATER INDEPENDENCE AND JOY IN THE PRESENT.

✻✻✻✻✻✻✻✻✻✻✻✻

interest in the Tarot, and our modern Tarot market was created by a new group who associated the cards with many esoteric metaphysical systems such as numerology, the Kabbalah, astrology, magic, alchemy, and the entire history of occult thought up to that time.

In England, MacGregor Mathers and his secret metaphysical

group, the Order of the Golden Dawn, included members such as W.B Yeats, Arthur Edward Waite (who cocreated the Rider-Waite deck), and Aleister Crowley (who cocreated the Thoth deck). Waite and Crowley were major pioneers in the field of Tarot, and today, the Rider-Waite deck remains as the most popular Tarot deck in the world and the Thoth deck is widely admired for its revolutionary artwork. In America, C. C. Zain created the Egyptian Tarot and established a spiritual study group called the Brotherhood of Light, while Paul Foster Case and his esoteric association, the Builders of the Adytum, developed the first correspondence course taught on the Tarot.

By the 1960s and 1970s, the Rider-Waite and IJJ Swiss Tarot decks could be found for sale all over America, and books on the Tarot began to appear in the marketplace. Since that time, hundreds of books and decks of every imaginable type have been produced in an astonishing array as the Tarot reaches its pinnacle of popularity with the new millennium.

## Fear and the Tarot

Some people are terrified to have their cards read, though the Tarot might intrigue them. This fear is usually based on a lack of experience with the cards or having had a previously negative or disappointing reading from a card reader. Many people are concerned about getting bad cards—like the Devil, Tower, or Death trumps—or being told of a horrible future or that the person they love does not know they exist. None of the cards are bad, and a reading should never scare anyone away from the Tarot. Once acquainted with the positive purpose of the cards, most people are eager to learn more about the Tarot. The Tarot is fun; it was never meant to be dark or scary. This is the most common misconception about the cards. Owning a deck is not a sign of worshipping the occult or being into witchcraft or satanic worship.

The Tarot is designed to be a powerful force of evolution toward all

✼✼✼✼✼✼✼✼✼✼✼

THE READING IS NEVER THE FINAL WORD ON WHAT WILL HAPPEN; IT MERELY ILLUSTRATES THE OPTIONS YOU HAVE CONCERNING A PARTICULAR MATTER AND WHAT SORT OF BEHAVIOR YOU CAN EXPECT FROM EVERYONE INVOLVED.

✼✼✼✼✼✼✼✼✼✼✼

that is good and sacred. It is one of the most useful mediums for the development of human consciousness and healing the individual psyche through the revelation of universal truths encoded in the cards. Those who assume the Tarot cards are not of god are wrong—the insight and information of the readings come directly from the heart and mind of the godhead. The fact that many of the trump cards are biblical in origin cannot be denied. You have to be pretty ignorant to be afraid of a little deck of cards from ancient, ancient times. If you know the Tarot well, it is hard to comprehend why for hundreds of years the cards have been guilty of so many imaginary crimes against humanity. Amazingly enough, during many eras of civilization, you could be forced into exile, jailed, or even killed for possessing a deck.

If you are sincere as you read the cards, the experience will be uplifting and mind-expanding. The secret to clarity in a reading is belief. No matter how incompetent you feel as you begin to work with the Tarot, if you trust your deck, the cards will speak to you as they have to people throughout the centuries.

Readings may often draw blanks or not make complete sense, but each reading represents one step toward the process of learning about the Tarot. Also, the full impact of a reading may take time to become completely obvious. There is no limit to the knowledge you can acquire about the Tarot; there is always something new to discover about the cards. They are a wonderful tool that can be used for guidance your entire life.

✠✠✠✠✠✠✠✠✠✠

THE TAROT IS DESIGNED TO BE A
POWERFUL FORCE OF EVOLUTION
TOWARD ALL THAT IS GOOD AND
SACRED. IT IS ONE OF THE MOST USEFUL
MEDIUMS FOR THE DEVELOPMENT OF
HUMAN CONSCIOUSNESS AND HEALING
THE INDIVIDUAL PSYCHE THROUGH THE
REVELATION OF UNIVERSAL TRUTHS
ENCODED IN THE CARDS.

✠✠✠✠✠✠✠✠✠✠

# CHAPTER TWO
## THE TAROT DECK

### The Pip Cards

The Tarot deck consists of 78 cards; 56 of these are called the pip cards, or the minor arcana.

The pips are divided into four suits similar to a modern playing card deck. Instead of diamonds, spades, hearts, and clubs as suits, the Tarot has swords, disks, cups, and wands.

SWORDS build toward increased wisdom and knowledge. DISKS build toward physical comfort and security. CUPS build toward loving others and emotional fulfillment. WANDS build toward creative and constructive passionate energy.

The four suits of the Tarot deck correspond to the four elements and are associated with the following types of activities:

> ✻✻✻✻✻✻✻✻✻✻✻✻
>
> **THE TAROT IS A FORCE OF EVOLUTION FOR THE GOOD OF THE WORLD AS A SOURCE OF COMFORT WHEN INNER GUIDANCE IS NEEDED TO ANALYZE YOUR PSYCHOLOGICAL AND SPIRITUAL DEVELOPMENT.**
>
> ✻✻✻✻✻✻✻✻✻✻✻✻

| Suit | Element | Activities |
|------|---------|------------|
| sword | air | realization; obstacles to growth; spiritual sacrifice; reason; logic; adaptability; versatility; skepticism; restlessness; awareness; self-consciousness; alertness; the mind and intellect; communication; thought processes; decisions |
| disk | earth | actualization; the world of matter; cooperative activity; refined affection; dogmatic spirituality; the physical body; the necessities of existence; solid construction; completion; property; money; prosperity; talents; material things |
| cup | water | receptivity; soulfulness; development of the inner self; the unconscious mind; sensitivity; emotions; dreaminess; fantasy; inertia; intuition; psychic abilities; love; sympathy; understanding; peacefulness; devotion; imagination; visualization |

| Suit | Element | Activities |
|------|---------|-----------|
| wand | fire | creativity; sexuality; impulsive behavior; enthusiasm; independence; dynamic force; assertive energy; heroic action; courageous drive; passionate desire; humor; positivity; inspiration; compassion; enterprise; spiritual growth |

In each suit, there are ten numbered cards (ace through ten) and four court cards (King, Queen, Knight, and Page). The ace is the earliest, most primordial form of the element, and the ten of each suit is the maximum manifestation of the quality of the element. The two through nine are valuable lessons that nurture a slow evolution or ripening as the individual gains consciousness of and control over the activities of the element. Here are the meanings for the ten numbered cards:

| Number | Meaning |
|--------|---------|
| ace | the deity; beginnings; new ideas; pure potential; initial impulse toward action; unity of force available; sowing seeds that pave the way for the harvest of the ten; the arrival of something new and powerful; the archetypal character of the suit |

| Number | Meaning |
|--------|---------|
| two | simple, pure, easy, and early combinations of the element; dynamic tension; the sacred couple; duality in nature; polarities of energy; balancing opposing forces; making important choices; coming together with others in relationships |
| three | the trinity; strong creation through the medium of the element; advancement and growth; partial completion; wholeness; laying a solid foundation for the future; seeking perfection; mind, body, and spirit; growthful activity; successful collaboration; creative expression of the element |
| four | stability and structure developed through the element; full integration of the element; accomplishment; a solid conclusion; establishing boundaries; putting order to things; being practical about the future; creation of the home environment |
| five | unusual demands and challenges; unstable forms of the element; uncertainty; annoying obstacles; difficulty connecting with others; wanting more than your current reality allows; fluctuating ideas, emotions, thoughts, and feelings; change occurs beyond your control |

# The Tarot Deck

| Number | Meaning |
|--------|---------|
| six | great usability through a connection of all forces in a suit; achieving a sense of balance; heightened fulfillment; easy transition to a new level of activity; the inclusion of others in your plans; sharing whatever you have; battles won; enjoying hard-earned blessings |
| seven | individual application of the suit; the unfoldment of new plans; spirituality; mysticism; personal vision and power; development of the imagination; many potential options are available; unique creative contributions to the world; special talents are recognized; a particular point of view |
| eight | a serious intensity of the suit; relationships of a permanent nature; more work to do; revision of plans; personal values under examination; preparing for action; awaiting a new cycle of activity; letting go of the past |
| nine | substantial and long-lasting expansion of the element; accomplishment; personal fulfillment; an opportunity for spiritual maturity; great soul gifts and creative talents; moving out into the world; deep involvement with others; integrating different aspects of your life |

ten           maximum, firm, and fully developed manifestation of the suit; completion of a cycle of growth and activity; the finished form at the end of the process; achieving a whole personality; abundance on all levels; accumulation on the material; reaching for perfection

## The Court Cards

Within each suit there are four court cards: King, Queen, Knight, and Page.

KINGS are commanding male figures, mature rulers. QUEENS are commanding female figures, mature rulers. KNIGHTS are active male figures, more servile than Kings. PAGES are youthful and devoted apprentices or messengers of their element.

************

THERE IS NO LIMIT TO THE KNOWLEDGE YOU CAN ACQUIRE ABOUT THE TAROT; THERE IS ALWAYS SOMETHING NEW TO DISCOVER ABOUT THE CARDS. THEY ARE A WONDERFUL TOOL THAT CAN BE USED FOR GUIDANCE YOUR ENTIRE LIFE.

************

Court cards represent how other people and different facets of your own personality will affect the outcome of the reading. A King and a Knight will not necessarily symbolize a male, nor will a Queen always symbolize a female. The behavioral descriptions of the court cards signify dispositions and temperaments regardless of gender. An abundance of court cards indicates the involvement of many people with the subject of the reading.

# The Tarot Deck

## The Trump Cards

The remaining 22 cards of the Tarot deck are called the trump cards or the major arcana. The trumps have their own numerical hierarchy and are numbered 0 to 21 (or 1 to 22), beginning with the Fool and ending with the Universe or World card. Both the names of the trumps and their order can vary from deck to deck. Following are the most common numbers and titles:

0   The Fool
1   The Magician, Magus, or Juggler
2   The Priestess, High Priestess, Juno, or the Female Pope
3   The Empress
4   The Emperor
5   The Hierophant, Jupiter, Priest, or the Pope
6   The Lovers or Love
7   The Chariot
8   Justice
9   The Hermit
10   The Wheel of Fortune
11   Strength, Force, or Fortitude
12   The Hanged Man
13   Death
14   Temperance
15   The Devil
16   The Tower or House of God
17   The Star
18   The Moon
19   The Sun
20   Judgement
21   The Universe or World

The trump cards are more enigmatic and visually complex than the pip cards. It is believed that the symbols and figures with which they are decorated project a wide range of cultural and mythological associations. The clothing that adorns them and their postures and gestures are all considered important to their interpretation.

The major arcana carry spiritual force wherever they appear in a Tarot reading. The events they represent are destined; they are inevitable lessons that guide a thinking, feeling soul toward maturation.

## Choosing a Tarot Deck

A PERFECT TAROT READING IS A MAGICAL SESSION WHERE THE CARD READER USES THE DECK AS A TOOL FOR GLEANING KNOWLEDGE FROM THE CARDS IN ORDER TO GAIN INSIGHT.

For the most part, the standard 78-card Tarot deck has survived virtually unchanged for at least five hundred years. Since the 1960s millions of Tarot decks have been sold. Today, over one hundred different decks are mass-produced for distribution in the United States alone. Artists continually reinterpret the ancient imagery of the cards for new decks at a time when the Tarot is undergoing a renaissance of interest worldwide that is not abating. The Tarot is in demand internationally and has strong audiences in Canada as well as in every European country, Japan, South America, India, Australia, New Zealand, and many other places. In almost every major city in the world, you can find Tarot classes, readers, and decks available for sale, often in more than one location. The Tarot has come into its own as a multicultural, multiracial, and multinational intuitive art and divination tool. It is important to under-stand that any Tarot deck can be used in conjunction with this book to give a Tarot card reading.

Some readers choose from a variety of decks for doing Tarot readings while others read with only one type of deck. The art-work on the cards is a major factor in drawing people to a par-ticular Tarot deck. The image on a card influences how you interpret it, and many readers prefer to utilize the simplest, least cluttered decks.

When you begin to read, you may find it helpful to start with a highly animated deck like the classic Rider-Waite Tarot Deck where the pip cards are brought to life in scenes depicting human activities that give you an idea of what the card means. For example, instead of starting out with a deck like the Swiss IJJ Tarot Deck that has two crossed swords as an illustration for the two of swords card, you might choose the Rider-Waite pack, which shows a blindfolded woman balancing two swords on her shoulders as she sits on a bench with her back to the sea under a crescent moon. The more detailed visual associations of the Rider-Waite Tarot deck give clues to the novice Tarot reader on how to interpret the card, as the picture helps the reader iden-tify and recall the meaning of the card whenever it appears in a spread. Some decks attribute extremely complex visually symbolic associations to each card. The Church of Light Tarot Deck, for example, assigns planets, numbers, Hebrew letters, and zodiac signs to the 78 cards.

You may wish to buy a deck that appeals to you aesthetic
ly, or you may select the deck that another card reader has uti-lized when reading your cards. You should feel comfortable

with the deck and find it user-friendly when you begin to read for yourself and others. Many people receive their first deck as a gift or buy one on a whim and then stick with that type of

✶✶✶✶✶✶✶✶✶✶✶

READINGS ARE IMPRESSIONISTIC IN NATURE, AND LEARNING HOW TO BLEND THE COMPONENTS TAKES PRACTICE AND REQUIRES IMAGINATION AND INTUITION.

✶✶✶✶✶✶✶✶✶✶✶

deck for life. Some card readers work with decks that are missing cards or with regular playing cards with suits of spades, clubs, hearts, and diamonds or even with Tarocchi decks. Some Tarotists own a collection of different decks and use one or the other depending on their mood. The main thing with choosing a deck is that you feel a connection to whatever type of cards you use and they work for you in a reading.

In many Tarot decks, the names of the four pip suits have been changed, as have the titles of the court and trump cards. The following list includes some of the decks that contain modifications to the traditional 78-card Tarot deck:

Crowley Thoth Tarot Deck—the Pages and Kings turn into Princes and Princesses here, and all 56 pip cards bear descriptive terms on the bottom of the card, such as "Peace" for the two of swords. This deck changes Justice to Adjustment, the Wheel of Fortune to Fortune, Strength to Lust, Temperance to Art, and Judgement to the Aeon.

Voyager Tarot Deck—the court cards are Man, Woman, Child, and Sage here. Suits are crystals (mind), cups (heart), worlds (body), and wands (spirit). The Voyager deck is composed of collages of photographs and other printed matter.

Karma Tarot Deck—Juno or the High Priestess becomes Wise Woman, the Empress turns into Lilith, the Emperor here is called Osiris, and Jupiter or the Hierophant is titled the Grand Master.

# The Tarot Deck

Herbal Tarot—the Hanged Man is the Suspended Person in this deck and the Devil is referred to as Pan.

Native American Tarot Deck—some changes in trump titles are Hosteen Coyote (Juggler or Magician), Corn Maiden (Juno or High Priestess), Medicine Woman (Empress), Council Chief (Emperor), and Shaman (Jupiter or Hierophant). The suits are blades (swords), pipes (wands), vessels (cups), and shields (disks). The court cards are Matriarch, Chief, Warrior, and Maiden.

Motherpeace Tarot Deck—this deck of round cards replaces the Hermit with the Crone, and the Hanged Man becomes the Hanged One. The court card titles undergo a change as Kings, Queens, Knights, and Pages of the traditional deck turn into Daughters, Sons, Priestesses, and Shamans. The court cards are referred to as the Daughter of wands, the Son of wands, the Priestess of wands, the Shaman of wands, and so on.

Merlin Tarot Deck—the pips in this pack are called by the suit names of birds, dragons, fishes, and beasts.

Tarot of the Ages Deck—the trump cards are representative of Egyptian civilization. The pip suits are Vikings (swords), Africans (wands), Aztecs (cups), and East Indians (disks).

Angel Tarot Deck—though the pip suit titles are swords, wands, cups, and disks, the artwork of each of the pips contains the symbols of spades, hearts, clubs, and diamonds incorporated into the design.

✷✷✷✷✷✷✷✷✷✷✷

TAROT READINGS CAN CHANGE THE
COURSE OF YOUR DESTINY OR BRING TO
LIGHT THE PSYCHOLOGICAL AND
SPIRITUAL TRUTHS BEHIND THE DRAMA
OF YOUR EXISTENCE.

✷✷✷✷✷✷✷✷✷✷✷

Norse Tarot Deck—in this pack some of the trump titles are Balder (Fool), Odin (Juggler or Magician), Frigga (Juno or High Priestess), Freya (Empress), Tyr (Emperor), and Thor (Chariot). The court cards are Kings, Queens, Princesses, and Princes.

Cat People Tarot Deck—the suits are called rubies (swords), emeralds (wands), topazes (cups), and sapphires (disks). The trump cards are associated with diamond gemstones.

Mayan Tarot Deck—twenty of the trump cards in this deck are called by the names of the days of the Mayan month. The pips are titled in five different languages: French, English, Spanish, Italian, and German.

Knapp-Hall Tarot Deck—the court cards are named King, Queen, Warrior, and Squire. Each trump card is inscribed with a Hebrew letter and a heraldic emblem.

Robot Tarot Deck—all the card titles are in Italian, and the pip suits have been altered to *laser* (swords), *nulla* (wands), *scarabee* (cups), and *luci* (disks).

The Medicine Woman Tarot Deck—the four minor arcana or pip suits are called arrows, pipes, bowls, and stones. The court cards are defined as Exemplar, Harvest Lodge, Totem, and Apprentice. Each trump card contains a single-word description across its base, such as Harvest for the Wheel of Fortune.

Visconti-Sforza Tarot Deck—this ancient deck has some unique trump titles and stands out from other antique decks for this very reason. The Mountebank (Juggler or Magician), the Old Man (Hermit), the Traitor (Hanged Man), and the Angel (Universe) are the titles this deck has changed. The court cards are referred to as Kings, Queens, Knights, and Jacks (Pages).

# CHAPTER THREE
## THE TAROT CARD READING

## What Is a Tarot Card Reading?

Tarot card readings can help you align with your deepest dreams and become more self-reliant about choosing which way to go in life. They can show, with uncanny accuracy, what is happening to you at the time of the reading and what to expect in the future. In this way, they give you a sense of direction and assist you in understanding the way things work so you can find greater satisfaction romantically, financially, and spiritually.

A perfect Tarot reading is a magical session where the card reader uses the deck as a tool for gleaning knowledge from the cards in order to gain insight. The reader, the deck, the collective unconscious, and the inquirer must all be functioning on the same wavelength for this miraculous meeting of minds to take place. Until you reach this stage, you will need to utilize this book to identify how each card should be interpreted in a spread. Eventually you will reach a point where you will remember what the 78 cards mean and will not have to completely rely on this book when you begin to read for others.

The information that comes through a reading is extremely valuable to the development of your soul because the inner voice that speaks to you through the cards is the best guidance to be found anywhere. A clear reading will always push you toward who or what is really right for you based on destiny requirements of which your higher self is aware, even if you try to avoid your proper path in life.

> THE TAROT ENLIGHTENS YOU INTELLECTUALLY, ETHICALLY, IDEOLOGICALLY, PSYCHOLOGICALLY, AND SPIRITUALLY THROUGH PROFOUND AND POWERFUL READINGS THAT SERVE AS POINTS OF CLARIFICATION TO PROPEL YOU INTO ACTION AND STEER YOUR HEART, MIND, SOUL, AND BODY TOWARD ACHIEVING YOUR GOALS FOR THIS CURRENT INCARNATION.

The Tarot reading can also help you change old patterns and habits that are comfortable and uncomfortable at the same time. Although you feel discontented, you may have trouble seeing your own destructive tendencies. The Tarot can show you how to replace deadening activities with satisfying, simple, and natural alternatives.

The symbiotic relationship that develops between you and your Tarot deck keeps reinforcing your belief in the ability of the cards to help you comprehend the spiritual story behind your existence. A good reading always fills you up with positivity and hope for a better future for yourself and others. Tarot readings never fail to tell the truth to an inquiring individual who desires to see things as they absolutely are. The cards continually direct you toward the highest and the best the world has to offer, so that you can make good use of your incarnation and leave behind a history of creative activities that were in harmonious alignment with the cosmos.

## *Steps for a Tarot Card Reading*

A Tarot reading takes place when you interpret your own cards or you translate a reading for another person who is known as the "inquirer." The reading consists of shuffling the cards and laying them out into systematic patterns called spreads. Spreads create the scenario of the reading and place the cards in a time sequence. The meanings of the cards are interpreted in conjunction with their placement in the spread in an effort to answer the inquiry brought to the reading.

## Finding the Significator

Before you begin to read the Tarot cards, you must find the significator. This card represents the inquirer while establishing the subject-combination of the reading. If you want to do a complete reading, your instructions begin here. Otherwise, if you only want to lay out Tarot spreads in response to specific questions, you can skip this initial step of the reading and turn right to the section of this book devoted to Tarot card spreads.

To determine the significator, one of the eight King or Queen court cards is chosen to symbolize the inquirer. This is done astrologically. Ask the inquirer what his or her zodiac sign is; if the inquirer does not know this information, use this table to discover it:

| Birth Date | Zodiac Sign |
|---|---|
| March 21—April 19 | Aries |
| April 20—May 20 | Taurus |
| May 21—June 21 | Gemini |
| June 22—July 22 | Cancer |
| July 23—August 22 | Leo |

| August 23—September 22 | Virgo |
| September 23—October 23 | Libra |
| October 24—November 21 | Scorpio |
| November 22—December 21 | Sagittarius |
| December 22—January 19 | Capricorn |
| January 20—February 18 | Aquarius |
| February 19—March 20 | Pisces |

When you have determined the sign of the inquirer, use the following table to identify his or her significator. If you are reading your own cards, apply this same method to ascertain your significator. For those born on the cusps of signs (very early or very late in a sign), choose the sign that you feel most in tune with.

| Zodiac Sign | Female | Male |
| --- | --- | --- |
| Aries, Leo, Sagittarius | Queen of wands | King of wands |
| Taurus, Virgo, Capricorn | Queen of disks | King of disks |
| Gemini, Libra, Aquarius | Queen of swords | King of swords |
| Cancer, Scorpio, Pisces | Queen of cups | King of cups |

Therefore, if the inquirer is a man born on March 18th, he is a Pisces, and his significator is the King of cups. If the inquirer is a woman born on January 4th, she is a Capricorn, so her significator is the Queen of disks.

# The Tarot Card Reading

## Notes on Shuffling

You begin every card reading by shuffling the Tarot deck before you lay the cards out into Tarot spreads. The instructions are the same whether you are inter-

preting your own cards or reading for an inquirer. The only difference is that the inquirer shuffles the deck *after* the reader shuffles and *before* the cards are laid out into the Tarot spreads. The last person to shuffle the cards before they are laid down is *always* the person whose cards are being read. The shuffling process is *always* used between spreads in a reading.

Try to keep the cards facing in the same direction when you shuffle the deck. If the cards become a mixture of right side up and upside down, simply put them right side up as you turn them over into a spread. The cards are always laid out facing the reader. The inquirer should sit directly across from the reader, even though the cards will appear upside down from his or her vantage point.

## Establishing the Subject-Combination of the Reading

After the significator has been identified, the reading begins and the subject-combination must be established. If you are reading for yourself, take the deck in your hands and concentrate on the matter you want information about as you ask the cards for clarity and guidance.

Shuffle the deck three times. If you are reading for an inquirer, ask him or her to shuffle the deck three times after you do.

Once the cards are shuffled, separate the deck into the four subject piles:

Work and Business
Love and Relationship
Trouble and Conflict
Money and Material Matters

The reader lays the deck face down and cuts it twice from right to left:

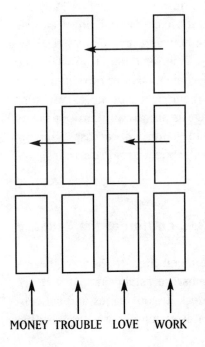

Take the top half of the deck and place it next to the bottom half of the deck, forming two stacks of cards.

Move the top half of each stack to the left, making four stacks of cards.

Now you have the four subject piles.

MONEY  TROUBLE  LOVE  WORK

Once you have divided the deck into four piles, pick up a pile, turn it over, and sort through it. Go through each stack until you find the significator. In the case of the Pisces man, you would search through each pile, from

right to left, until you find the King of cups.

If you find the significator (in our example, the King of cups) in the Work pile, this will become the first subject-combination of the reading. Now put all the cards together again and shuffle them. Ask the inquirer to shuffle them, too. Then break them up once more into the four subject piles. If, during your second subject search, you find the King of cups in the Money pile, the subject-combination will be a blend of these two areas, Work and Money.

These subjects are topics, or categories, that represent problems, activities, and concerns that the spread will illustrate and further define.

## The Meanings of the Subject-Combinations

**Work and Work:** emphasis of reading is work and occupation; it will discuss specific action to take on a matter

**Work and Love:** the reading will show what effort is required in your relationships with other people; there is a need to ascertain how a love alliance affects your work; your behavior as it influences your partnerships

**Work and Trouble:** changes necessary at your workplace, where problems arise over your output or involvement; difficulties you have working with others; cause of disharmony and possible solutions; you need to analyze and adjust how you apply your creative energy

**Work and Money:** making substantial gains in your work; receiving money or other rewards for your dedication to a project; realizing how you can develop your talents; dealing with ordinary things on a practical level; taking constructive action

**Love and Love:** unions emphasized; reading will be a complete discussion of a love relationship or partnership

**Love and Trouble:** crises, problems, and changes in love relationships and partnerships; disharmony in unions or alliances

**Love and Money:** symbolizes a need for a deeply devoted union or a firm partnership; indicates that a relationship is finally materializing

**Trouble and Trouble:** problems caused by your behavior; disturbances in interpersonal relationships; major changes underway, which reading will illustrate

**Trouble and Money:** financial issues need examination; concerns about proper utilization of talent; reading will analyze money difficulties

**Money and Money:** emphasis of reading is accomplishment, making things happen, and actualizing desires; a chronicle of your movement toward personal success; your current material circumstances

Once you have ascertained the subject-combination, the reading moves on to the spreads.

# The Tarot Card Reading

## Laying the Cards into Spreads

There are many Tarot spreads to choose from, depending on what you want to discover through a reading. In this section of the book, you will find 14 spreads: Grand Cross Spread; One Card Spread; Four Card Spread; Past, Present, Future Spread; Master Spread; New Relationship Spread; Soul Mate Search; As Above, So Below; Money Spread; Three Card Spread; Problem/Solution Spread; Astrological Spread; Elemental Spread; and Lifetimes Spread. The instructions for laying the cards into spreads, the meanings of the placements, and the interpretation of each arrangement are included in the "Fourteen Tarot Spreads" section, which follows.

To interpret the spread, you must read carefully through the explanation of that spread and look up the meaning of each card in the section of this book called, "The 78 Tarot Cards and Their Romantic, Financial, and Spiritual Interpretations." Find the descriptions of the card that apply to love, work, money, or personal growth problems that you are examining through your card reading, then fit the definition into the position in the spread where the card surfaces. Where the card lands in the spread placement defines how you apply the meaning of the card in the scenario being created by the spread. The descriptions of the cards are based on similarly abstract concepts and are intended to set off multiple triggers in the mind of the card reader.

Read through the spread as though the cards are the details of a story held together in a plot represented by the Tarot spread. Look at the cards as forces within a reading that are separate in meaning but form a message collectively. Readings are impressionistic in nature, and learning how to blend the components takes practice and requires imagination and intuition. Random images and associations that pop into your mind are *always* important. You should acknowledge them and tell the inquirer about them.

Continually pay attention to cards that appeared earlier in the spread and tie their meaning into the developing scenario. As you analyze the spread, look at the spread placement and blend it together with the definition of the card that most applies to the matter being examined through the reading. Move your eyes around the spread, registering in your mind the types of cards represented and their juxtapositions to each other. Be aware of combinations of the same suit or type of card within a reading. All trumps in the positions of the Grand Cross Spread would indicate a reading of monumental importance. A spread containing a majority of wands would emphasize the passionate and creative nature of the inquirer due to the meanings associated with the wands suit. All four seven minor arcana cards in a spread would stress challenges that need to be overcome, and symbolize taking action when you least care to. Also acknowledge which types of cards are *not* represented in a spread. A lack of cups would indicate little emotional involvement in a matter; an absence of disks would show little grounding in reality concerning the subject of the reading; a trumpless spread would indicate a fairly pedestrian reading.

As you now know, the first step in a Tarot reading is to take the deck into your hands and shuffle it three times. If you are reading for an inquirer, have him or her shuffle the Tarot deck after you shuffle it. Then lay the cards down in the spread positions according to the order in which they appear, drawing one card after another off the top of the deck. When you have interpreted a spread to your satisfaction, gather all the cards and bring the deck back together. Again, try to keep the cards facing in the same direction. When you read for another person, the cards usually get mixed up, but you can turn them right side up as you turn the cards over to interpret the spread. Remember, if you are reading for an inquirer, you (the reader) must collect the cards between spreads and shuffle the deck three times before handing the deck over to the inquirer. The cards are placed into a spread after the inquirer has shuffled. The reader should ask the inquirer to concentrate on his or her question as he or she shuffles the deck. The cards that appear in the spread respond to inquiries posed to the deck during the shuffling process.

When you sit down to read, ask the Tarot deck for specific advice about your problems. Mentally focus on receiving good information and wise guidance during the shuffling process, so your interpretation will be authoritative. Do not feel put off by the enigmatic pictures on the faces of the cards as you turn them over in the spread. Remember, all you have to do is look up the meanings of the cards in this book and follow its simple instructions to give a decent Tarot reading.

The Tarot is articulate to the point of eloquence once you know what the cards mean and how to utilize a deck in a reading. When you properly connect the visual attributes of the cards to their meanings, and can translate what they symbolize in the people, events, and circumstances of your life, you can give Tarot readings that can change the course of your destiny or bring to light the psychological and spiritual truths behind the drama of your existence. Do not be fatalistic with a reading; look forward to the prospect of using the cards as a tool for finding out what is really going on behind the spectacle of reality. You will grow to love the Tarot as you receive uncanny, nearly miraculous readings that accurately describe what is happening in your life and what will come to pass in your future.

## Fourteen Tarot Spreads

### Grand Cross Spread

The most classic and well-known spread is the Grand Cross or Celtic Cross. The layout for the Grand Cross consists of 11 cards.

When you read through any spread for an inquirer, you should verbalize the names of the spread positions as you lay the cards down or as you turn them over.

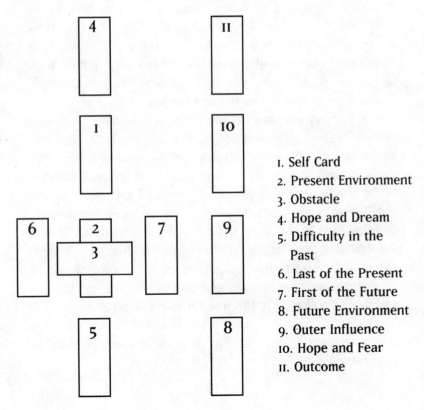

1. Self Card
2. Present Environment
3. Obstacle
4. Hope and Dream
5. Difficulty in the Past
6. Last of the Present
7. First of the Future
8. Future Environment
9. Outer Influence
10. Hope and Fear
11. Outcome

# The Tarot Card Reading

## The Meanings of the 11 Positions in the Grand Cross

**1. Self Card:** The self card symbolizes the inquirer at the time of the reading and describes his or her current state of mind or position in the matter.

**2. Present Environment:** This card represents the atmosphere at the time of the reading and how the general environment influences the self card.

**3. Obstacle:** Any card in this position is an immediate obstacle in your path, and you must acknowledge its influence on the course of the reading. It is important to accept this card even if you ultimately decide to ignore, fight, or enjoy what it symbolizes. The obstacle can be a block in your way of thinking or an activity you must undertake reluctantly in order to meet the outcome of the reading.

**4. Hope and Dream:** This card indicates what you want more than anything and what you should be striving for, or it can represent wishes fulfilled in their purest form without any compromise. This position is separate from the rest of the spread. It carries the force of a delicate dream that you maintain, regardless of what is happening in reality.

**5. Difficulty in the Past:** You have to meet the challenge of the card that falls in this position. A past event has been causing trouble and making things hard for you even though you have grown through the difficulties. This position indicates that whatever is symbolized by this card will no longer be a hindrance but will give you support in the future.

**6. Last of the Present:** The card in this position stands for whatever has happened just prior to the reading.

**7. First of the Future:** This card represents what will occur immediately after the reading.

**8. Future Environment:** The card that falls in this spot symbolizes the atmosphere surrounding the matter in the future.

**9. Outer Influence**: The ninth card stands for the effect that other people have on the outcome of the reading. The card indicates what you can expect from family, friends, and acquaintances.

**10. Hope and Fear**: This position carries a sharp, decisive warning and is the turning point of the reading. You should work to attain what this card represents if you wish to meet the outcome of the reading. It is the resolve that you fear most, although it would successfully conclude the matter that so concerns you. This is the moment of truth and the ultimate decision you would rather put off indefinitely.

**11. Outcome**: The card in this position signifies the end result of the scenario of the reading. It sums up the entire situation. It is also the lead card for your next reading on the same subject.

✶✶✶✶✶✶✶✶✶✶✶

THE MOST POWERFUL AND ACCURATE
READINGS OCCUR WHEN YOU ARE
ENERGETIC, INSPIRED, AND AT
PEACE WITH YOURSELF.

✶✶✶✶✶✶✶✶✶✶✶

*Some Hints For Interpreting The Grand Cross Spread*

1. See how the obstacle and hope and fear compare to each other. How does the obstacle create a testing ground for what you must resolve with the hope and fear?

2. Compare the first of the future with the outcome to get a sense of direction about where the story is leading.

3. Compare the present environment with the future environment to see how the changing atmosphere around the inquirer will affect the outcome of the reading.

### One Card Spread

Some beginning readers like to shuffle the deck and choose one card to answer a specific question or to define their day ahead. As an even simpler exercise, other people enjoy flipping through the definition section and randomly landing one finger on a line of writing in response to an inquiry.

### Four Card Spread

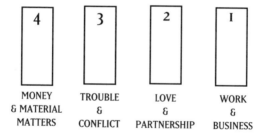

| 4 | 3 | 2 | I |
|---|---|---|---|
| MONEY & MATERIAL MATTERS | TROUBLE & CONFLICT | LOVE & PARTNERSHIP | WORK & BUSINESS |

For the Four Card Spread, you lay the top four cards out from right to left. The meaning of the card that falls in each position will define a certain area of your life and how it influences the subject matter of the reading.

## Past, Present, Future Spread

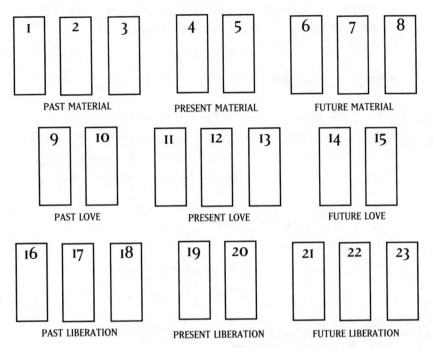

This layout utilizes 23 of the 78 Tarot cards. It makes an excellent exercise for learning how to combine your interpretations of two and three cards as they fall close to one another in a common corner of the spread.

This spread is read like a graph in the numerical order outlined above. Lay the cards out face down in this pattern and then turn them over (in the same order) two and three at a time. Learn how to combine the meanings of each group of two or three cards on the three horizontal rows of the spread. After a little practice, this will come quite naturally.

Interpret this spread by beginning with the past material grouping (cards 1 to 3). Then move to the right into the present

(4 and 5) and future material (6 to 8). Now, move down to the past love group (9 and 10) and on to the present (11 to 13) and future (14 and 15) love groups. Finally, go down to the bottom row and move from left to right through the past (16 to 18), present (19 and 20), and future (21 to 23) liberation groups.

This spread is especially helpful in that it provides a complete picture of a troubling matter on three levels: what is really happening (material), what is being felt by those involved (love), and what is happening to free everyone to move forward (liberation). You can see how things that happened in the past have influenced current issues at the time of the reading (the present) and what changes will occur at a future date.

❄❄❄❄❄❄❄❄❄❄

READING FOR OTHERS IS ALL ABOUT
HELPING THEM GAIN AN
UNDERSTANDING OF WHAT IS GOING
ON BEHIND THE SCENES OF THEIR LIVES,
AND THAT SHOULD ALWAYS BE YOUR
FOREMOST REASON FOR BECOMING A
TAROT CARD READER.

❄❄❄❄❄❄❄❄❄❄

## Master Spread

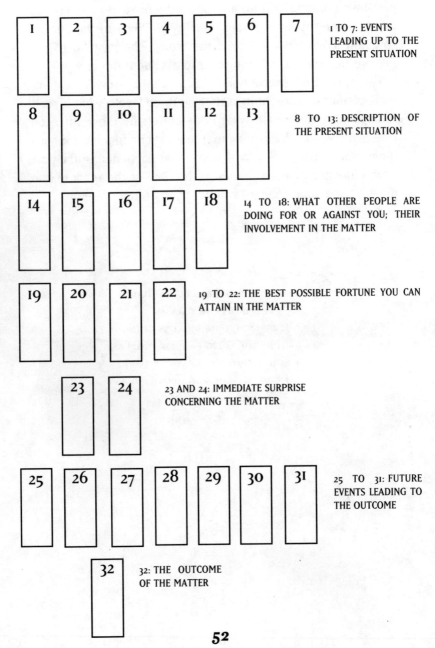

1 TO 7: EVENTS LEADING UP TO THE PRESENT SITUATION

8 TO 13: DESCRIPTION OF THE PRESENT SITUATION

14 TO 18: WHAT OTHER PEOPLE ARE DOING FOR OR AGAINST YOU; THEIR INVOLVEMENT IN THE MATTER

19 TO 22: THE BEST POSSIBLE FORTUNE YOU CAN ATTAIN IN THE MATTER

23 AND 24: IMMEDIATE SURPRISE CONCERNING THE MATTER

25 TO 31: FUTURE EVENTS LEADING TO THE OUTCOME

32: THE OUTCOME OF THE MATTER

# The Tarot Card Reading

You will use 32 cards in this spread. First, lay them out face down from left to right. Then turn them over and read them in numerical order, line by line. This spread will discuss and illuminate the widest range of variables that are affecting a matter. As in the Past, Present, Future Spread, you must learn how to interpret the meaning of a group of cards that fall next to each other. This spread may be too complex to read for another person at first; use it as a quiet internal meditative tool when you want a great deal of information on what is happening with a particular situation.

## New Relationship Spread

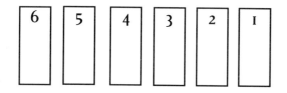

This spread utilizes six cards to help you get immediate information just after you meet someone new who interests you. Simply read the cards from right to left, turning them over as you go. Card 1 shows how he sees you; card 2 symbolizes what he needs relationship-wise at this point in his life; card 3 represents other women as current factors in his romantic world; card 4 signifies the fate of those connections; card 5 gives clues as to his amorous or friendly thoughts concerning you; and card 6 suggests where your interaction with him is headed in the future.

## Soul Mate Search

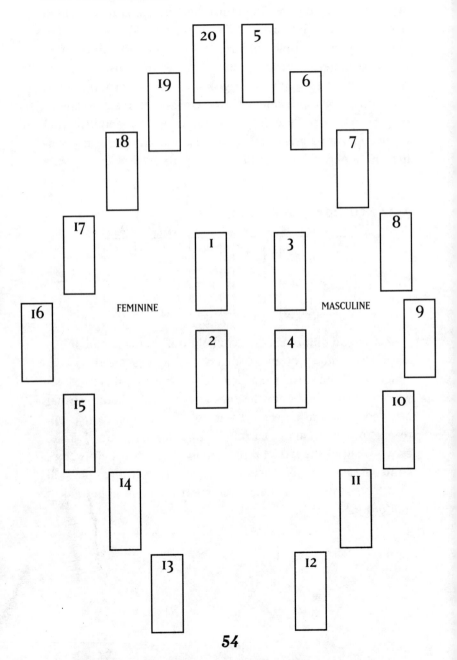

# The Tarot Card Reading

This layout examines the stages of development in your relationships with those of the opposite sex in terms of karma brought forth from your childhood experience (cards 1, 2, 3, and 4) with your parents, guardians, or figures of love and authority and how this has influenced your subconscious self-image. Implied in this spread (cards 5 through 20) is the pathway to the ideal person, or soul mate, with whom you could share a mature commitment without repeating as an adult the identical imbalanced union that your parents may have had and move on to create a relationship that reflects the highest aspirations for your deeply loving self.

To interpret this spread, begin with cards 1 and 2, which indicate your self-image as a female. The Tarot cards that fall in these two positions show the way you see yourself due to karma taken on from the maternal energy in your life.

For a woman, cards 3 and 4 on the masculine side of the spread symbolize her animus, the male archetype that she attracts to herself naturally, based on her experience with the paternal energy in her life, which has played a large role in establishing the level of her self-esteem. Cards 1 through 4 show the karma taken on through the parents, for better or for worse.

For a man, cards 3 and 4 on the masculine side indicate his self-image due to the karma taken on from the fatherly influences in his life. Cards 1 and 2 describe his anima, the female archetype that he unconsciously seeks, based on his experiences with female energy in his past. If he has already released any negativity inherited through the parents, cards 1 to 4 would take on a higher level of meaning and would be indicative of his search for the most pure and complementary soul mate and would show him animating cards 3 and 4 in a highly spiritual manner. This man would find his true consort through the activities of the cards that surface in positions 1 and 2. This would, of course, apply in reverse for a woman reading her cards.

For a female, cards 5 through 12 symbolize what her man has to accomplish psychologically, emotionally, spiritually, and materially on his path to meeting her and through the earliest stages of their relationship, with card 12 defining the nature of the union in its ultimate conclusion. Cards 13 through 20 show what she has to go through in her romantic experience until she is secure in her connection to the right man (card 20).

For a man, cards 13 through 20 depict what his soul mate is doing to find him and at what level her male archetype is currently functioning. Cards 5 through 12 show how he his proceeding on his path to his one true love.

### As Above, So Below

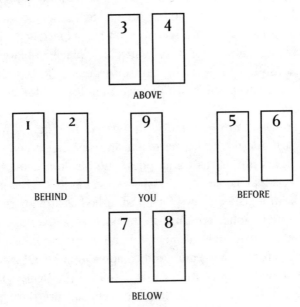

56

# The Tarot Card Reading

This directional spread examines the spiritual forces that surround you, influencing your movement out into the world and defining the quality of your daily life.

To use this spread, lay the top nine cards out, as shown in the illustrated arrangement. Cards 1 and 2 symbolize your past experiences with those who no longer influence you or what is behind you and has lost its power over you. Cards 3 and 4 describe what crowns you (is above you), environmental factors affecting you, and how you merge with society in general. Cards 5 and 6 have to do with what is before you in your future, what is ahead of you, the outcome of the subject of the reading, and who or what is growing more dominant along the horizon of life yet to come. Cards 7 and 8 show what is below or beneath you, what you already have under control, and the people who are your constant source of support. Card 9 represents you, or the inquirer, and depicts the core experiences that you are undergoing at the time of the reading.

## Money Spread

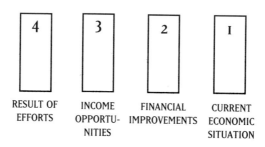

| 4 | 3 | 2 | I |
|---|---|---|---|
| RESULT OF EFFORTS | INCOME OPPORTU-NITIES | FINANCIAL IMPROVEMENTS | CURRENT ECONOMIC SITUATION |

Card 1 symbolizes your current economic situation; card 2 shows where you can expect financial improvements and indicates who will help you; card 3 represents income opportunities you do not expect; and card 4 symbolizes the result of your efforts.

## Three Card Spread

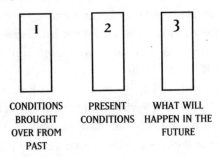

| I | 2 | 3 |
|---|---|---|
| CONDITIONS BROUGHT OVER FROM PAST | PRESENT CONDITIONS | WHAT WILL HAPPEN IN THE FUTURE |

This is a quick spread designed to answer the most specific questions posed to the deck in the least amount of time.

Read this spread from left to right, interpreting card 1 as conditions brought over from the past as they affect the issues brought to the reading, card 2 as present conditions, and card 3 as the outcome of the matter or the direction your involvement will take depending upon the nature of the Tarot card that surfaces here.

❊❊❊❊❊❊❊❊❊❊❊

YOU LEARN TO FACE ADVERSITY WITH
LAUGHTER AND HOPE FOR THE FUTURE.

❊❊❊❊❊❊❊❊❊❊❊

# The Tarot Card Reading

## Problem/Solution Spread

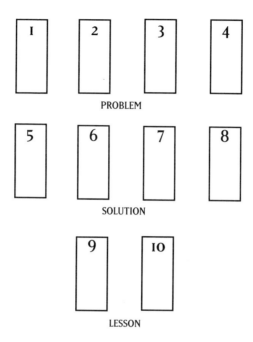

This layout helps you get to the heart of the reasons why certain challenging people and situations happen for a purpose in your life. It analyzes how you can first identify the nature of the problem and constructively deal with it through positive action to resolve old issues that you have chosen to deal with at the time of the reading.

Lay out the ten cards in the above arrangement. Cards 1 through 4 symbolize the current status of the situation and focus attention on the problem you are currently facing. Cards 5 through 8 show you what course of action will lead to a satisfying solution to the situation. Cards 9 and 10 depict the karmic lessons inherent in this obstacle that you need to comprehend to change the course of your life for the better.

## Astrological Spread

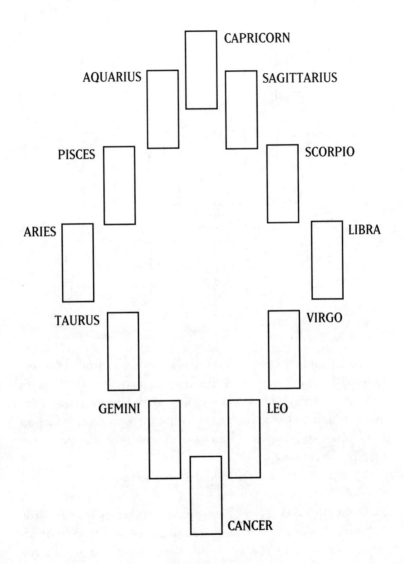

# The Tarot Card Reading

There are two different ways to utilize the following layout of 12 cards.

This spread can be used to forecast the year ahead as you would throw this spread only once a year with card 1 symbolizing the month you are in at the time of the reading. Place one card down for each of the following 11 placements that correspond to the remaining months. Record this reading so you can refer to it monthly to see how the Tarot card for each month represents lessons, issues, activities, and people that will dominate your life during that period of time.

The second method of application for this spread would emphasize your natal astrological chart. Again, place one card down on each of the 12 positions. This time the card would illustrate the 12 houses of the horoscope: card 1 corresponding to the first house in the astrological chart, card 2 corresponding to the second house in the astrological chart, and so on. The Tarot card that appears in the house placement of the reading symbolizes the nature of your experience and involvement with the area of life defined by the 12 house system of the science of astrology. For those unfamiliar with the meanings of the houses, here are the following definitions for you to use when you employ this second method.

| House | Meaning |
|---|---|
| first | your physical appearance and outward personality; the way you move, speak, and act; the vibration you communicate through your facial and body expressions |

| House | Meaning |
|-------|---------|
| second | your resources, talents, and abilities; your experience of personal values; your sense of responsibility; how you attract money and possessions to yourself |
| third | short journeys; early life conditions, especially your environment; siblings, relatives, and neighbors and their influence on you; the quality of your conscious mind and intellect; your communication skills; your exposure to knowledge during early education |
| fourth | the more passive of your parents; your home life and property; your self-image; your sense of personal security |
| fifth | your love life; children; personal pleasure and enjoyment; entertainment; self-expression and creative abilities; speculation and risk taking |
| sixth | your physical needs and domestic environment; conflict as it affects your health or employment; your ability to serve others; your work ethic |
| seventh | partners in marriage or business; your team members in life; those who oppose you as enemies or antagonists; legal matters |

# The Tarot Card Reading

| House | Meaning |
| --- | --- |
| eighth | death; material inheritance; spiritual legacies earned in other lives; joint resources; your sexuality; the field of parapsychology |
| ninth | long journeys; foreign lands and people; higher education; philosophical interests; the superconscious mind; visions, dreams, and symbolism |
| tenth | your more active parent; your career direction, reputation, and public image; your outer world pathway that defines who you are |
| eleventh | friendships and social life; ambitious long-term goals and objectives; humanitarian impulses; looking forward to the future |
| twelfth | what you keep hidden from others; your need for privacy and secrecy; your limitations, frustrations, and confinements; your subconscious mind; the karmic conditions of your soul; the quality of your spirituality; reaching perfection in this lifetime |

## Elemental Spread

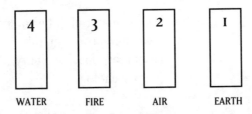

| 4 | 3 | 2 | I |
|---|---|---|---|
| WATER | FIRE | AIR | EARTH |

To utilize this spread, lay the top four cards out in the four placements shown in the illustration, and interpret the cards from right to left in the proper numerical order.

Each of the elements has the following correspondence to the four suits of the Tarot and generates the following activities in your life.

| Element | Suit | Activities |
|---------|------|------------|
| earth | disk | the body and all physical sensation; material expression of spirit; money, talent, and a constructive building up of practical ability |
| air | sword | the mind, thought, and intellect; making plans; sudden realizations; communication; facing challenging decisions |
| fire | wand | passion and desire; creative force; the spirit in action; life-giving energy; what you strive for and believe in |
| water | cup | the subconscious mind; soul qualities; emotional nature; receptivity; imagination and visualization |

# The Tarot Card Reading

## Lifetimes Spread

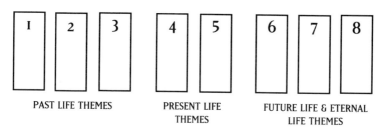

| I | 2 | 3 | 4 | 5 | 6 | 7 | 8 |

PAST LIFE THEMES          PRESENT LIFE          FUTURE LIFE & ETERNAL
                            THEMES                   LIFE THEMES

The eight cards that make up this spread are laid out from left to right in this simple self-explanatory spread.

This spread should not be done too often and should be recorded for future reference.

✻✻✻✻✻✻✻✻✻✻✻
ALL THE CLEAN ENERGY YOU PUT OUT
COMES BACK AS COSMIC REWARDS.

✻✻✻✻✻✻✻✻✻✻✻

❋❋❋❋❋❋❋❋❋❋❋

IT IS A HUGE MORAL RESPONSIBILITY TO
SET YOURSELF UP AS A SPIRITUAL
AUTHORITY WHO PRESENTS THE TRUTH
TO PEOPLE AND SUGGESTS A COURSE
OF ACTION WHILE TRYING TO MAKE
ACCURATE PREDICTIONS CONCERNING
THEIR FUTURE.

❋❋❋❋❋❋❋❋❋❋❋

# CHAPTER FOUR
## TECHNIQUES FOR THE
## TAROT CARD READER

### Preparing for a Card Reading

You must approach the Tarot reading with an open mind and heart and a readiness to accept the truth without fear. Never read the cards if you feel incompetent or anxious. Give readings only when you feel confident and have complete faith in the ability of the cards to clearly define the people, activities, and potential concerns and problems that are brought to the reading. If you sit down to read when you are afraid, depressed, or in a negative mood, the reading will reflect your dark projections. Ironically, when you are feeling down, that's usually when you need a reading the most!

Do whatever is takes to reach a calm and mellow state of mind before you read the cards. To find the answers you seek, you need to reach into the depths of your being and lock into a higher wavelength, where your senses are alert and aligned with a favored source of ancient wisdom. Some card readers meditate, breathe deeply, do yoga, or pray in order to achieve a relaxed but heightened consciousness. The most powerful and accurate readings occur when you are energetic, inspired, and at peace with yourself. The more positivity you bring to the reading, the more intelligible, helpful, and right on the information will be that you receive. Of course, you may have to read cards for someone when you do not want to, so go with the flow and trust the Tarot to provide healing on all levels—hopeful messages as well as unavoidable truths.

The mood of the reader and the atmosphere of the reading influence the depth and accuracy of the message in the cards. Try to be in an environment that is free from disturbance. If you find yourself reading for reluctant inquirers, do not try to convince them of the validity of the reading. If they are skeptical or testy—do not worry—relax and the reading will be educational for both of you. If their questions are ridiculous or they ask for lottery numbers or want to know when someone is going to die, you have the right to not read for them. It seems that more spiritually advanced people are the easiest to read for, as they are in touch with the hidden momentum of the forces at work shaping their lives. Thoughtful, growthful people tend to live in alignment with the highest principles and have historically sought out insight through intuitive readings.

As you speak, the inquirer listens to everything you say, even if he or she does not seem to be paying attention. Do not be overly concerned by any lack of reaction. Concentrate on your interpretation of the cards and do your best. Accept that the cards always discuss events and attitudes that are hitting home on conscious or subconscious levels. Also remember that the inquirer is eagerly listening for what he or she wants to hear, and if you see obvious signs of dissatisfaction with the reading, do not be discouraged. The wisdom brought forward through the Tarot will expand in significance as the future unfolds, though it is important to keep in mind that the beginning reader will find limits to the amount of information available without total reliance on the card definition section of this book.

It is a huge moral responsibility to set yourself up as a spiritual authority who presents the truth to people and suggests a course of action while trying to make accurate predictions concerning their future. Reading for others is all about helping them gain an understanding of what is going on behind the scenes of their lives, and that should always be your foremost reason for becoming a Tarot card reader.

✶✶✶✶✶✶✶✶✶✶✶✶

THE ULTIMATE TRANSFORMATION IS
ACCEPTING THE TRUTHS SPOKEN BY
YOUR INNER VOICE.

✶✶✶✶✶✶✶✶✶✶✶✶

## *The Hazards of Speculation*

One of the major dangers of card reading occurs when readers consciously or unconsciously project aspects of their own lives into a reading they are giving for an inquirer. Inexperienced card readers often make this error and should not read for the general public until they become more detached from their own emotions and more skillful with their deck. All Tarot readers have to be careful not to invent information that is not directly related to the meaning of the cards as they fall in the spread positions. Unfortunately, some readers invent material to tell the inquirer when their mind goes blank during a reading, and they quickly think up something to say in order to fill the awkward silence. These false interpretations can render a reading nonsensical and can destroy the uplifting nature of the reading. If you encounter this problem, simply look up either the love, money, or spiritual definition phrases that correspond to the card in the chapter entitled "The 78 Tarot Cards and Their Romantic, Financial, and Spiritual Interpretations," where you can always find the right words to describe any card as it applies to the matter under examination.

Reading the Tarot requires intuition and imagination to unlock its system. Because the Tarot is inventive by nature, you are constantly walking the thin line between fantasy and reality due to the mysterious symbolism of the cards. Stop yourself from being manipulative or control- ling when you read for others, as that lowly

\*\*\*\*\*\*\*\*\*\*\*\*
**THERE ARE NO ROAD MAPS TO OR FROM THE HEART.**
\*\*\*\*\*\*\*\*\*\*\*\*

behavior is not suitable for a real Tarot reading. Your innate goal should be to expand your authentic understanding of the cards through sincere, fulfilling readings that inspire you and satisfy those who are ultimately helped by your accurate inside information.

## How Often Should the Cards Be Read?

Another precarious situation arises when you read the cards too often. If you constantly read about the same subject, you may fail to correlate what comes to pass in your life with read- ings that you have given because of information overload. When you read too frequently, the power of the reading is diluted, and your ability to pick out the incidents, people, and activities that the cards refer to gets muddled because you are flooding your mind with endless and ultimately pointless spreads. The Grand Cross Spread uses II cards whose interpre- tation should be enough for one day of Tarot work.

When you begin to read, you should ascertain the subject- combination of the reading using the significator and then throw a Grand Cross Spread once a day. This will help you maintain a balanced perspective on reality and assist you in doing readings that give correct predictions for the future as well as truthful assessments of the past and present. Weekly, try some of the other Tarot spreads found in this book, such as the Three Card; As Above, So Below; or Problem/Solution spreads. Utilize the Soul Mate Search and the Master spreads more rarely and read the Astrological and Lifetimes spreads only once a year.

When you are new to the Tarot, it is helpful to read regularly if you can handle it and it does not interfere with your daily activities or blot out the more rational faculties of your intellect. You know you have overdone your readings when your interpretations get mixed up and your predictions become messy. You can grow confused about who or what the steady successions of pips, court cards, and trumps symbolize in your life. If you repeatedly ask the same question of your deck, each successive spread on the same subject defeats the austere clarity and poignancy that one single spread could offer you. Use repetitive spreads only when you are in control of your card-reading skills and need more information on a particularly prominent card or to expand on an aspect of a previous spread. The original reading is always easier to decipher and apply to the comings and goings of your life, because focusing on one or two spreads gives you just enough material to form a story.

If in desperation you throw spread after spread, the truth of the reading will become so weak as to demoralize you or disappoint your inquirer. If you have done readings repeatedly, put your deck away and wait awhile before attempting another reading. Break your Tarot card routine and return to making completely conscious choices without the assistance of any divinatory tools. You need to reaffirm your self-reliance and let life pass by without the constant crutch of doing Grand Cross Spreads over and over until neither the cards nor the spreads make sense. It is infinitely better to study the Tarot slowly and surely, using this book as your guide, and do a moderate number of readings to master the Tarot system.

## How Long Does a Reading Take to Come True?

One of the most commonly asked questions is when will a reading become reality. Readings vary in how long they take to come true. Often you find that a reading will last until the next time you read on the same subject. Sometimes you receive a lifetime reading that totally examines the complete range of what will happen to you as your destiny unfolds. The cards most often symbolize what you can expect to have happen until a successive reading on the identical topic, though there are no set boundaries around how long information derived from a reading will apply to your life. If you are doing the cards too frequently, it becomes extremely difficult to ascertain what is really going on because you are not giving the cards enough time to come true. It is best not to be so overly concerned with when events will occur in the future; instead, study the cards and wait to see what materializes. Note the conspicuous cards that surface in the past when you choose to examine the same issue.

## The Timing of Events

Ascertaining the correct timing of future events is a huge problem with Tarot readings. The most irresponsible thing a reader can do is give dates that do not deliver. Sometimes the nine days a reader tells you that an event will occur can turn into nine years! Often predictions can take years to

✽✽✽✽✽✽✽✽✽✽✽✽
THE PURE OF HEART HAVE AN INBORN
LOVE OF HUMANITY.
✽✽✽✽✽✽✽✽✽✽✽✽

materialize because the inquirer is slow to make the personal changes that would lead to a fulfillment of the prognostication. Always be more general when stating for a fact when something will happen. Study the cards whose definitions relate to matters of timing in the section of this book entitled "Tarot Cards with Similar Meanings." The Chariot, the Wheel, the ace and eight of wands, the Knight of wands, the Knight of swords, the ace and the six of swords, and the Page of swords are cards that indicate a faster speed of activity. Temperance, the ace, two, and seven of disks, the Universe, and the eight of swords are usually signs of delay. Some card readers like to attribute one day to the aces, two days to the twos, and so on in the minor arcana, but it is rare that a prediction can be so easy. Only give specific dates when you are totally sure at a gut level that you are right.

If you insist on determining when a matter will happen in actuality, you need to look at the cards that fall in the future placements of a spread that reflect what will occur later on. Cards in impending positions always seem strange, because what is yet to come is unknown at the time of the reading or has not been decided upon by the principal players represented by the court cards in the spread.

## What If a Reading Does Not Make Sense?

Sometimes readings do not make sense, but they are usually unbearably correct and informative as they give you the inside story on any subject you wish to explore. Some readings do not come true, and others are extremely difficult to interpret. This occurs when your mood is off or the cards are functioning at a level you cannot decipher at the time of the reading.

Readings can fail when you are reading for inquirers who are afraid of the cards because they have no knowledge of the Tarot or have been exposed to the negative cartoon imagery of card readers. Some people are so undeveloped spiritually that they cannot understand the language you are using to explain their reading. This makes it even more impossible for you to give them a proper reading, and it is best to abandon the idea of doing cards for such individuals unless you can handle criticism that could interrupt your careful synthesis of the spread and its components. The only solution to the challenge of reading for a reluctant inquirer is to delineate the spread in the simplest of terms.

❋❋❋❋❋❋❋❋❋❋

YOUR POSITIVE ATTITUDE AND SENSE OF CERTAINTY ABOUT YOUR UNIQUE DESTINY LEADS YOU ALONG A PATH OF EXPERIENCE HARMONIOUS TO THE NEEDS OF YOUR INNER SELF.

❋❋❋❋❋❋❋❋❋❋

## Hints for Interpretation

When you begin to read the cards, you have a fixed notion of what each card symbolizes, courtesy of the card definitions in this book. Do not be put off because every card has so many love, money, and spiritual meanings. These different facets of their meanings and explanatory portrayals are not contradictory, but are actually complementary to each other. Each card has a wide range of interpretations that share a similar conceptual base because of the overall ideas and images associated with the card. As you read through the descriptive paragraphs that correspond to each of the love, money, and spiritual definitions of each card, you will easily choose which phrase best illustrates what that card means in the spread position in terms of what is happening in your life. Keep mentally scanning the lists of phrases until you find the ones that fit into the subject matter of the reading and make perfect sense to you.

Once the cards are shuffled and dealt into the spread positions, you can create an interesting commentary on the entire picture of what the spread signifies. Look at the spread placement and blend it together with the definition of the card that lands there, which you can look up in this book. Eventually, you will commit the meanings of the cards to memory and rely on the book less and less when giving a reading.

If you have specific questions for the Tarot deck, you can omit the search for the significator through the subject piles. There is no need to pinpoint what the reading will explore because you are set on finding out more about a particular matter, rather than getting an overall analysis of your entire existence. If you want a picture of the general forces that are influencing your reality, stick with the subject-combination step at the beginning of the reading, as described in Chapter 3 of this book.

## The Questioning Process

The questioning process has everything to do with how you interpret the cards. By formulating empowering inquiries, you can have more fulfilling and accurate readings. The Tarot provides the true details that are not readily available elsewhere, and the key to stimulating the investigation is to make your query as clear as possible. Decide ahead of time what you want to ask the cards before you begin shuffling. Interrogating the

deck with questions is the
heart of the reading, and it
helps if you are specific
with your inquiries. When
you are extremely emotional about the subject of the

✸✸✸✸✸✸✸✸✸✸✸
TRYING TO UNDERSTAND THE MEANING
BEHIND YOUR DESTINY LEADS
TO GREATER WISDOM.

✸✸✸✸✸✸✸✸✸✸✸

reading, be more passive and less victimized about what you
ask the deck; request guidance about what you should do or
how you can best prepare for future developments. Being less
fatalistic always helps you get a clearer reading. Remember, the
main line of thought before spreading the cards should be: Why
am I in this position now, where do I need to go, and what
adventures will I encounter along the way? The Tarot cards in
the spread represent people and events that move you forward
as the Fool with total trust in the universe.

Here are some sample questions that are most commonly
posed to the deck:
What is going to happen to me regarding the area of my life
as defined by the subject-combination of the reading?
Who is this person in my life?
What should my attitude be toward this person?
What is the best way to act in this situation?
At what stage is my relationship with a certain individual?
Does he have anything to do with my future?
Will I get the business deal?
Will I be successful with a particular project?
Is it worth taking this trip?
How can I make more money?
Is this a safe investment?
How long will it take to sell my property, and will I get my
asking price?

How can I find a more satisfying career?

What should I do to find my soul mate?

How old is my future mate and what does he do for a living?

When will I meet someone new?

Will he call?

What is he thinking of me?

Will I ever get married?

Will I ever have children, and how many?

Who is he sleeping with?

What is the best way to approach this person or situation?

What does this person think about me romantically?

Will he leave his wife or girlfriend?

Will I see him today?

What is his basic psychosexual orientation?

Will he evolve and change?

If I move, where should I go, and will the location be right for me?

Should I continue with school?

What is the spiritual lesson behind this situation?


## *Throwing Consecutive Spreads*

If a card is surprisingly prominent when you throw the Grand Cross Spread in response to a specific question, and you want to examine it further, go right into a brand-new Grand Cross. Gather up the cards and reshuffle the entire deck while mentally asking who or what this particular card represents. The second Grand Cross Spread would define what you can expect from the involvement of this card in the drama of your life. Asking a long series of questions and throwing a spread to answer each of them can be highly illuminating detective work.

It is easier to do consecutive spreads if the first spread does not make sense or you posed a precise inquiry to the deck at the beginning of the reading. The Grand Cross is the best spread to use for clarifying the message of the spread, but you could also try the Problem/Solution; Three Card; and As Above, So Below layouts found in the Tarot spread section of this book.

## Looking for Indicator Cards

Indicator cards are those that are constantly prominent in your spreads whose presence helps you identify what person or event is going to manifest what the cards are talking about in reality. Tarot cards move around in the time sequences of the spread positions, forming logical patterns that reflect what is happening. If you throw a Grand Cross on Monday and the Hierophant or Jupiter is your outcome, and by Thursday the same card surfaces as your self card, you can assume that whatever the Hierophant symbolizes has gone from being a goal to becoming part of your personality in how you approach the issue of the reading. Another example would be the King of wands as your first of the future on Monday, and by Thursday, he is in the last of the present position. The cards are saying that in just a few days you encountered the person or situation that the King of wands symbolizes in both readings. Or the Tower appears for several weeks every time you do the cards and always in a future placement of the Grand Cross. Then, suddenly, a totally shocking truth is revealed to you at the same time that the Tower begins to show up in present tense positions in the spread. One day a woman can get the two of cups as her future environment even though at the time of the reading her life seems pretty loveless; but with the King of disks as her first of the future placement you can be sure of the type of man she will meet.

✣✣✣✣✣✣✣✣✣✣

FOLLOW YOUR OWN INNER VOICE BY SURRENDERING TO THE DIVINE.

✣✣✣✣✣✣✣✣✣✣

Tarot cards can also disappear from your readings altogether, and you realize, for example, that the Emperor or the Empress has not been in your cards for months. When you finish interpreting any spread, glance over it, and mentally tally how many swords, disks, cups, wands, court cards, and trumps are present in its design. Also, if the spread lacks a certain type of card, it would indicate that your life in terms of the subject of the reading is deficient in the missing element. For example, no swords would signal that your intellectual functions are not being used to solve the situation that the reading characterizes; no trumps would emphasize a lack of spiritual significance in the matter that the reading examines.

## *Achieving Greater Accuracy with a Reading*

Being an accurate card reader is your first responsibility and because hearts and minds change every day, readings can lose their validity quite quickly. Some days your intuition is dead on and other days you do not have a clue as to what the cards mean. Also, Tarot gives you a greater range of options to choose from and is never the final word. Even if a reading is not one hundred percent right on, it still helps you see things from a more spiritualized angle. Often a reading reflects what you want at that time; for example, one day you are madly in

love with a guy and he is
all over your cards and
then you begin to detest
him and he disappears
from your cards. Your
inner intention pulled

✳✳✳✳✳✳✳✳✳✳✳✳

A GOOD RELATIONSHIP UPLIFTS YOUR
VIBRATION AND IS HEALING TO THE
ENTIRE PLANET.

✳✳✳✳✳✳✳✳✳✳✳✳

him into your Tarot readings because you thought you loved
him, but you were wrong about your own feelings.

Confidence in your own inner authority is crucial to giving
readings that come true, and a good interpretation should tell
you what you already know anyway. It also helps to maintain a
level of purity and honesty and avoid the impulse to control the
cards and only hear what you want to hear. We all want to
believe readings when they tell us only good things. Every card
reader should give the same identical information to any one
individual, and if you spent a thousand dollars going to ten
readers, they should all tell you the same thing. There is only
one truth available at any one given moment and your objective is to go to that source for your predictions. If one reader
tells you she sees a husband and children for you and another
insists you will be childless, then somebody is obviously wrong.
Once you believe the forecast of a reader, you have already
altered your future. Do not place too much value on readings
and never make life-changing decisions based only on the
words of a psychic. Listen to what the reader says, weed out
what is obviously wrong, see what happens in reality, and then
make your big choices. It is not recommended that you seek out
romantic advice from a reader who is down on men or obviously psychologically imbalanced.

## Why Is It Hard to Read Your Own Cards?

This is by far the number one complaint lodged by card readers everywhere. It is so bad a problem that many incredible Tarot readers who read with authority for others, have to seek out the advice of another intuitive for confirmation of what is already in their cards. The worst objectivity, of course, comes when you read your own cards about love. It is just the hardest thing to do and yet reading for yourself is how you learn about the cards. It is nearly impossible to get an unbiased opinion from the cards because you are so busy projecting what you want to have happen.

This difficulty seems epidemic and rarely does the reader exist who is capable of analyzing his or her own love life as romantic matters mess with the logical mind. Instead of questioning the deck to death about some guy who you desire as a potential partner, if you throw the Moon, Devil, and Magician trumps or the three, nine, and ten of swords or the five and Knight of cups—the guy is not happening! If you remain attracted to him after the reading, why bother with the Tarot? The signs are too clear that he is a mess!

The best advice seems to be to approach a reading as a detached, passive agent and adopt an emotional distance toward the person or the issue. Surrender to the universe and ask what you need to do to meet the right person or how you can best deal with someone you are already involved with. And, of course, the number one question of all time is: when will he call? No matter how evolved the woman, and how in control of her life she may be, almost everyone asks this at least one time per reading.

**All relationship lessons help you further understand your ever-developing love nature.**

# CHAPTER FIVE
## THE 78 TAROT CARDS AND THEIR ROMANTIC, FINANCIAL, AND SPIRITUAL INTERPRETATIONS

## THE SWORDS

### Ace of Swords

The ace of swords symbolizes the power of a directed mind. All ideas are consolidated into one major line of thought, as you make a firm decision concerning the subject of the reading. By relying on your own judgement, you confront opposing opinions and create a clear channel between thought and action. You know what you want and how to proceed with any matter to champion your own interests and move forward on the clearest path to your future.

*R*omance:
   deciding to look for someone new * letting yourself believe in love again * old ways of thinking about relationships must go * breaking out of antiquated behavioral patterns * getting over the past * exploring dating opportunities through increased socializing * dealing with early psychological issues by clearing your life of ambivalent men * a piece of truth illuminates your vision of him * telling him exactly what is on your mind * making your own plans regardless of him * beginning or ending a

relationship with a man based on an intellectual decision ✳ letting him know verbally how you feel about him ✳ he decides to move forward with you ✳ both of you are certain about starting up a romance ✳ he knows exactly what he wants to do with you ✳ he could contact you at the beginning of the day, month, or year in question ✳ he is going to give you important information ✳ establishing a home together ✳ preparing a leading question to ask him next time you speak with him

## *Work & Business:*

following a predetermined career no matter what the cost ✳ being motivated to move forward ✳ business ideas will come to you directly ✳ wanting to make a deal really badly ✳ pushing your agenda through regardless of any opposition ✳ influencing others at work by communicating exactly how you think ✳ trying to figure your way in or out of a deal ✳ breaking the news about a project in the best possible way ✳ announcing a new career direction ✳ getting rid of burdensome employees ✳ eliminating unnecessary expenses ✳ cutting back on overhead and superfluous perks ✳ deciding to go for the gold ✳ entering a new cycle of determination ✳ developing a futuristic facet of an existing business ✳ setting your purpose and establishing career goals and direction ✳ the time draws near for a new job ✳ calling on clients early and often ✳ moving quickly to accomplish certain tasks ✳ possessing enough confidence to feel capable of achievement ✳ receiving new and obvious perceptions about a definite career goal

## *Spiritual Growth:*

learning how to live in the present ✳ trying to concentrate by centering your conscious powers ✳ believing in your ability to generate positive change in your environment ❋ getting your head together after a confusing period of time ❋ struggling to be more honest and true to your word ❋ seeing the obvious path before you and following it ❋ staying optimistic and proceeding energetically in the right direction ❋ following a cherished dream ❋ making the right decisions to accelerate spiritual growth ❋ by choosing a higher path you always win ❋ breaking with an entire karmic group ❋ being able to completely own your own information ❋ beginning an investigation into a religious or spiritual tradition ❋ taking a giant leap forward in consciousness ❋ giving up that which holds you back spiritually ❋ mentally preparing for immersion into a field of metaphysical study ❋ losing your sense of feeling separate from others ❋ a message from the universal source gets through to you ❋ thinking about joining a formal group with whom you share a similar ideology

## Two of Swords

The two is a quiet card where you uphold the decision of the ace of swords. It represents reliance on blind faith to deliver a preferred result in a matter at a time when nothing seems to be happening. This card urges you to trust in your power of concentration to reach a goal and apply yourself with intense certainty about what will occur in the future.

## Romance:

feeling relaxed when you are single because you are at a place of peace within yourself ❋ being absolutely convinced that you will meet the perfect person when the time is right ❋

knowing that your love life will improve no matter how long the wait ✳ holding out until somebody worthy shows romantic interest in you ✳ to initiate change in an existing relationship stay put and keep your insights to yourself ✳ slow surrender to a realization about a guy ✳ taking time to find out what he wants ✳ not forcing any issues when he is not verbally forthcoming about his feelings ✳ he may be open mentally to what you are saying but he is hiding his feelings ✳ a relationship without emotional content ✳ listening quietly to your lover as a sign of true friendship ✳ wondering if two people can ever really trust each other ✳ a relationship that preserves the independence and individuality of the couple ✳ staying alert during a period when he is testing you ✳ feeling as though you have nothing to say to him ✳ realizing that he has not shown interest yet ✳ meeting of the minds in a romantic arena ✳ forcing yourself not to lose faith in him ✳ understanding that trust takes time ✳ sharing the same values and beliefs as him ✳ getting to know him first as a friend for self-protection

## Work & Business:

hesitating about moving forward with a project ✳ waiting until the pieces fall into place ✳ supporting a business venture before you know if it is genuine or not ✳ waiting to hear about a job, school, or project acceptance ✳ holding out until you know how to proceed during a time of very little activity ✳ internally preparing for future manifestations of business plans ✳ adopting an unwavering belief about your business potential ✳ carrying on with self-confidence when there is no real evidence of success ✳ going through the motions to launch a project even though funds are not available ✳ upholding your deepest dreams and beliefs about your creative abilities ✳ people working together based on principles of trust * being awfully quiet about your finances * knowing you have strong guidance concerning your outer world destiny * staying positive and concentrating on the results you want even if the inherent business structure does not exist yet

## *Spiritual Growth:*

listening to your inner voice and the timing of its revelations * a profoundly moving soul experience * living on faith and a prayer * making a decision to take a break and gain clarity by doing your spiritual work * controlling your thought patterns * replacing negative attitudes with more positive, hopeful projections * exercising vigilance over your darker emotions * being honest with yourself and not avoiding personal issues * mastering the balance of spiritual and material life * having extremely high ideals * making peace with the reality you have created * astral travel * a clear telepathic connection with another * two people who share the same religious beliefs based on faith and patience * removing the concepts of time and space from your conscious reality * prayer gives people urges and guidance leading them in the right direction * spiritual practices that encourage your ability to detach emotionally * developing integrity of soul * gleaning knowledge from other realms in quiet meditation

## Three of Swords

The three of swords introduces emotional depth to the intellectual world. This card traditionally represents a physical separation that leads to a lack of communication between two people and creates sensitive feelings bordering on self-pity, sorrow, and despair.

### Romance:

wanting more from a situation than he is willing to give * having trouble being apart from your sweetheart * in a place or situation where the beloved one is absent * love elates us when shared and destroys us when unrequited * realizing that a guy cannot care easily or normally * falling in love with someone who does not exist * watching a relationship go bad from too much physical separation * being totally hurt and disgusted by his behavior toward you * game playing during courtship based on pain, fear, rejection, and intentional misunderstandings * faithless people shock your personal integrity * being romantically drawn to someone who most certainly will deeply affect you and may break your heart * his psychological damage prevents him from believing in relationships * realizing that he has absolutely no experience in love * he may be having trouble locating or reaching you * he is sad because he cannot be with you and misses you * becoming attracted to someone who has suffered much internal turmoil * childhood heartbreak and abandonment issues preventing intimacy * he suddenly rejects you and is no longer available * still being deeply affected by someone on an emotional level * becoming vulnerable due to your feelings for him * sadly recognizing that you must end a relationship with great reservations

# Work & Business:

job loss ＊ being laid off at work ＊ moving to a new job location ＊ losing coworkers with whom you are extremely close ＊
somebody is fired who you depend on for support ＊ a job that
is physically isolating due to either the hours or location ＊ missing the camaraderie of others while working out of the home ＊
being hard-pressed to find anything beneficial in a business
deal ＊ having trouble believing anything good will ever happen
＊ a business person does not return your phone calls ＊ a job is
like doing penance to you ＊ releasing personal sorrow through
mindless activity at work ＊ turning into a workaholic to avoid
the challenge of romantic intimacy ＊ the right road in business
is often the hard road ＊ having ambitions to help heal all the
suffering in the world ＊ assisting the poor in society, whether it
is the hungry and the homeless, orphans, refugees, or those
generally disenfranchised ＊ a card of music, poetry, and the
written word inspired by a true love of humanity ＊ emotionally cathartic, creative work that changes the lives of its audience
＊ aspects of entertainment businesses that deal with caring for
the planet and its people ＊ fundraising events and charitable
work that benefits those in need

# Spiritual Growth:

being tuned in to the suffering of humanity ＊ time is volun-
teered to take care of others ＊ having compassion for those you
meet in your day-to-day reality ＊ healing misunderstandings
with others by apologizing to them ＊ creating a lifestyle that
reflects the true you ＊ letting go of people who hurt your feelings and delay your spiritual growth as a happy person ＊ soulful melancholy based on heavy thoughts about the troubled
state of the world ＊ difficult periods when karmic debts come
knocking ＊ the hurt you have inflicted on others comes back to

you * problems in this lifetime as a result of misuse of others in your past * a new level of vulnerability emerges after a grueling ordeal * having a tough time during a spiritual transition * harboring grief based on an unrequited relationship compels you to do inner work * sorrow in this lifetime connected to losing the love of your life in the past * deep acts of betrayal that place your soul in despair * having trouble imagining who will rescue you from the karma of a broken heart * thoughts of life being over * feeling alone, unloved, and abandoned * wondering how you will find the spiritual strength to carry on * weeping as a form of soul purification * loss of a loved one sends you on a new religious or spiritual journey

## Four of Swords

The four of swords represents withdrawal from social activity in order to experience uninterrupted thought as an exercise to strengthen your own viewpoint on any given matter. Through this sword, you gain mental clarity and become intellectually certain of how to proceed after this silent and serious time.

### Romance:

realizing this is not the time for a relationship in your life * using the solitude available to casually review the learning experiences from past romances * thinking a lot about the who, what, where, when, and why of your requirements in a man * breaking out of a period of being alone * waiting to discover whether a friendship will evolve into a love affair * thinking through a potential commitment to someone about whom you are uncertain ✳ you need to get a clearer picture of what exactly is going on with him ✳ he may require time to organize his thoughts and feelings about you ✳ his complete silence and absence may be an indication that he currently has nothing to talk about ✳ he is quietly analyzing his position with you ✳ leaving a relationship for awhile ✳ time spent alone for a couple ✳ the value of reflection while being apart ✳ retreating from him to avoid emotional collapse ✳ he may be totally holding himself back ✳ he is not discussing you with anyone ✳ a warning against interfering with his current relationship if he is not available ✳ healing him of his sense of isolation and loneliness is a possibility if he has emotional breakthroughs ✳ rethinking your priorities ✳ wondering whether he is truly worth the effort ✳ marriage based on friendship only and not a sexually active union

## Work & Business:

sorting out career options and choices ✳ setting your mind straight on business plans ✳ can indicate a period of unemployment where you spend a lot of time at home ✳ work that physically isolates you ✳ a deal may be on hold and you should use this break to reevaluate your plans ✳ getting into a thinking zone will help you to discover business solutions ✳ sorting out your strategy in order to be in the right position financially ✳ holding onto your savings ✳ trying to reserve as much cash as possible while negotiating a deal ✳ somebody is not telling you everything about their economic situation ✳ withdrawing an offer ✳ your vision of a project is limited because all of the data is not in yet ✳ retirement and consideration of business activities in your later years

## Spiritual Growth:

retreating into the sanctity of your own self ❋ a period of spiritual seclusion ❋ dropping out of society in terms of a chosen lifestyle ❋ working to heal and balance your soul ❋ making space in your life for quiet and meditation ❋ realizing that the answers are within you ❋ focusing your conscious psychic powers on a given effect ❋ days of listening only to the inner workings of your mind ❋ lacking distractions that intrude upon your concentration from the world of reality ❋ solitary times strengthen the soul ❋ ultimately, in the end, we are all alone, in silence ❋ confinement is necessary for recovery or convalescence ❋ sitting still and detaching your intellect from your body during prayer or meditation ❋ having the ability to control your thought-form projections ❋ creating effect from the silence of sanctuary where you pull yourself together into a stable mental state

## Five of Swords

The five of swords challenges you to recognize your own truth regardless of what others may think. By relying on the opinions of your inner dialogue, you will come to dominate your turf and make absolute decisions. As a card of deliberation and discrimination, this sword helps you consider the views of others without weakening your own intellectual force.

## Romance:

being attracted to someone who is your opposite ❋ scheming and head games as a part of courtship ❋ somebody you rely on will not come through in the end ⁂ the necessity of compromise in a relationship ⁂ fighting with him over who is right ⁂ bickering every day and having communication problems with him ⁂ deciding you do not want to live his life or deal with his people ⁂ carrying around anger toward him and projecting it onto others ⁂ how you see him interacting with others is not of your own integrity ⁂ his controlling nature and competitive attitude toward you is suffocating ⁂ only the couple knows what is really happening ⁂ he is being fed information about you from others ⁂ he may be using your mutual friends to spy on you ⁂ he may be inquiring about you behind your back ⁂ other people oppose the relationship and he listens to their opinions ⁂ meddling friends and family members tell you he is not right for you ⁂ do not believe the gossip you hear about him ⁂ juggling more than one lover at the same time and hoping nobody finds out ⁂ fighting is creating serious intimacy problems between you ⁂ letting him talk though whatever he says will not improve relations ⁂ relying on hearsay during dating to gain an understanding of his feelings for you ⁂ getting rid of bogus people who are trying to come between you ⁂ having to ignore sexist remarks ⁂ his self-centered approach to life ignores your emotional needs ⁂ deciding whether he is truly worth the effort

## *W*ork & *B*usiness:

financial problems are driving you crazy ⁂ do not participate in office gossip or politics ⁂ keep your eyes and ears open and your mouth shut ⁂ time constrictions may prevent you from completing a project ⁂ hassles and fights with coworkers ⁂ seeking an office atmosphere that is conducive to mental clarity ⁂ not working a normal nine-to-five job ⁂ figuring your way out of an aggravating misunderstanding with an employer ⁂ back stabbing, double-crossing colleagues ⁂ rumors of mergers, layoffs and buyouts breed distrust amongst workers * someone is calling your bluff during negotiations * questioning the validity of a business deal * uncertainty about a source of future earnings * not hearing what you want about a business deal * experiencing an erosion in your share of the market * disappointing news may or may not be true * deciding against the grain of the suggestions of others * what you do is controversial in the eyes of the status quo * a standoff that makes it impossible for you to proceed in any one direction * discord needs to be replaced with harmony, cooperation, and teamwork * learning to say no to people and activities that waste your time and creative energy * how other people do things as opposed to how you do things * you must tell someone the score to advance * as an employer, laying down the laws of expected behavior with employees

## Spiritual Growth:

standing up to others who question your spiritual ideology * if you are not being honest with yourself, expect some mental instability * living a lie is painful * pretending to follow a traditional religion, but your heart is not in it * finding your own path and truth * someone is challenging your belief system * accepting that you cannot help someone you care about evolve spiritually * removing all obstacles to personal growth * letting go of those who refuse to understand your point of view * feeling a lack of compassion from those closest to you * changing religious affiliations * not caring what others think about the spiritual teachings or traditions you enjoy * not following the religious upbringing of your childhood * stop listening to the prognostications of others * get rid of gurus, psychics, psychiatrists, counselors, and religious leaders who no longer serve your personal growth * trying to avoid sociopathological tendencies in yourself * having trouble playing by the rules spiritually * understanding the moral shortcomings of others without taking their behavior personally * staying away from those who play destructive mind games * learning to have stronger mental boundaries with those who act against you

## Six of Swords

The appearance of this sword rushes you forward, swiftly and easily, on a solo journey along the pathways toward your goals. You possess all the necessary information and connections to create a strong network of people, activities, and communications that supports your personal evolution.

## Romance:

after a period of confusion in your love life, you begin to think clearly again * starving to death for intellectual union with another * being able to speak freely with your lover * a relationship that is easy from the start * past misunderstandings clear up * the courtship moves in the right direction at the proper place and the perfect time * instant rapport with another due to similar interests * sharing creative and cultural tastes with him * retaining your own mental space within a relationship can be taken for granted * a couple achieves excellence through clear channels of communication * you are closer to him than anyone else in your life * you have told him all of the details about your past and have no reason to ever lie * the way that he relates to you is the most important indicator of future happiness * the more information he gives you, the more easily you can begin to relax and trust him * the sooner he confides in you the better * he has reached the point where he is ready to tell you everything * if he is attached, part of his plan has been to cross over to you * he is completely aware that he needs you * he wishes to create a more formal union * if you tell him honestly what you require, he will meet your demands * maybe you are both thinking the same thing * he has covered the territory in his mind already * he will definitely call or contact you soon * you may be traveling to where he lives or meeting him in another location * he may invite you on a vacation and make the journey easy for you * he is telling everyone about you in the most respectable way * a relationship that is so effortless, there is no turning back

## Work & Business:

deals move forward easily * people arrive to assist you with business plans exactly when you need them * maintain a positive attitude toward future prospects * talking to the right person will lead you to good information * having to travel for work * a new position opens up at your current job * possessing the right background and training for a career promotion * being the connecting force for a group collaborating on a project * increasing earnings by going back to school to learn about new technology * anything and everything to do with computers * breaking out on your own by starting a new business * setting up an efficient system for financial records * income correlated to technical skills * somebody clearly got your message * business ideas derived from the influence of a great conversation * mental breakthroughs help to improve your attitude toward your job * easy communication of data * you know where a project is headed and who else is involved * writing

and lecturing or attending or giving workshops ❋ a conference
or retreat that is career-related

*Spiritual Growth:*
   studying a wide range of belief systems ❋ spiritual travel you
make on your own can represent a turning point in terms of
spiritual commitment ❋ making a decision to take a particular
course of training ❋ feeling a sense of belonging amongst kindred spirits ❋ receiving the exact universal guidance that you
need ❋ networking with those of similar beliefs ❋ using all of
your divine senses ❋ an easy journey in consciousness ❋ feeling
better about yourself and your position in life ❋ old memories
that hold back your development fade at last ❋ conscious technology ❋ beingness enters the hi-tech world ❋ using the Internet
to search for information on healing, religion, and spirituality
❋ intricate intellectual systems that delineate universal force ❋
taking off by yourself to explore interests ❋ visiting locations
that are dear to your soul ❋ formalized prayers, mantras, sacred
books, and texts as well as oral religious traditions passed
down through the generations ❋ inner journeys launched that
help you listen to and receive guidance ❋ consciousness expansion ❋ total awareness of past life experiences ❋ physical movement that leads to a healing on all levels ❋ increased mental
powers ❋ the path of least resistance is always the best path ❋
rushing forward on the quickest roadway to your spiritual goals
❋ enlightenment grants the ability to read the unwritten books
of primordial history

## Seven of Swords

This is the card of the individual, the eccentric, and the iconoclast as the mind here is liberated to pursue original or unusual intellectual paths. You have the freedom to express your own ideas and ideals regardless of opposing societal conditions or opinions, and by challenging the status quo, you find security in your own viewpoint.

*R*omance:

being attracted to wild, offbeat, radical, activist, or counterculture characters * he has his own way of doing things in a relationship * his self-absorption may be a sign that he cannot achieve true intimacy * establishing your own identity in his world * he will always make his own interests paramount * a nontraditional commitment * an unconventional marriage * someone who loves you for who you are * he will not reject you if you respect his intellectual freedom and never censor him * at the initial meeting you connect in the most abstract manner * looking for a new type of relationship that may not be what anybody thinks * say it to him as you see it * try one more time with him, and if he says no, close the door * being with someone regardless of your marital or romantic status * his lack of feelings makes him no emotional prize * he is not classic marriage material * somebody who is all talk, no action * new attitudes changing a long-standing union * he could be taking a trip away alone * romantic dyslexia * erasing societal scripts that limit the development of a romance based on true love * he is living the way he wants to live * he has his own reasons for being rebellious

# Work & Business:

a self-made person who has not received help from anyone * wanting to pursue unorthodox dreams * desiring to be more of your real self at work * breaking away from the pack to try something different * staying true to yourself and keeping on course * inspiration and enthusiasm for a new career direction and purpose * unique applications of business principles * a project will develop differently than you think * not feeling compelled to follow tried and true methods * stalling for time on a project * structural reforms need to be implemented at work * feeling renewed ambition for a deal that is on hold * living by your own business code * alternative investments * operating an illegal business * keeping the details of a financial transaction to yourself * nothing is easy if you insist on following your own unique working arrangement * being extremely brilliant but confused about how to apply your intelligence * an activist, radical, or revolutionary person who initiates change through their occupation * eccentrics who express their true selves in a particular creative medium * nonconformists who achieve personal goals that highlight their own individuality * searching for unique solutions to the problems of the world

# Spiritual Growth:

living by a purely personal philosophy * liberation from old ways of thinking * not wanting to talk about inner changes you are experiencing * keeping spiritual information to yourself * being programmed against any one type of religion * owning your own brand of higher faith * restless souls who are ahead of their time * trusting in your personal method of healing * having the freedom to think for yourself * the liberation of spirit from the physical body * establishing an unusual moral code to live by * making your way down the road of evolutionary progress toward a greater knowledge of self * someone who operates inside and outside of a formal religious system * discovering your own interpretation of the universal law * release from a time period plagued by suffocating ethical hypocrisy * loss of people and responsibilities that are preventing your evolution * utilizing psychic self-defense * calling on the white light of protection as a force field when in challenging situations * misunderstood renegade spiritual or religious leaders who break from tradition * cosmic outlaws * underground theological movements * unusually small religious spinoffs * weird, obscure cults with eccentric or fanatical leaders * radical changes made to existing doctrines * unorthodox healing treatments * alternative medicine

## Eight of Swords

The eight of swords is a card of limited communication and interpersonal misunderstandings. This sword creates a predicament where your freedom of speech or movement is impaired and prevents you from taking action on a matter or receiving information that could help you move forward. Though this card implies restrictions, it also signals release from this isolating period of time.

## Romance:

trying desperately to trap a man * feeling as though you could be stuck with him at the same level forever * he may not know what to do about you for awhile * being enormously limited by the way you think about him * finally getting information about him that others have been keeping from you * he has been thinking about you but has not taken action yet * he had a lot of great ideas he presented to you that have fizzled out * meeting someone at the wrong time or when they are with another person * not being able to act out your feelings due to existential circumstances * he may be psychologically enmeshed with a crazy or unloving woman and needs to let her go * it is his loss if he cannot be kind * he has not realized yet that he can have you * choosing chaotic people as romantic partners * the full picture of the relationship needs to be revealed * he is having trouble moving forward and needs to liberate himself * your vision of him may be incomplete or warped * you have had enough of his convoluted behavior * your romantic problems are all in your head * how hard it is to rearrange your thoughts about a guy * releasing your fears of self-expression in relationships * coming through as a different person in how you handle men

## Work & Business:

getting ready to make important contacts or phone calls * rethinking your game plan * using your intellect to break through career limitations * a major issue is about to be resolved that will move the deal forward * the release of valuable information helps you resolve financial problems * plotting your way out of a business black hole * inner vision helps you see around corners in negotiations * feeling restricted at work * quietly ruminating strategies * waiting for the right time to strike * having trouble getting through to someone and then, suddenly, they become available * stepping back from a deal to await more favorable timing * keep your eyes and ears open so you do not miss the details * being set free from a project that is ruining your life * complications arise over utilizing good ideas * nothing happens prematurely with this card * stalemate broken * end of labor strike * fearing failure or that you will never be successful * a confusing career transition * check all messages and phone numbers twice for accuracy

## Spiritual Growth:

releasing yourself from a limited way of thinking * breaking free of those who hold back your personal growth * having trouble coping with reality * cleansing your physical body for a period of time * learning how to use different parts of your mind * you need a mental amputation or a brain transplant * obsessive compulsive disorders that compel the repetition of actions to fulfill uncontrollable impulses * opening up mentally to the highest truths of evolution * difficult times when you go within for clarity * soul boredom when nothing seems to happen * relying on your inner life when the outer world seems oppressive * pain leads to knowledge * confusion leads to clarity * anxiety leads to peace * the build-up to a spiritual wake-up call * avoiding getting sucked into the karma of another* not using higher principles in your life though you have knowledge of deep truths * letting others be themselves with their own beliefs * stop projecting your inner anxieties on others * feeling that real life is threatening and retreating into a world of fantasy or spirit * phobias are exaggerated fears about the future * getting ready to end a period of isolation * gaining complete liberation from an entire karmic trip * your spiritual development is on hold until you resolve certain issues blocking the evolution of your soul * being afraid of changing daily patterns that make you feel protected but trap you into a boring life * unrequited love as a religious icon * blinded by your love of a god or goddess * being surrounded by negative or hypocritical spiritual messages * learning about the enlightening value and uses of emotional detachment * becoming trapped in a cult-like group and having trouble seeing your way out clearly * abandonment or rejection by a religious group * the loneliness of the exile and the refugee apart from the land of their beliefs * not the greatest time for psychological clarity * opening up to people or groups who could help you organize your life

## Nine of Swords

This sword represents an overload of mental activity and increased intellectual sensitivity. The message here is to remain positive and strong even if you lack the support of others. The nine of swords teaches you to accept criticism without resorting to self-victimization and to use the verbal input of others to gain a greater awareness of your true self.

### Romance:

a private sense of shame due to a personal past * reviewing why you have feelings for broken men * damage attracts damage * the psychologically destructive nature of unrequited love * your mind is still stuck on your last relationship * an agonizing time of unsettled emotions * accepting that the person you love cannot change * an affair is causing extreme disturbance * the experience with him is not easy * being humiliated by his behavior toward you * a definite card of estrangement * a challenging time when your life is a mess * having stress-filled, sleepless nights due to him * doubt and confusion come up because you have trouble with the harsh aspects of his personality ✳ perpetually unsure if the two of you are on or off ✳ feeling guilty about dropping a guy who is mentally too far gone ✳ he projects his neuroses on you ✳ his pain is way too deep and may lead to cruel or potentially sadistic behavior ✳ both of you have been badly hurt by previous lovers ✳ he is emotionally defeated in a bad relationship with another ✳ he is afraid to sever his connection with a woman who will not let him go ✳ he chooses women who make him suffer ✳ he lies to hurt you and get a reaction from you ✳ a man who is cynical about marriage ✳ you need to let go of a union that is tearing you apart ✳ a guy is completely flipping out over you ✳ he secretly wonders whether he can handle falling in love ✳ wanting to wound him as you leave him behind ✳ it is hard to face being separated from the one you love ✳ realizing that you are infinitely smarter than him

## Work & Business:

business interactions with others are getting to you psychologically ✳ mean bosses or colleagues are causing problems for you ✳ you could be stabbed in the back over a deal ✳ a job that is no fun at all due to an environment of rivalry ✳ frying enemies in the world of finance ✳ using methods of abuse and humiliation to get what you want ✳ having a hidden lack of self-esteem regarding your performance ✳ the agony of sitting still and finishing a project on a 24-hour-a-day schedule ✳ exercising extreme caution in negotiations ✳ feeling as though the whole world is against you professionally ✳ making a commitment to a work-related opportunity that will force you to deal with unkind people, difficult circumstances, or a miserable location ✳ transforming emotional pain into a career that deals with processing the grief of others, like a priest, rabbi, shrink, or counselor ✳ worrying about manifesting income ✳ being scared to death about starting something new ✳ getting closer to gaining the information you need ✳ having a huge amount of work to do on a short deadline ✳ the business of intellectual properties

## *Spiritual Growth:*

thoughts overwhelm you on the limitations of earthly life ✳ feeling lost and helpless in the face of adversity ✳ wondering if you are losing your mind ✳ phobias that prevent you from living a normal life ✳ an extended time of emotional anxiety or panic attacks ✳ having trouble sleeping due to nightmares, trauma disorders, or physical pain ✳ nervous exhaustion ✳ the damage of stress ✳ depression ✳ glorified forms of self-mutilation ✳ someone who is moved sexually or psychologically by pain ✳ illness brought on by cruelty or abuse from others ✳ the onset of an episode of mental illness ✳ confronting personal demons during the dark night of the soul ✳ paranoid people are usually guilty of past life crimes against humanity ✳ the negativity of others ruins your vision of heaven on earth ✳ resisting the value of a rich inner spiritual life ✳ getting rid of toxic people ✳ wasted self-sacrifice in this lifetime for those who are not worth it ✳ apocalyptic visions of prophets and doom sayers ✳ fear of the future-based disaster scenarios ✳ the end of the world as we know it ✳ technology turns against our modern way of life ✳ psychic violence ✳ learning how to protect yourself from harmful energy ✳ reject those who hold back the collective spiritual growth of humanity ✳ a horrifying awareness of the pain you have caused others

## Ten of Swords

The ten of swords reminds you that nothing of intellectual value is easy to attain. The ten signals that you must conclude your involvement in a matter that has reached a permanent stalemate. You move on with increased awareness and knowledge, having achieved the broadest possible integration of wisdom and mental power concerning the subject of the reading.

*R*omance:

you do not want to repeat bad relationships * deciding never to put yourself through a tormented affair again * emotional, mental, and physical draining from a tumultuous romance * you do not want to deal with men from the past anymore * realizing how much you both need to change for a successful partnership * having trouble feeling attached to a future with anyone * end of an era of habits that isolate you from others * you need to pull out of a relationship that is dead, gone, and over * a man who has outrageous obligations to a family that has never-ending crises * the exhausting details of life that ruin romantic impulses * do not discuss love problems with your family * his people freak out over you * apologizing to those close to you for past rude behavior * a relationship where the issues will never change * you need to let go of an abusive man * a union dissolves on its own that has reached the end of the line * as great as he may be, the intense drama of the love affair is killing you * if you get back together, you could experience all the same problems * one or both of you may become homeless due to your breakup * realizing that the people he brings into your life are complete strangers * he could just be a bum or burnout who has no intention of changing his economic status * being stuck with kids in a bad marriage * you may know too much about him to take him seriously * a guy feels like he blew it with you * a committed couple who are not having sex with each other or anyone else * not wanting to take on his problems anymore * total exhaustion from the constant strain of a complicated love affair

## *W*ork & *B*usiness:

leaving your current job on bad terms * being taken to the edge at work * on the verge of physical collapse * getting nailed financially by many business people or coworkers * feeling burned out and like you cannot take it anymore * being too tired from the daily grind to do anything but sleep * letting go of a job that is pure torture * conflicting interests will never change with a boss * it is time to join the human race professionally * money earned takes a great toll on your quality of life and health * feeling so trapped by financial demands * opportunity is coming to an end—either get in or get out * having trouble getting the information or support you need * useless, deadbeat employees that should be let go * trying every avenue to find work * current business plans are shattered * money-wise, the arithmetic becomes impossible * having almost too many career ideas you want to actualize at once * you cannot go any further in your current profession * a backward progression in a job choice will lead you nowhere * your working hours are not in sync with your natural body clock * you need to put in mandatory overtime hours and wonder where you will find the strength * too many details to oversee in a project that must be totally organized * sacrificing private activities for the sake of fulfilling professional responsibilities

## Spiritual Growth:

someone you have helped spiritually turns against you * outgrowing certain dogmatic beliefs * you could make a huge mistake by choosing the wrong spiritual affiliations * reviewing the deeds of a lifetime * the end of a long, exhausting cycle that has depleted your spirit * you need to stop personal entanglements that suffocate your soul * making a major spiritual decision to end an unloving relationship * too many voices * too much socializing * craving quiet, private time away from others, especially family * walking away from someone you have tried to help in every possible way * realizing, with a sickening sensation, that you cannot force anyone to evolve * coming to the end of being connected to a spiritual group * being frustrated, in retrospect, that you wasted time with others engaged in a cult-like mentality * clairaudience * the channeling of multiple disembodied beings * the draining effects of giving psychic or intuitive readings * people wait anxiously for the outcome of the prayers of their spiritual leader * resynchronizing past life abilities that blossom as current soul gifts * possession of an enlightened vision that grants you total recall of akashic history * not remembering dreams * waking exhausted due to lack of restorative sleep * your body craves tranquillity for healing * warning against too much exercise * you must end a long period of negative lifestyle habits

## *Page of Swords*

The Page of swords is a master of observation and communication whose role is to witness interactions between people, gather ideas and knowledge, and report back to the world at large. The Page can represent a message, phone call, or conversation that serves to further the subject matter of the reading.

### *Romance:*

studying his behavior before you decide to go out with him ∗ trying to get a complete take on him ∗ you need to have a conversation with him ∗ he knows he has to listen to you ∗ he has to call if he wants to develop a connection ∗ his friends play a little game with you to protect him and prove their loyalty ∗ finally hearing the truth about some guy you like ∗ he is not ready to get serious ∗ he just wants to socialize ∗ he is thinking about you but is not ready for a relationship ∗ can be a card of a marriage proposal or him telling you he loves you for the first time ∗ you are worried that he will not let you into his life ∗ you suddenly get the message behind what he has been saying all along ∗ when you meet a new guy, take the initiative to talk first ∗ a guy who stares you down whenever you meet ∗ a phone call from a man whom you are interested in romantically ∗ you are a sitting duck because he has easy physical access to you ∗ someone with a stalker mentality ∗ a guy who is voyeuristic when it comes to sex ∗ he is extremely nervous around you ∗ to be open, free, and available for a relationship ∗ a new man in your life who asks you a thousand questions ∗ relying on rumors and offbeat informers to gather information about him ∗ a guy who is extremely cautious about making any verbal commitments before he can act on them * he is testing your reaction to dramas he has created for this purpose * if he is not forthcoming about his feelings, consider dating other people

## Work & Business:

raising money by meeting people and talking to them * you need to review your financial plans to ensure future benefits * someone gives you a loan when you need it most * you could have a quick conversation where a business deal falls into place * you are being guided to bail out and avoid involvement in a potential fiasco * peering into the future for career ideas * having to spy around undercover for inside information * using the Internet, detectives, or a financial agency to check the credit rating or financial status of a potential partner * have all paperwork looked over by a trusted ally * get the word out that you are seeking employment * make that important phone call * receiving a message that changes the course of your career * to have your own voice in business dealings * a coward who plays both sides in a negotiation * communicating with an entirely new group of coworkers * make alternative job plans * a challenge coming up at work where you offer your services out of loyalty to your employer * filing for a loan or monthly payment plan for a large-ticket item * anything to do with computers, faxes, and telecommunications * to see the big picture in terms of investments * utilizing caution while checking things out before you jump in * someone who helps guide you in the right direction professionally

## Spiritual Growth:

a general curiosity about the world of spirit * being an outspoken supporter of your particular brand of beliefs * gaining great spiritual insight * total awareness of the angelic protection surrounding you * someone out of the blue presents you with the exact guidance you seek * being cosmically connected * calling someone psychically to you to reassure them they will be okay * if you need to receive information, it may be time to get yourself a reading * advice from on high * the word of God * a call from the heavens * the one and only truth gleaned from the highest source * a disembodied entity from the spirit world is trying to contact you * an intuitive person who can help you communicate with deceased beings * universal memory * the essence of your soul quality and experience * searching for your spiritual identity * someone who watches over you and guides your destiny * strong protection around you that prevents stagnation in your process of enlightenment * a person with whom you share mental telepathy * no longer feeling alone or ignored but part of a larger spiritual network * guardian angels * your higher self that contains your genius, intuition, and creative intelligence

## Queen of Swords

The Queen of swords has a cold, detached way of dealing with the world at large. She is primarily interested in seizing power through the use of her extraordinary intellect and is willing to fight to gain control of any situation and manipulate conditions to her own advantage. In a reading, the Queen of swords speaks of standing up to others, making demands, and being clear about your own needs.

*R*omance:
  a strong probability that you will give him the boot and reject him * you are doing all the talking in a relationship * positive romantic choices may not be happening now * your intelligence may be difficult for him to accept * his perception may be that you are persecuting him * you need to let him know how you feel * during separation tell him that you miss his friendship * keep calling him and staying in touch * you become the initiator in love * use gossip to check in and see if he is all right * the other woman as a negative force in his life * caught up in jealous trips with another female * a girl is hanging on to him though he wants to end the relationship * a woman who clings to and claws into a guy as she leaves his life * a high-maintenance woman with an agenda * his girlfriend or wife is studying you to see why he is attracted to you * a jealous and difficult mother, sister, ex-wife, or ex-girlfriend who tries to interfere with your romance * a woman who is mentally unstable, manipulative, or abusive * venting your emotions out on another * you have to pull him in line * each time you turn him away, it strengthens your clarity about relationship issues * unmar-

ried, separated, or divorced women * life as a single mother * avoid being emotionally defensive or verbally abusive * a gossipy female friend who tells him everything you told her * you have to constantly fight with him because he is not fulfilling your needs * his attitude toward you hardens your normally loving personality * asexual women * utilizing time alone without a mate to actively improve yourself * avoid repeating the emotional failures of your mother

## *Work & Business:*

a brilliant administrator * an overbearing boss * lawyers, career managers, literary agents, or personnel people * networking with others is crucial to your career success * make those phone calls and try again if they are not returned * an intensely pushy woman who delegates responsibilities * an independent woman with her own income or business * a woman who runs the show behind a wealthy or powerful man and orders him around * being nasty and mean by forcing someone out of a job * having to fire an employee * tough financial negotiations * push for your own equality as a woman * you need to make the effort and be the aggressor to get what you want * only you can make things happen for yourself * asking for a new job title, raise, or promotion * gathering information on alternate employment opportunities * be realistic about the facts * doing things your way without listening to others * a woman gives you the inside scoop at work * your boss hopes you will break the bad news to others * being a forceful fighter until the battle is won * creative inspiration as a result of escaping mentally from an intolerable relationship * computer programs unforgiving with mistakes * getting your message across * pushing for your demands * arguing your case on your own behalf * negotiating a deal * working as a therapist or counselor * people who forge ties only to further their own ambition

## *Spiritual Growth:*

the dilemma of having all the information at your disposal but you are still unenlightened * having studied every new age trend but still not being a nice person * emphasis on a solo evolutionary path about which you keep quiet * a female elder who is respected and revered for her knowledge * a woman who is connected to the divine source and brings forth words of encouragement and enlightenment * working as an advisor or counselor gives you confidence in your own spiritual authority * giving psychic readings to others always mirrors what you need to hear personally * disturbed women who play mind games as self-styled spiritual authorities * manipulative female operatives in the religious world * setting your own rules for a spiritual journey * claiming your birthright to soul development * anti-abortion protesters who are jealous because others are having sex, unlike themselves * women who cannot reproduce because of hormonal or fertility problems * sterility caused by poor diet, stress, too much exercise, or loss of a regular menstrual cycle * hormone replacement therapy * fertility treatments * women with type-A personalities that damage their physical vitality * a woman who is sadly trying to attack you psychically * voodoo queens * witchy women

# The Swords

## Knight of Swords

The Knight of swords symbolizes the insecure mind who refuses to listen to the feelings or opinions of others. He is certain only he knows best and knows everything, but deep down he lacks confidence in his own ideas and beliefs. This card can also signify being totally directed toward a goal without any distractions.

### Romance:

toughness as a mask for secret helplessness * feeling lost due to a lack of love in your life * you are off and running, checking this one and that one out * it is up to him whether he goes for the relationship or not * he cannot be close to you when he needs to think * the minute he got you interested, he ran away * a big talker who tries to sweep you off your feet with false flirtations and projections of his own fantasies * a guy who plays romantic games only to sleep with you and afterwards runs away or completely disappears * craziness may be all he has ever known in relationships * men that do sick girls only * a guy who is emotionally detached and has trouble feeling anything * he does not recognize you for who you are * he may have trouble remaining engaged in any real intimacy * he could be terrified because you two are moving too fast * he may be compelled to always tell you the exact opposite of what he feels * a guy may be too busy for you * he has not called because he is not interested in you * he already knows the relationship is over but he has a sickening sensation about ending it * he only chases after women who are unavailable * he cannot physically stand his current partner and will eventually break up with her * he needs to get off his high horse and stop blaming you for his problems * a man who fears women emotionally and physically and will do anything to avoid sex * a guy who has never ever been in love before * he will make it clear when he is ready to get closer * he will move fast if he decides to go for you * he could be pulling away from your energy * you see him as the heartless skeleton that he has always been * a sudden and strong repulsion toward someone you were once deeply attracted to due to their unkind and uncommunicative behavior * an angry man who revenges you for abandoning him, emotionally or physically * if he rejects true love, he will be a mess and deteriorate psychologically * he is undermining your own sense of authority * he may be having a mental breakthrough and is finally deciding who is real to him romantically * rage and hostility toward women as expressed by his rudeness, disinterest, or tendency to silence your feelings * if he does not return your calls, forget him * if he does not show up for a date, forget him * if he does not care about you, forget him * a man who is not easily affectionate and may not like being touched * a guy who pretends to be dating other women just to get rid of you * his obsession with other emotional entanglements prevents you from being his romantic priority * not verbalizing his desires is a sure way to lose your interest

## Work & Business:

the intensity of your ideas impresses others * you will go to any lengths to learn more about a subject or project * rushing into a deal without practical considerations * someone you need for financial help will not give you the time of day * a person is not returning your calls, letters, or e-mails * you may need to defend yourself at work * a job that requires constant travel * employment that forces you into a mindless, repetitive routine * someone rushing in to grab you for a position * using professional training as a public defender ✶ a man who does not have the business connections you want ✶ once partners get their cut they will disappear ✶ someone involved early on in a deal who will not last ✶ feeling free to be exactly who you are at work ✶ a con man who rips you off and leaves town ✶ can mean hitting bottom financially if cash has been scarce ✶ an unfriendly or difficult coworker who you cannot reason with because they are crazy ✶ someone who is in your face begging for money or a loan ✶ do not delay business plans ✶ get to it, go for it ✶ your talent and intelligence make you a quick and productive worker ✶ launching a tour or traveling campaign on short notice

## *Spiritual Growth:*

immersing yourself in mindless distractions to avoid bigger personal issues ✶ a time for inhibition and saying no to people ✶ lying to others as a total waste of energy ✶ being sucked into the chaos and madness of a crazy person who is trying to control you personally or spiritually ✶ someone who is not interested in the sacred intuitive arts ✶ if you resist acceptance of the god force you could grow mean-spirited and socially isolated ✶ anxiety at crisis times with no beliefs to turn to for soul comfort ✶ conquering self-doubt and a negative self-image on the path toward wholeness ✶ religious leaders who judge, compete, condemn, criticize, and terrorize those who follow other spiritual practices ✶ you need to take your focus off an uninterested man so a more positive, healing relationship can evolve ✶ if stuck in a cult, just get out ✶ violence launched in the name of religion ✶ adamantly defending your own beliefs and not being open to dialogue ✶ someone who is so lost in their hi-tech world that they have no spiritual life whatsoever ✶ physical and mental abnormalities as a result of abusing others and all forms of life in the past history of your soul * helping heal yourself by getting into a health plan immediately * reaching a new level of consciousness if you have already begun your journey toward enlightenment * you need to learn how to enjoy life more and not rush through your days in mindless haste

## King of Swords

The King of swords uses intimidation, game playing, and the condescending side of his personality to help gain intellectual power and self-control over his emotions. He is an authority figure and an acknowledged leader in his field who thrives when involved in mentally stimulating pursuits or educating others in his environment.

### Romance:

he rejects you romantically before you dump him * he is checking you out in his own ridiculous fashion * you may have to play his mind games if you go out with him * a jerky guy who knows he cannot win your heart * an emotionally cold man who shuns involvement * he likes to imagine romance more than act on it * a chronically aloof man uninterested in real intimacy * someone who has never placed women on a pedestal * he is afraid of letting go and opening his heart * you may never be number one in his life * you may meet a core of resistance in him that criticizes, judges, and distrusts you * a man who knows going into a relationship that he will stop and flee * he has empty rationalizations about why he cannot be with a woman ❋ he had made up the mental part that your affair is over ❋ let him talk things out while you listen ❋ he would rather chitchat with you than sleep with you ❋ a man who is reluctant to have sexual relations ❋ he cannot deal with his own emotions ❋ a man who is faultfinding with everything you do ❋ he may need a woman who looks up to him and does not try to change him ❋ he may trust you more, but will never tell you everything ❋ he verbalizes his fears through negative statements he makes about you ❋ he either opens the door wider to let you in or closes the door forever ❋ he is only used to having control issues with women ❋ a macho guy who may not want an equal woman ❋ a rough guy who can be brutal ❋ a cranky, spoiled man who expects a woman to be subservient to his moods ❋ someone who goes hot and cold with you ❋ he may have trouble fitting a relationship into his work schedule ❋ a man comes forward with plans for your future together ❋ looking for a mate who shares your intellectual interests ❋ a man who is playing out an old flame by ignoring her ❋ his first step toward intimacy is asking you dozens of questions out of curiosity

## Work & Business:

taking advantage of your knowledge of human behavior in negotiations ❋ a business man who comes through for you if he wants to ❋ a very experienced expert who is the best in his field ❋ a lawyer, professor, scholar, mentor, doctor, employer, diplomat, politician, philosopher, law enforcement person, or intelligence officer ❋ playing games to stall for time in a deal ❋ learning the rules of business ❋ growing more powerful financially ❋ a strong leader with a sharp, analytical mind ❋ seriously considering an offer of employment ❋ learning discipline and focus through your job ❋ working on a plan you cannot tell anyone about yet ❋ a powerful figure with ideas and plans seeks a promotion * using a defensive buffer with colleagues * do not doubt your own authority * aggressive tactics with sales and marketing efforts * someone to whom others listen * using humiliation to get what you want from others * an egotistical competitor who is smarter than you * a counselor, teacher, or mentor who trains you the hard way * a brilliant guy who is difficult to get along with on a personal level * critics, editors, publishers, studio executives, film producers, public relations people, or gallery and theater owners who exercise power over creative artists and those in the entertainment field

## *Spiritual Growth:*

acting according to dogmatic spiritual principles * deep sorrow at a soul level is released through angry behavior toward others * trying to rid yourself of anxiety and possessive or controlling attitudes in your personality * acting selfish in your attachments with people * narcissism to the point of completely ignoring your spirit * the lifetime mistake of staying with an abusive man who holds back your spiritual evolution * researching by reading up on several traditions and finding one that appeals to you intellectually * eccentrics who live longer because they do not care what others think * an ego-driven religious figurehead who makes his own rules of morality * the karma of the hardened heart * serve or suffer * a man close to you has had a spiritual awakening he wants to tell you about * he who passes judgement on others * the logical or skeptical mind of the atheist * alternative health practitioners * intuitive yet grounded therapists and counselors

## THE DISKS

### Ace of Disks

The ace of disks begins a cycle of material change and the development of constructive opportunities that will further your talents, abilities, and financial status. The ace is the seed of its suit, and with the proper nurturing, this earliest, slowest form of activity ensures future fruition of the ripest of harvests.

*Romance:*

an initial encounter with someone who is a potential suitor * do not judge someone by their appearance or your first impression of them * a relationship is developing, though you cannot see the whole picture yet * finding someone who is real * first meeting, first date, or the first time you see him * going slowly and becoming more familiar with him * being present and in the moment about your feelings * a couple who is always there for each other * a quick meeting with someone who becomes more than a casual acquaintance * beginning again with him after spending a growthful period apart * giving a guy a chance who is just starting his career * having only tasted the future with him * there will be many more wonderful moments with him as the relationship develops * he has the potential to become a King of disks type of guy * do not assume his current romantic behavior is his only way of being with a woman * you only get one small glimpse of a guy and are deeply affecting on a physical level * a time for dating and meeting new people * more than one guy may be coming into your life * a commitment too early in youth cuts off many other opportunities * he may not be mature enough or established enough for you but give him a chance ✳ a major indicator of sperm as an impregnating force ✳ living in the moment with him, not the past or future ✳ someone you admire drops in on you unannounced ✳ preparing for a relationship before the right partner appears ✳ working hard to build a strong foundation with him ✳ exercising patience and acceptance with your man

## Work & Business:

steady work at a base level ✳ small efforts could reap large rewards later ✳ the importance of how you set up a new business ✳ past events give rise to your current financial status ✳ more than one direction to take for developing future projects ✳ searching for employment by checking out many potential employers ✳ a time to stay open to changing professional fields entirely ✳ moving forward with a grounded stability ✳ the money comes in to fund your lifelong dreams ✳ a window of opportunity to build up capital ✳ run with the chance being presented to you ✳ knowing how to get things going ✳ an important early stage of seeding projects ✳ long-term investments begin with a small amount of money ✳ a job that does not appeal to you at first captures your growing interest ✳ receiving an offer on a building, property, or business for sale ✳ having a creative work in development with a financial backer ✳ looks can be deceiving as the wealthiest of people adopt a simple lifestyle ✳ a nest egg ✳ putting assets into a program with an increased savings rate ✳ to get past step one you must put time, energy, and money into a plan ✳ someone notices your potential and helps you develop ✳ the appearance of ability and how you can nurture it ✳ setting up a strong foundation for the future ✳ acquiring knowledge in different fields of interest that will be valuable to your eventual choice of profession ✳ short-lived jobs that provide you with skills and information you will use at a later date * getting control over assets that belong to you but are in the trust or possession of another

## Spiritual Growth:

the beginning process of a complete change of lifestyle * slight hesitance toward a commitment to follow a higher path * dropping in on a mentor, place of worship, or spiritual event without warning * the divine origin of earthly life * experiencing an epiphany * using creative energy to connect to the earth * maintaining balance as a materialistic person with regards to nature and the environment * being guided toward the study of a particular religion * wicca, paganism, druidism, and other forms of Earth-centered worship * opportunities abound for enlightenment * finding incredibly evolved people in the least likely of places * your initial introduction to a spiritual path that eventually becomes a huge part of your daily life * struggling to integrate more cosmic viewpoints into your reality * permeating inanimate objects with universal energy * feeling as though things used for rituals have an extremely powerful and positive effect on your personal healing * sacred pieces of art * objects that are on altars or utilized in a formal religious service * a sign from above arriving in the form of a tangible item and seen as a confirmation * your current, high level of consciousness has been earned in a previous existence * the ground you cover in your evolution today will be a part of future reincarnations * old soul gifts resynthesized and resynchronized into the psyche of your current outer-world path work * awareness of eternity forces you to do the right thing and get your life in order * a sign of a disembodied entity returning to a human form at the moment of birth

## Two of Disks

This card traditionally indicates travel, change, and movement in your life. The two of disks can also signify making a decision to leave your current environment, job, or relationship. It is an unstable disk that finds you caught in a material limbo without long-term security or deep resources.

## *R*omance:

not sure how a relationship will work out in practical terms * you need to resolve your uncertain feelings for someone * staying loose and not making a commitment at this time * being in a transitional period between lovers * caring about another person but having trouble making up your mind * being confused about how to proceed with a guy * in the morning you love him, by the evening you hate him * he may not know what he wants yet * not needing someone in your life to contribute to living expenses * he moves to another location far away from you * a long-distance relationship that requires a commute * he invites you to meet him for a brief rendezvous that involves travel * he may be in a holding pattern about leaving his current partner * a guy who is broke because he is supporting children, ex-wives, or girlfriends * he feels wishy-washy about you * he does not know what to do * he gets close and then pushes you away * he may want it both ways with you and another woman * a man who divides his time between two home environments with two different women * he proposes to you and then loses interest * his intentions go back and forth between two extremes * if he does not move forward, find someone more stable * being caught in the middle of a feuding couple * he is used to very little happening in his life * a partnership based on small, noneventful daily routines ∗ avoid merging with him financially unless you like a struggle ∗ trying to find cash to finance practical dreams you share ∗ having trouble choosing between two great men ∗ you may have to change your residence to be with him ∗ having trouble getting him to make specific plans with you

## $W$ork & $B$usiness:

your career is in a constant flux and you have no control over it ∗ working hard in one direction and suddenly going a different way with a project ∗ short-run financial support ∗ small loan, quick payback ∗ self-correcting mechanisms in the market ∗ having money to cover basic living expenses only ∗ a credit crunch may hobble your ability to purchase large ticket items ∗ projects launched on a tight budget ∗ having to scrounge around and beg from a group of people to fund an expensive undertaking ∗ investment bankers ∗ money from clients in distant places ∗ finding practical solutions to shipping needs ∗ goods and services found at a better price at a different location ∗ changing the address of your business ∗ transportation issues that surround getting to work ∗ the necessity for a commute ∗ the possibility you will be reporting to a different neighborhood for employment to continue ∗ treading water while staying at your current job ∗ travel is extremely important for business ∗ a back and forth day trip ∗ taking several part-time positions here and there ∗ being sent on a journey by your employer ∗ a job opportunity that forces you to run around all day ∗ being offered a spot in a branch of your current company that requires a move ∗ pay-as-you-go financing ∗ layaway payments and purchasing items on credit ∗ slow negotiations over a deal that is in limbo ∗ you need to go looking for money during a time of fluctuating fortunes ∗ dispersal of income distribution * watching the stock market from the sidelines * economic opportunities would increase in a different place * money comes in and is quickly spent * working very hard without receiving proper monetary compensation for your efforts * learning how to be flexible and share your resources with others

## Spiritual Growth:

definition of the natural law of motion and change in the universe * a lifetime spent repeating religious rituals of youth without any deviation from the rules * geographical solutions to your personal problems do not work * feeling life would be better in a different location but it is hard to decide when and where to go * the prime mover is cause and effect because the soul is eternal * reincarnation as a great force keeps you coming back again and again * the cycle of rebirth explains vague nostalgia about the land, cultures, and characters of long ago * not the best time to make a huge transition unless the finances are in order * being hesitant about your spiritual loyalties * confusion over what to do to improve your lifestyle * nothing ever really changes with problems caused by our insecure natures * feeling unsettled, restless, and anxious about the future * the immortality of all beings as manifested in the human spirit since the beginning of all creation * a small moment in the journey of a soul during one sojourn as compared to the greater history of all time

## Three of Disks

The three of disks represents physical accomplishment by bringing to completion a phase of work to which you have applied time, energy, and spirit. This disk also refers to long-standing employment or owning a business that flourishes through intense labor and personal commitment.

## Romance:

end of an era for a troubled partnership * closing a cycle of a relationship experience * growing up and becoming more responsible to someone special * receiving a concrete confirmation that a casual crush could be a bona fide love affair * friendly coworkers whose familiarity creates a strong foundation for something more serious * you could meet your mate on the job or socially through those at work * a close friend at your place of business sets you up on a blind date * attend all extracurricular events that colleagues invite you to, as a great man could be there * when your career is in order, you will meet your equal partner * couples who run businesses together * a marriage where the husband and wife stay together to maintain a joint venture or to avoid the lowered standard of living common to divorce * finish up issues with past lovers so you can be totally available to him * a grounded union where both people live in the reality of the moment * he could become a part of your daily life and share the most basic activities with you * he is committed to making the relationship work * drawing up a formal legal agreement with him concerning money, business, or property rights * a special site for a wedding * going to the chapel, temple, mosque, or other house of worship to exchange vows * holding the ceremony at a favorite sentimental or traditional location ✳ he asks you where you want to raise the children ✳ you decide together how your job schedules will change when you start your family ✳ a couple makes long-term investments with an eye toward retirement ✳ remaining together takes a ton of energy and effort ✳ the financial aspects of a divorce are agreed upon and settled amicably and for all time

## *Work & Business:*

wearing many different hats professionally ✳ multitalented individuals who utilize their expertise on the job ✳ a possibility of owning a few different businesses or expanding an existing operation into new locations ✳ purchasing or leasing a franchise or dealership ✳ expect more than one offer of employment ✳ having to multitask to become familiar with all aspects of a project ✳ that work takes precedence over your personal concerns ✳ turning into a workaholic ✳ joining a small group of partners to develop specific business plans ✳ service-related industries that offer the public basic necessities ✳ you may become so busy you need to hire interns, apprentices, or paid assistants ✳ agreements reached ✳ contracts signed ✳ financial matters settled ✳ rights on a creative project sold as a development deal that includes future options for new product ✳ solid job offers ✳ employment agencies ✳ headhunters ✳ many professional options available to you ✳ serious money coming in due to extremely hard work ✳ growing more powerful on the material due to the intense application of your abilities ✳ practical solutions to the most common business problems ✳ planning for retirement and earmarking funds for living expenditures ✳ finishing an enormously complicated project ✳ receiving a commission for creative work ✳ talent being recognized and developed through the help of others ✳ you may need to add

employees, collaborators, or partners to an expanding undertaking ⁕ you could benefit professionally by joining a team,
group, association, community, or company with whom you
share common interests ⁕ ending a job on excellent terms with
your employer and armed with solid references

## *S*piritual *G*rowth:

cleaning up your past mistakes ⁕ experiencing closure over
unfinished business concerning misunderstandings with certain
people ⁕ settling old karmic debts by being of service to humanity ⁕ helping others gain growthful employment as a mission in
life ⁕ finishing up a course of spiritual study ⁕ incorporating a
few different healing techniques into your practice ⁕ lifestyle
requirements and practical rules of an organized religious
group ⁕ communities whose daily labor reflects the principles
of their beliefs ⁕ communal people who live off the land and
build their own shelters in a sacred space ⁕ the erection of
monuments, signposts, and architectural ruins that bear witness to the higher consciousness of ancient civilizations ⁕ building housing for the disenfranchised and assisting them with
food, job training, and the basic requirements for a decent life
⁕ the intentionally holy design of churches, temples, mosques,
and any and all places of worship ⁕ businesses that give freely
to charitable causes ⁕ long-standing foundations that provide
support for the needy ⁕ to be in alignment with your true
nature and purpose ⁕ the reality of your life is the most important spiritual test you need to pass ⁕ your current existence is
exactly what you prepared yourself for in a previous lifetime ⁕
your deep inner being is expressed through your profession ⁕
all artists leave behind works that are immortal ⁕ your job is
completely about using your healing skills ⁕ if your deepest
desire is to find work that is soul satisfying, the universe will

lead you to the right place ❋ refine your lifestyle, focus on self-improvement, activate creative productivity, and await the arrival of the true soul mate

## Four of Disks

The four of disks emphasizes concern over financial security and highlights money and possessions as material testing grounds. The value of acquisition is the lesson here, as you focus on establishing a solid base with powerful resources at your disposal. This card also helps to increase your spiritual strength and stabilize your creative ability regarding the subject of the reading.

### Romance:

staying in a marriage for financial security only ❋ he may primarily be interested in you for financial gain ❋ remaining in a relationship because of comfort and familiarity, but you are not in love ❋ the only common ground a couple shares revolves around superficial material appearances ❋ you want a new kind of intimacy with secure friendship as a permanent foundation ❋ romantic compromise to maintain the status quo ❋ love cannot be created on a balance sheet ❋ a relationship with a solid and mature partner ❋ he may want a more committed relationship ❋ the person who is meant for you will court you instantaneously ❋ a guy who clings to you or you being too needy with him ❋ even if a couple is going through a bad period, hang on to each other ❋ feeling totally comfortable and having complete trust in your man ❋ his greatest dream is to support you financially ❋ peace, comfort, and security in a relationship where your practical needs are taken care of ❋ a grounded union capable of living powerfully on a daily basis ∗ do not expect separation or divorce ∗ sex is definitely not the most important aspect of a relationship where materialism rules ∗ an incredible love affair with a solid partner ∗ be careful that a lover does not threaten your financial security or hit you up for money ∗ property and retirement funds completely protected for a couple ∗ making him feel an enduring sense of safety with you

## Work & Business:

wealth and financial security restored ∗ you need to manifest more material power in your life ∗ clinging to people who have money ∗ safeguarding your possessions against loss ∗ get your budget in order ∗ having access to incredible resources ∗ having a great desire to purchase major items ∗ not wanting to part with anything you own ∗ fear of having to liquidate or sell off property and valuables ∗ keeping your material appetite from overwhelming you ∗ reaching a point in your life where you want the security of ownership ∗ keep savings and long-term investments in place ∗ solid businesses that will grow in the future ∗ you will not get ripped off financially ∗ all the pieces are in place for a project to be launched ∗ establishing boundaries ∗ deals involving land that is headed for development ∗ having a protected living arrangement that cannot be challenged ∗ in a dispute, your assets will not be threatened ∗ you need to manifest more material power in your life ∗ discovering the one talent you have that has the potential to earn you serious money ∗ maneuvering your own advancement professionally ∗ being approached about a job by people already well-established in their field or business ∗ it is not the time to take risks with your investments

## Spiritual Growth:

if you want to initiate personal change, stay put * when fear and doubt arise, draw on your inner wisdom and stay centered * your material concerns may encroach upon spiritual beliefs * do not be afraid to let go of habits that block your evolution * releasing antiquated attitudes from the past * never take miracles for granted * always be grateful for money that allows you time to pursue creative pursuits * amazing blessings come in the form of financial security * receiving funding for establishing a place of worship or distributing literature concerning a spiritual system * greedy leaders who pilfer the savings of their followers * can be a card of true fulfillment through the grounding nature of your beliefs * a miserly attitude as an obstacle to soul development * being guarded with others in traditional religions about your real faith * pretending to follow a certain theology to appease your family * never lose sight of the many paths available for enlightenment * a sincere and genuine seeker of the truth * repeating old spiritual crises * accepting a religion at face value and enjoying the solid comfort of its long history * focusing on strengthening your physical body as an important step in your personal growth

# The Disks

## Five of Disks

The five of disks depicts a simplified lifestyle and the adoption of a value system that you establish based on your own material principles. This card typically symbolizes a strain in your money supply and warns against not developing your creative abilities or your spiritual nature.

## Romance:

coming out of a heavy relationship where you were needy and emotionally dependent * a man who is making you pay for the crimes of other women who have hurt him * undergoing a desolate phase in the aftermath of a breakup * dating someone who is beneath you socially, spiritually, or financially * not getting the passionate goods from him * feeling unloved, misunderstood, and not respected for your true self by him * stripping away false behavior to arrive at what is real between you * struggling with the most basic and essential physical necessities together * partners going broke due to loss of energy from fighting over personality clashes * helping each other through bad times * until he loves himself he cannot love another * he needs to recover his sense of trust in women * a couple who, due to circumstances, has no private place to meet * keeping your romance a secret from his previous partners is unhealthy for your self-esteem * being hurt because he hides you from his family, friends, and coworkers * he may feel he does not deserve to be loved for himself * he may be coming from a place of neediness and have nothing to offer you * he may not be used to being with someone decent * his perception of you is limited * a guy who cannot beat his own insecurities * his rejection of you is his loss, though he may not realize it yet *

133

he may be no bargain * he may not have a dime to his name * a guy who pretends to be a struggling artist or impoverished to protect his true assets * do not lend him money or buy him expensive gifts because you will regret it * being the mistress of a married man and feeling left out in the cold because his wife is always number one * needing him so badly that the relationship is crucial to your survival * someone who has spiritual values and is with you for the right reasons * one of you is hiding wealth or poverty * two lost souls find each other and fall in love * hanging out with a man because you are homeless * relationships with drifters and deadbeats * his miserly attitude and a lack of generosity is squeezing you * his living arrangement is not good * he may be a stranger in exile in his own home * a couple who shares charitable work

## Work & Business:

keeping expenses and expenditures to their very minimum * realizing you do not need luxuries to keep up with illusory appearances * dwindling savings * taking great risks and putting your money on the line * you may not receive the amount of cash that you anticipate * if you do not use your talents, you will lose them * waiting or wading through financial problems * goods and services going out exceed capital coming in * a rise in debt cannot continue indefinitely * those who work at minimum wage need to develop skills through training * having trouble starting your own business due to lack of monetary backing * you need to lower your overhead * sub-optimal standards of living * government borrowing public funds to pay for programs * corporations charging clients for their increased operating costs and extensive losses * government not meeting financial needs of retirees as a cause for alarm * not having enough money to invest in a project or complete a deal * you are in the process of paying your dues professionally * having trouble finding employment and feeling worthless * a time period of hardships and career setbacks * someone with money sickness who hides wealth and lives like a pauper * being deprived and underprivileged as a child * hoarding money for the future * being judged by your monetary status or lack of it

## Spiritual Growth:
coming out of the atheistic cold to the warmth of spirit * a complete lack of moral conscience or an overload of soul energy * the hypocrisy of self-styled authorities who judge others by their physical appearance, social class, or economic circumstances * you could receive philanthropic assistance from an agency, individual, or association * having trouble transcending feelings of unworthiness or failure due to the psychology of your childhood experience * unconsciously repeating financial mistakes of your parents * reality hits and breaks the bubble of a beautiful though unrealistic dream * simplicity of lifestyle feeds a spiritual life * you need to do more and give more to others * charity in all forms * volunteers who feed, clothe, and house the poor * someone whose life revolves around doing good works for others * like-minded individuals get you through tough times * seeking out spiritual asylum * leaving a cult with nowhere to go and no sense of self-worth * going so low that acceptance of a higher power is your only springboard back to health and harmony * losing everything you have and starting over with only faith in heavenly guidance * when challenged with practical problems, you make the right higher choices and the money comes through effortlessly * make taking care of yourself a priority * rid your diet of foods with no life force and go natural and organic * seek out information if

you lack the skills to keep yourself healthy * being taken care of through divine providence

### Six of Disks

The six of disks offers a lesson on balancing the material you exchange with others through shared resources; when you give of your time, energy, knowledge, and possessions, you receive exactly what you need in return. Your core desire is to utilize your assets for personal success but to also enrich the lives of those with whom you work and live.

### Romance:

recreating what you once had romantically with another * giving of yourself through actions, not just words * understanding and nurturing the gifts of your partner * always assisting the one you love without hesitation * getting what you need in a partnership that is equal and fair * he may be ready to share his life with another again * career compatibility or having mutual interests with your mate * being accepted for your authentic self and the sense of security that generates * really great sex where neither partner holds back emotionally * a couple that almost always experiences simultaneous orgasm * he does such nice things for you * he only wants to make you happy and satisfied * a man who is generous with you financially * he constantly buys you gifts * enjoying simple, basic pleasures together * you are a real part of his daily life * living together and sharing meals, events, and activities as a committed couple * the comforting intimacy of mornings spent at home alone * sharing your residence with a new man * merging bank accounts and other financial resources * learning not to take him or the relationship for granted * he has come through for you before when you most needed help * you want him to be as happy and comfortable as possible * a well-liked man who does good deeds for everyone around him * someone who is a giver to your friends and family* an excellent friendship deepens into mature love * practicing unconditional acceptance of each other * a guy who is spoiling and flattering you for mercenary purposes that will be revealed later

## Work & Business:

a dramatic increase in trade * a fair price for goods exchanged * the way to go in business will become clear * a windfall * a payoff * good connections come to you * a partnership where one person provides money and the other possesses skills and know-how * you may need to invest more cash before fruition of a deal, but it is worth it * a loan or financing comes through * renewed ambition * a fair promotion is at hand * a job that provides a good salary and excellent benefits * a lucrative business transaction * being offered an opportunity that is too good to pass up * your work environment gives back to you * actually liking your employers or managers * you are a valuable asset professionally * foundation grants * philanthropic assistance * scholarships * student loans * prize awards * your company offers you educational benefits or stock options * a good time to ask for a pay raise or a higher-level job title * everybody supports you for an independent project * people will come through and give you what you need * social security, pension, and other benefits due to you from the government or big business * the welfare system and food stamp programs * increased income helps you enjoy richer daily activities * the formation of a new company where all workers find the perfect place to showcase their talents in a learning working environment * an excellent time to call in your debts or cash in your chips

## Spiritual Growth:

money comes to you from the universe when you are in the flow * someone whom you have selflessly given to in the past suddenly returns the favor * reaping what you sow on every level * taking responsibility for your actions toward others * being given access to sacred knowledge that increases your practical understanding of the cosmos * making financial contributions to people and causes that promote peace, tolerance, and global healing * sharing your daily life with others who have similar beliefs and follow the same ritual habits * trying to live in balance with the environment as much as humanly possible * a real giver whose first impulse is to help those in need * a humanitarian who dedicates their lifetime to contributing to the advancement of the planetary soul * any and all charitable efforts * the communal movement where like-minded individuals create self-sustaining communities * making donations to local organizations * it is okay to seek help from others when you are struggling

### Seven of Disks

The task of the seven of disks is to lovingly care for every stage of your own development as a creative person. This disk teaches patience because the process of real growth cannot be rushed, but by working hard to establish optimal conditions, you ensure a fruitful future harvest. You gain ground by moving closer to your goal at a steady rate until you feel confident enough to establish your outerworld destiny.

### Romance:

you want to meet somebody responsible and hard working * trying to release an old relationship and struggling for closure * you may need to disengage from someone temporarily in order to grow * it might be best to return to the safety of your own world and do things by yourself * keep plugging away with a new guy and take it one step at a time * if you rush things with him, your business plans could be ruined * it may be hard to maintain a connection with him unless you take it really slow * getting to know each other gradually, so intimacy can grow naturally * he wants to spend more time with you in the future * you need to challenge him to meet your demands * he may want to see you briefly just to check you out * he definitely will figure his way through any obstacles to your union * you know the truth about his situation, and reality demands that you be forbearing * be willing to compromise to make him feel comfortable with you * you want to see each other but cannot be together at this time * a relationship could work out if you both focus on taking care of daily responsibilities * having to wait a long time before you see someone again

## Work & Business:

protecting assets * guarding over treasures * there may be a false sense of security with present conditions * opening up new avenues to creative development * steady economic growth * be patient for best results * deal with basic tasks at hand daily to avoid frustration * a deal is in the process but not complete or final * the monotony of attending to paperwork each day * going through a time when you doubt your own abilities * hoping to make more money and develop new talents * a slow but steady promotional ascent professionally * the wait and the work will be worth it later on * you may need to buy your own freedom financially * you experience a material increase through small gains, not from impulsive get-rich schemes or easy money * making steady progress on many different creative projects * you reap greater rewards by waiting for the right time to move forward * staying longer than necessary at a job that keeps you in economic limbo * keep track of a creative work in progress by taking notes on conceptual development * letting your assets mature slowly by investing according to a responsible life plan * the more you are willing to work toward a goal, the more you will ultimately benefit * a transitional time where you adopt a more disciplined approach to completing important projects

## Spiritual Growth:

do not worry about what you cannot control * building up a strong knowledge of the self * a simplified lifestyle as a source of a deeply satisfying happiness * cutting back on clutter and acquisition makes it easier to survive slow financial periods * lack of ownership compels you to focus on what is really important * awareness of your own inner wealth * increasing your connection to the cosmos * you never lose on a spiritual path, you only learn more as you go ❋ true soul development takes time ❋ nothing important ever happens quickly ❋ in the midst of confusion, sit tight and watch how problems resolve themselves ❋ not having the right physical space to do healing work on yourself ❋ living in harmony with the natural cycles of growth ❋ sensitivity to plant and animal life ❋ gardening, hiking, and a love of the outdoors as deeply healing experiences for the soul ❋ recycling man-made products ❋ hoarding food and other supplies against imaginary disasters ❋ transforming derelict land and buildings into thriving environments ❋ gaining knowledge about a healthy lifestyle ❋ dropping out of a hectic reality to discover yourself spiritually

## Eight of Disks

The eight of disks finds you diligently laboring to reach a level of perfection in your work. You must be patient and apply yourself steadily toward your goals by repeating certain tasks and steps to increase your abilities and establish yourself as a capable, creative person.

## Romance:

struggling to get a relationship off the ground ❋ in retrospect, feeling you could have tried harder and done more with him ❋ re-creating your family drama repeatedly with him ❋ trying to always do the right thing ❋ a couple going through the motions of a shallow union ❋ a marriage based on economic necessity where the husband and wife are consumed with material considerations ❋ two people who are emotionally like ships passing in the night ❋ laying the groundwork for a future romance

* if you two get back together too soon, you could repeat the entire melodrama again * you mutually decide to build a life together on a practical level * creative people who share an artistic talent or interest in the same crafts * he wants you to be involved with him on a project that requires much planning * he needs to change his unconscious habitual response patterns * let him know he matters to you * good relationship skills need to be developed * he is calling in all his favors and resources to make life happen with you * he may have done a lot of work on himself but he is not through yet * you need to resolve communication problems with him * he does feel a vested interest in you * a card of family restructuring * heavy domestic responsibilities weigh you down * be patient while he develops his own career * there is another round coming with a guy * couples counseling

## *Work & Business:*

putting creative ideas into a practical form * finishing up the details on a major project * being buried under the weight of your tasks * your whole life feels like endless labor * the daily grind that revolves around caring for family members * working hard for income or to advance your position * construction or remodeling of a home * financing or hard work needed to improve a property * commissioned work * highly skilled craftspersons, especially sculptors, architects, jewelers, and furniture and instrument makers * all forms of manufacturing * learning a practical skill or trade * electricians, carpenters, car mechanics, computer operators, chefs, and secretaries * musical and theatrical performers who repeat the same repertoire day after day or year after year * becoming an apprentice to a mentor or expert in your field * on-the-job training goes up substantially in all income groups * you need to refine your plans and technique for a project ❋ covering the same territory over and over professionally ❋ manual labor ❋ overcoming financial hardship through hard work ❋ grabbing any employment available to get quick cash ❋ a loan helps increase educational opportunities or leads to a new training course that could boost your earnings ❋ colleagues are quietly waiting for the completion of your massive undertaking

## *Spiritual Growth:*

serious dedication to the task of enlightening others ❋ repeating the same mistakes until the soul gets it right ❋ an ability to decipher what works for you spiritually ❋ skills that follow you from lifetime to lifetime ❋ memory imprints of past-life abilities that account for prodigal and precocious talent ❋ how arduous the path to discovering the truth about yourself ❋ more work needs to be done on the journey you have undertaken ❋ religious rituals repeated ad infinitum ❋ being a constructive tool in the healing of others ❋ having the gift of patience and compassion for those just beginning their spiritual path ❋ master/apprentice relationships and organizations that promote same ❋ you need to evolve more and gain wholeness in your character ❋ chop wood, carry water ❋ hand to eye clairvoyance with cards, runes, or other divination tools ❋ sacred works of art crafted by evolved beings such as sand mandalas, fetishes, altar materials, Tarot cards, astrological charts, and statues of deities ❋ déjà vu experiences ❋ building shelters as a healing process or charitable act ❋ working at a soup kitchen to feed the hungry ❋ it may be difficult to see where all your spiritual studies are leading ❋ wanting to become a better person ❋ going to therapy on a regular basis ❋ a knowledgeable person transfers wisdom to you ❋ procuring a skill to meet your outer-world destiny ❋ a spiritual leader or teacher puts you through your paces during the memorization of scripture

## Nine of Disks

This powerful disk attracts money and possessions and symbolizes spectacular talent and strong ability. You shine in the world by realizing your dreams to their greatest capacity and are capable of receiving both spiritual and material rewards because of the level of perfection you have reached.

## Romance:

he really appreciates where you are coming from ❖ he understands all the nuances of your personality with ease ❖ everybody is preparing for a solid future ❖ a successful relationship that is rich with shared values ❖ a person of substance whom you like immediately ❖ he thinks you are great and does not want to change you ❖ someone from your identical cultural background with whom you feel comfortable and familiar due to equal experience ❖ a man who is well-established in his career ❖ he has a lot to give, almost too much ❖ he enjoys making you happy ❖ he does tangible and helpful things for you ❖ a guy who is fully aware of his own self-worth ❖ a man who wants a partner who has money ❖ you both live in the world the same way ❖ enjoying each moment by making it count ❖ a relationship can proceed if he gives you what you want ❖ a quality individual with whom you have a real connection ❖ a couple who has it all and shares their blessings with others ❖ taking for granted that he is always there for you ❖ he admires your creative or business abilities ❖ he loves to see you enjoy the life you have together

# Work & Business:

your talents are respected and enjoyed by others ✳ realizing how hard work builds up your self-esteem ✳ your work environment is a reflection of your true self ✳ getting your wish by attaining the career of your dreams ✳ making money from your own investments and properties ✳ having control of your estate as a creative person ✳ a constant flow of funds ✳ your holdings dramatically increase in value ✳ maximum sustainable growth ✳ do not sell stable assets ✳ you receive your price in a real estate deal ✳ the products of your talent make you a valuable commodity ✳ beautifying your place of business ✳ career efforts pay off and result in self-employment ✳ you have reached a salary ceiling at your current job ✳ you have proven how good you are to your employers ✳ be confident about your professional performance ✳ rights of stockholders ✳ long-term financial planning ✳ political ideas and a social conscience permeate your work ✳ having total faith in your own ability ✳ your self-worth is highly developed, resulting in special and unique opportunities for advancement ✳ request the payment you rightfully deserve for your sophisticated creations ✳ your source of inspiration is dependable and overflowing ✳ enjoying life to the fullest degree possible ✳ being independently wealthy

# Spiritual Growth:

feeling that you will be okay no matter what happens ✳ having the strength and courage to change your life ✳ being a valued member of a spiritual community ✳ reaching higher ground in your behavior ✳ establishing a study group around the subjects you enjoy most ✳ receiving recognition for all you have given others ✳ surrounding yourself with equals to raise your vibration ✳ someone who is beautiful inside and out ✳ the wealth of the inner life ❋ all of your actions reflect a morality that respects others ❋ being secure with your spiritual viewpoint ❋ your innate sensibilities ❋ being born conscious with wisdom at your disposal in youth ❋ others look to you for grounded advice ❋ a talent for comprehending divination ❋ a deeply devoted person who is the central pillar of their spiritual group ❋ building strength of character ❋ desiring to heal the planet rather than add to the forces of destruction ❋ a wealth of goodness ❋ a sense of well-being ❋ finding acceptance for your religious beliefs within your family ❋ all of your actions are extensions of a really ethical system

## Ten of Disks

The ten of disks refers to utilization of your talents to establish structure in the outer world and for all time. This is the most major disk of wealth and the inheritance of money, values, and knowledge from ancestors, mentors, and guides who connect your inborn talents to their lifetime accomplishments to build a better world.

## Romance:

a socially desirable person ❋ a prosperous marriage ❋ he wants to settle down and start a family ❋ a couple with a deep love and appreciation for their children and parents ❋ a solid home life ❋ a relationship that effortlessly becomes serious due to a common plan for living ❋ only good will come from a righteous union ❋ shared resources ❋ dealing with society together ❋ participating in local or community activities especially due to children ❋ he could be the perfect biological specimen for reproduction ❋ a man with a secure job, a nice home, and a decent and somewhat normal lifestyle * taking care of family responsibilities * providing financially for blood relatives * being a full-fledged couple in public * living with those unrelated to you as a family unit * a man from the past remembers the rainbow of feelings you evoked in him * a sporting or cultural event involving parents and children * you both want to be fulfilled by your partnership * not being ashamed of romantic mistakes from the past * having group soul karma with a guy * your mate is open to new ideas about making money * a couple receiving financial support through the family * a home is bought with the assistance of parents or grandparents * two lives merge socially and materially * a serious proposal that includes the traditional package of marriage, home, and children * desiring only the best for each other * a man from a wealthy background * a man who is extremely close to his parents and siblings * raising your children in the town where you grew up

## Work & Business:

a special project of yours is well-received and brings in big bucks * being loaded with talent through genetics or a rich cultural environment developed by self * following a traditional profession from your background * a parent gets you started in a business * personal resources are extremely secure * a major job offer puts you at the top of the heap * having a lot to accomplish professionally * there is unlimited money to be made * an unbelievable opportunity to get in on the ground floor of a future business bonanza * inheriting money, stocks, or property * working for your father * building equity through land purchases * long-term capital investments * public pension programs * commissions earned from the sale of existing homes * the future growth of retirement funds * domestic gross product ∗ open markets in your own country, state, or town ∗ the social intelligentsia and cultural elite ∗ institutional funding ∗ multinational corporations ∗ mergers and acquisitions ∗ big business, big money ∗ buying and selling residential, agricultural, or commercial properties ∗ taking over a family-owned business ∗ you may have to spend money to make money ∗ becoming involved in the project of a lifetime ∗ management, employers, CEOs, COOs, and entrepreneurs ∗ taking serious responsibility for the material protection of others

## Spiritual Growth:

spiritual rewards from a lifetime of serious morals ∗ mastery of the material world ∗ a deep-seated contentment with your home life ∗ expressing soulful qualities in all you do ∗ being evolved enough to want it all ∗ the formation of a family can be an important step in your healing process ∗ you automatically give back to others as a reaction to your own prosperity and blessings ∗ having an inner family that supports you unconditionally ∗ having a whole and healthy sense of spiritual community ∗ people who share religious beliefs reside together in an extended society ∗ achieving the classic dream of the rare traditional grateful family ∗ a large religious group that is backed by government, the wealthy elite, or a corporate entity ∗ breaking free of childhood distortions to form a solid home based on mutual respect of the tenants ∗ accepting a religious package on face value or because your parents did ∗ awareness of cultures and civilizations you have experienced in past lives

## Page of Disks

The Page of disks is a messenger of information through the written word and rules over practical knowledge and the symbolic system of language. He is a youthful hard worker who is always willing to offer his assistance to any project. He often represents the student or the seeker who looks to his teachers or employers for a sense of material direction.

## Romance:

a younger person with whom you develop sexual chemistry * partners committed to making their relationship a success * a union based on trust, respect, mutual affection, and unconditional support * you may have to assist him selflessly to become an integral part of his life * being preoccupied with thoughts of him * a modest and humble guy who is struggling to adjust to your way of being * holding your own ground in his world * self-sufficiency in love * a man who is ready to make the preliminary moves toward asking you out * he is gathering information about you and reading up on subjects that interest you * he is asking questions to accumulate details about your life * his plan may be to work with you * he has practical ideas for your financial problems * he may not have experience with a mature woman * he may write you a letter or send you an e-mail * he could be capable of producing poetry, articles, or literature professionally * one or both of you may be a student * he is taking his time to develop his career * you may need to clarify something with him via a written agreement * he is not completely out of the picture yet * there may be a project you will share together * he does not feel ready enough to be with you * a marriage contract * he is playing a supporting role in your life ∗ falling in love with a guy through his creative work ∗ a man you meet on the job

## Work & Business:

practical assistance ∗ seeing to painstaking details concerning a project ∗ someone may be dragging their feet on a deal ∗ exercising diligence toward professional responsibilities ∗ waiting for agreements to be signed ∗ all paperwork, documents, contracts, and the recording and safeguarding of same ∗ all mail, packages, faxes, phone messages, data systems, and Internet-generated communications ∗ read all fine print with great care before committing yourself on paper ∗ book and journal publishing, manuscripts, editors, and bookstores ∗ interns, volunteers, students, and assistants ∗ someone who is dying to work with you ∗ those who watch over day-to-day operations ∗ educational opportunities abound ∗ you may need to take a seminar or workshop to get crucial information or connections ∗ in a dispute, legal documents help strengthen your case ∗ business enterprises will develop for you ∗ legitimate operations that launder illegal gains ∗ fine tuning purchasing, distribution, accounting, and administrative details ∗ bringing a large part of the population into the mainstream hi-tech arena ∗ using a corps of workers to change capital structure ∗ give people increased skills so they can function successfully ∗ training bright, young, impoverished children to become fruitful members of society

## Spiritual Growth:

making a long-term commitment to personal development ∗ getting the support and guidance you need from the universe ∗ someone seriously dedicated to doing inner work ∗ not being afraid to apply yourself with diligence to earn the rewards of spirit * you need to move outside of self for inspiration on a higher level * all and every type of spiritual document such as books, scriptures, scrolls, bibles, channeled material, automatic writing, and messages from the one true source and the scribes, scholars, and apprentices who work with the same * the preservation and protection of ancient religious documents * the incredible manifesting power of language * seeking a new level of mastery in a particular area of interest * emotional and psychological blocks are released, resulting in awesome spirit communication that will reach others * immersion in all material pertaining to a course of study * someone who is truly connected to Earth energy * gaining inspiration from the amazing beauty and perfection of the natural world * entering a spiritual apprenticeship as an absolute beginner * becoming a staff person for an alternative health practitioner * researching holistic data from print and Internet sources

## Queen of Disks

The Queen of disks represents comfort and happiness in the world of living things. She offers practical support, a nurturing, maternal calm, and common sense advice to those around her. This security-conscious Queen is primarily interested in money and talent being used for constructive purposes and is often found in business, where she takes stock of the moral and financial welfare of others.

## Romance:

realize you are perfect and not doing anything wrong * celebrating a lack of need for a man in your life * an okay stage of being single * not letting love distract you from your responsibilities * receiving admiration for who you are from men * no matter what happens romantically, you will survive beautifully * if a relationship fails, you will independently rebuild your life with grace * if he chooses you, he will have your unwavering support in the future * he may see you as a source of income * a guy who relies on you to run his business or his personal life * being a contented housewife * providing for others through domestic efforts to create a happy home * a woman who works professionally as a co-partner with her man * it may be best to leave him alone and let him figure it out for himself * do not feel insecure, you did not create his problems * he needs to fully comprehend what you have to offer * being left financially comfortable in the aftermath of a relationship * issues of alimony and child support * he may not be ready for love, but do not tell him * he needs to see you as a generous person * after your last encounter, he truly understood the parameters of your personality ❋ you may have to help him get rid of another woman ❋ stay on course and maintain financial independence ❋ being the woman behind the man ❋ sleeping with a man because he could help advance your career ❋ doing charitable deeds for others

## *Work & Business:*

taking control of your money ❋ seeing to a variety of practical needs ❋ you can be a homemaker and powerful in the business world ❋ to be completely successful in your own right ❋ self-employment or working from the home ❋ careers involving agriculture, food preparation, healing, mothering, philanthropy, banking, management, teaching, medicine, scientific research, geology, astronomy, botany, herbal remedies, the intuitive arts, or creative projects ❋ enhancing work environments with active participation and team work ❋ helping other people recognize their own talents ❋ having a good reputation as a hard worker ❋ women in powerful social, political, or governmental positions ❋ women who are big players in the business world ❋ an ambitious and security-conscious woman who gets deals and develops projects ❋ changing your lifestyle and going out into the marketplace after an absence or sabbatical ❋ staying focused on career goals during times of turmoil ❋ finding the perfect job that fits in with your existing domestic schedule ❋ projects generate friendships with great potential ❋ you are an instrument for the success of others ❋ earning enough money to purchase property or make long-term investments ❋ taking charge of the situation at work and demanding a pay raise

## *S*piritual *G*rowth:

adopting more healthful habits to feel better about yourself
* healing others of confusion and lack of purpose in their lives
* assisting everyone to reach a level of personal fulfillment *
being a caretaker of the earth who never exploits for material
gain * being grounded in your physical body * basic organic
foods bring energy and life force to the system * enjoying your
sensual nature * using health products and practices to
increase your vitality * achieving the perfect balance of diet,
exercise, and a positive attitude * investigating yoga, sacred
dance, reflexology, massage, or other forms of body movement
therapies * earning a living as a healer or intuitive arts counselor * a woman who feeds the hungry and the poor * being
totally financed to pursue personal growth * caring for all people without judgement or hesitation * channeling your money
toward groups that do good works * you give one hundred percent to others * the creation of a beautiful and serene living
environment is an important step in spiritual development *
taking grassroots action against poverty * founding your own
cause for assisting others with practical necessities * applying
logic to the supernatural world * practicing an Earth-centered
system of worship * claiming your right to live the way you
want * developing your creativity through a blend of intuition
and practical knowledge * in stressful times use your spiritual
awareness to stay grounded emotionally

# The Disks

## Knight of Disks

The Knight of disks lives within the laws of the natural world no matter where he is found. Like most of the other disks, he symbolizes hard work as the only path to financial gain and spiritual development. As the most normal man in the deck, he is loyal, honest, and always of service to others.

## Romance:

someone who is the nicest person on the planet * a regular guy who gets your phone number and calls to ask you out * he is not afraid to knock on your door * a man of his word who always comes through * a sensual man without sexual hang-ups or sick peccadilloes * a healthy and fertile man who is very active in bed * he may be pliable but never wimpy * he may appear subservient when playing the role of an average guy * he has a gift for enjoying a quiet, uneventful life * he is exactly as he appears * his personality is one dimensional * not a manipulating or controlling person * a guy who is interested in animals, agriculture, or the outdoors * a tranquil guy who is easy to please * he is pure in his intentions and will make his feelings obvious when the time is right * a guy who offers you emotional stability and a lifetime of security * he is looking for someone to share his life with * marriage, if you want it with him * a nice match * a good, sweet guy * he will offer himself in any way you will agree to * he is respectful of your feelings * he makes his plan with purpose and wants everything to be perfect * he takes care of all the details during the courtship * he will never blow you off or not show up * you could have an incredibly good life with a down-to-earth person * he is excellent husband and father material * if you reject him, you may have to give him money or valuable property you acquired together ✻ a strong possibility of impregnation ✻ a guy who is shy, kind, and without pride

## Work & Business:

financial stability ✻ steady income ✻ having a practical mentality toward hard work ✻ not an overly aggressive type ✻ you need to settle down and plant roots so business seeds can grow ✻ a low-maintenance job that is comfortable ✻ building up security through the slow development of plans ✻ a serious person at your place of employment ✻ everyday affairs and expenses ✻ the person with practical experience lands the job ✻ economic growth and fertility ✻ travel required for finalizing agreements ✻ trading commodities ✻ the availability of healthy food and clean air and water ✻ manufacturing ✻ labor relations ✻ field workers ✻ agricultural operations ✻ the food and restaurant business ✻ shifting to a more agrarian lifestyle ✻ all farmers, builders, contractors, carpenters, engineers ✻ animal breeders and trainers, gardeners, naturalists, and essential service workers ✻ getting a home in the country ✻ sticking to a basic budget ✻ the good life of a house on some land makes sense ✻ alternative energy sources that rely on sun, wind, wood, or water

## Spiritual Growth:

you deal with problems realistically ✻ a person who rarely asks for assistance from others ✻ saving your own soul ✻ to be more of your true self than ever before ✻ awareness that good behavior results in material rewards ✻ the simple life feeds the soul ✻ your love of nature and animals heals your spirit ✻ all living things respond to you with joy ✻ communing with ethereal beings * having a psychic connection to animals * community garden projects draw people together * volunteering to help feed and clothe the needy * you could replenish your life force by spending time in the country * a pet lifts your spirits and is healing for you * physical improvement begins with simple food choices, relaxation techniques, and systematic movement that releases energy in the physical body * an emphasis on right livelihood and positive career goals * Earth-centered religions * time in the wilderness during early enlightenment * spiritual markers left on Earth by previous civilizations as viewed from outer space, such as mounds, pyramids, lay lines, monoliths, crop circles, tombs, monuments, and temples that mark power points on the planet

## King of Disks

The King of disks is usually found in the business world as a successful and responsible person. He is an organized and efficient laborer who guides and protects those in his care by providing practical support for their many needs. This King has the maturation and staying power to see situations through to a growthful conclusion.

## Romance:

a conservative guy wants to make a commitment * he is in love in an old-fashioned way * his main attractions are his personal power and financial stability * to see security in a guy rather than adventure * not a very outwardly passionate person * someone who is emotionally detached but nice and caring * he wants to provide for you * a good man who is kind, gentle, and serious * he may seem withdrawn because his mind is on his money * getting ready to settle down * looking for a mate with common practical goals * falling in love with some-one who is financially secure is icing on the cake * his strongest desire is to do things for you * a gentleman who approaches you after he has completed his current relationship * he will repay you for all he has put you through * a serious marriage proposal * when he gets money he will pull himself together * feeling drawn to a strong, capable man * to want to own a man or vice versa * you may wish he was a little more dangerous * he wants to be with someone that shares his lifestyle * he wants to get closer to you * he relates to you in a practical fashion * he needs to discuss business with you * he asks you out and shows up * he is worth it in the most classical way * you may find emotional sparkle outside of your marriage * he will sur-vive monetarily in the aftermath of a divorce * a righteous part-ner who is solid, reliable, and capable of growing with you * he sees himself as a powerful provider and head of a family

## Work & Business:

a guy who is genuine * a deal that is on the level * an investor with cash * a man who does many things well * a wealthy or powerful business owner, corporate executive, politician, or patriarch * a man who knows how to manipulate his profes-sional network * workers rely on their boss for more than the delegation of tasks * being efficient when seeing to the neces-sary requirements for existence * having big plans for your future * you will be financially compensated * to take a job only for the income level * your ambitions are restored * you need to be more practical in your viewpoint on money * you resolve employment problems by starting up your own opera-tion * becoming an entrepreneur * knowing your market well * providing for yourself and making investment choices * a very

generous boss * an excellent bonus or commission check * a
father figure who sees to the welfare of his workers * a manager who is a grounding force by calming down or mediating
between his employees * a colleague who considers you part of
the family * taking on more material responsibilities in your life
* a job promotion that gives you more money, power, or a better title * successful self-employment * a very busy subcontrac-
tor * having a moral conscience as you build up assets * becoming a partner to someone already well-established in your field
* joining a business that is family-owned, has a long tradition,
or an incredible reputation

## Spiritual Growth:

a charitable person who donates large sums to less fortunate
people * someone who follows a simple but mature set of
morals * can indicate a marriage or business partner from a
previous lifetime * unbridled materialism prevents an increase
in consciousness * a spiritual leader or figurehead of a major
religion * an unenlightened but decent person * good past
behavior builds a positive karmic future * someone who is generally nice and sees to the physical welfare of others * an
activist who donates time, money, and energy to charitable
causes * a man who underwrites fundraising events * spiritual
gifts that appeal to a sense of honor and integrity * a whole
person who is not afraid to help others along in their soul
development * greedy people who become enlightened and
shift their focus toward helping others

# THE CUPS

## Ace of Cups

The appearance of this card signals falling in love and the ecstatic emotions associated with the earliest stages of intimacy, when two people experience a mutually deep affection. The ace of cups is a time for receptivity to all types of feelings and can inspire heartfelt creations, including children, if a reading is examining such a matter.

### Romance:

new relationships should be nurtured gently * there is potential for growth and fulfillment with the right guy * taking time for romance reaps rewards beyond your wildest dreams * an opportunity to enjoy a purely innocent flirtation * having a powerful instant attraction to another * he will be emotionally invested in all that you share * a classic case of love at first sight * the onset of a major affair of the heart * you are only looking for a real, rare, and pure connection with a man * having a big crush on another * a chance for intimacy without obstacles * new potential mates come into your life at this time * he cannot turn away because he is already totally enamored * experiencing sweetness and light with him * giving without hesitation to your man * feeling totally safe with him * being extremely nice to him * say yes to all of his invitations * telling him that you enjoy all that he does for the growth of the relationship * letting him know that you care enormously * a guy you just met suddenly opens up a whole new world for you * a marriage proposal based on a passionate commitment * fertility * pregnancy * you could have babies with this man * he brings up the subject of children * an unplanned pregnancy moves you forward together * feeling more feminine due to his attentions * renewing vows with your husband * love is at the heart of all you do * a deep and lasting happiness with another * a union that grows stronger in time * he is the only one you have eyes for * a man who opens you up sexually * being hit over the head by emotions when you first meet him * an immediate and total physical attraction to a guy * having an instant bond with a past life lover * enjoying a reunion with a man you have known previously

## Work & Business:

your romantic partner bestows a special gift on you * people will love what you have to offer * a positive reception to a business proposal * becoming intimate with a coworker * a new job or career in an area you enjoy immensely * having integrity with money * using your assets to finance soulful creative projects and events * feeling that you will be okay monetarily no matter what happens * a pending venture promises quick income * up-front sales before the products reach the market * easy and early profits * an excellent reception to a public offering * having immediate popular success with a new book, film, or record * a business that deals with emotional healing * the areas of pregnancy, motherhood, fertility issues, maternity needs, and child-care as career options * being able to purchase something you have your heart set on * money comes in for doing fun things for the family * how to balance raising children with a career * a business that caters to sexuality or sensuality * a shot of happiness from excellent financial news * finding money for renovating a room for your baby * paying for daycare and baby sitters * easily buying necessities for your kids * working as a teacher or youth counselor * making income from a business that caters to younger people * recreational and entertainment ventures that incorporate boating or water sports for the family * theme parks and tourist attractions * rebuilding your life socially and financially in the aftermath of a relationship that involves children

*S*piritual *G*rowth:
experiencing an opening of the heart * true liberation through spirit * deep subconscious memories revealed * spiritual ancestry * genealogical soul gifts * intuitive abilities inherited through the maternal lineage * the unconditional and indescribable ecstatic state of the death experience * surrendering to the tidal wave of emotion caused by the lunar cycle * rising above your childhood experience in your healing work * embodiment and disembodiment * water as a healing force when used for swimming, ritual bathing, baptism, or physical purification * intuitive visions seen in reflections from the surface of pools or bowls of water * an unconscious energy that travels between the body and the soul * the spirit leaves the material world and enters a new state of being * the divine origin of earthly life * taking to heart the religious training of your heritage * a new kind of spiritualized romantic vibration * all relationship lessons help you understand your ever-developing love nature * working to feel unconditionally for all beings * concentrating on getting that open heart feeling * having a great potential for psychic experience * utilizing your emotions as a tool for gleaning knowledge from other realms * the white light of healing and upliftment affects you positively on all levels * giving thanks for divine gifts and miracles brought in through prayer * respecting and admiring yourself before you can care for another * the initial meeting with someone sets the theme for the purpose of the connection * the blissfully unreal

state of passionate obsession ✷ finding kindred souls who understand the true you ✷ a lifestyle deeply devoted to a religious order ✷ the awesome spiritual awakening that accompanies giving birth to a child

## Two of Cups

The two of cups represents an equal emotional exchange based on purely good intentions and genuine mutual caring. This can symbolize a couple who strive to be together in a safe and happy relationship. In the material world, the two of cups shows how to achieve harmonious creative partnership and constructive teamwork with others.

### Romance:

showing you care by treating him well ✷ real feeling coming back at you for the first time from another ✷ there are no road maps to or from the heart ✷ true love is sacred and should never be interrupted ✷ similar soul qualities attract you to each other ✷ a man who makes you feel good ✷ you can trust your mate to be sensitive toward you ✷ the honeymoon phase of a relationship has the potential to continue long into the future ✷ an easy rapport with an emotionally accessible man ✷ he wants to make a sincere offer to you ✷ both of you are sensitive and vulnerable to moody behavior ✷ a real heart level connection to a kind and lovely person ✷ you may be his first and only sweetheart ✷ he knows what he wants and so do you ✷ a deep intimacy produces very lucky children ✷ if estranged, he wants to see you again ✷ he certainly has a rare affection for you ✷ being blinded by love ✷ joy and innocence pervade the best romantic match * holding a torch for someone special * he needs sympathy from you right now * intimacy expressed through cuddling and holding hands * two people experience true contentment when together * sharing a serene and enjoyable life with another * being friends helps a couple maintain long-term harmony

## Work & Business:

a pleasant and positive partnership that has lifetime potential * mutual attraction with a coworker is real whether anything develops or not * becoming inseparable friends with someone you meet in your occupation * having to put out constant good energy to customers * a business that requires excellent manners and interpersonal diplomacy * a job where you must remain courteous to everybody * a productive and harmonious place of employment * when asking for professional favors, be nice and you will get them * actively dating someone you met through work * you receive financial benefits through the employment of your romantic partner * getting along beautifully with your colleagues * career problems resolved by kind behavior toward others * coworkers take a healthy interest in helping you meet a compatible man * someone on the job has a crush on you * any business that deals with sex, romance, engagement, marriage, or honeymoon events * if two people desire the same goal, the project will come together * your lover supports and inspires your career * light entertainment and idealistic ventures that market fantasy to the public * forming a creative partnership with the person you sleep with

## Spiritual Growth:

life is a series of lessons in forgiveness and unconditional love * emotional bonding in the realm of spirit * if the heart is pure, the universe listens and provides * taking good care of another person is the ultimate spiritual goal * the entire quest of a lifetime may be to find your soul mate or twin flame * there is no one true path to a deeply passionate nature * a born-again pacifist * an ethical vegan who cannot eat or wear another living creature * sacred trust prevents unkind arguments in close relationships * you are worthy of assistance and compassion from others * those who radiate absolutely positive energy toward all * people who light up the lives of all they touch * loving someone with all your heart and soul * mantra recitation and prayer as projections of emotion from your heart to the ears of the godhead * natural psychic communication with an unknown intelligence * the healing power of a brain awash in the chemical release that accompanies falling in love * giving and receiving affection strengthens the immune system * a platonic relationship where no defensiveness or romantic expectations exist * having a genuine desire for everyone to achieve the best in life * intimate acts that focus on mutual ecstasy and satisfaction * a selfless union where both individuals break through their fears and expose their emotional vulnerabilities * a spiritual bond as the best beginning foundation for a connection that will grow out of control with insane passion

### Three of Cups

The three of cups represents a great party or collective social event on the horizon that will change the outcome of the reading. This cup can also indicate a pleasure trip or incredibly fun occasion that lifts your spirits and reconnects you to the celebratory tradition of all humanity, where community members gather to express the joy of being alive and escape the drudgery of material demands.

### Romance:

you need to find friends to socialize with to meet new men ✳ dating with a positive attitude while seeking the right mate ✳ going out and getting to know different people ✳ having a great time and enjoying yourself ✳ a relationship that is based on good moments shared ✳ a guy who makes time for sexual play✳ say yes to all his invitations ✳ a friendship that flourishes and develops into infatuation ✳ hanging out with a dud guy for his social connections ✳ using humor to make him laugh and cool out ✳ you only want him to be relaxed and happy ✳ not taking a flaky guy too seriously ✳ a large measure of being with him is to take a break from reality ✳ more than one man coming into your life ✳ having a choice between many potential partners ✳ thinking every person you meet has romantic possibilities ✳ he would not miss seeing you for all the world ✳ a strong signal that he is sleeping with more than one woman ✳ a casual attitude toward sexual encounters ✳ meeting someone new at a holiday celebration, party, wedding, dinner, reunion, barbecue, or other social occasion ✳ focusing on the positive aspects of a relationship, not the bad times ✳ traditional holidays used for the timing of events in an unfolding romance ✳ a large and splashy wedding ✳ playfulness and the pursuit of pleasure are a big part of a union that honors sensuality and life itself

# Work & Business:

you receive positive public recognition for your job performance * having a great time where you work * following your bliss professionally * not a serious or sacrificing position * amazingly good news about money coming to you * you are deliriously happy about the result of recent business deals * friendships formed at work that extend into your personal life * female colleagues with whom you are close outside of the office * forming an alliance, practice, or partnership with other women * wanting the good things in life without having to work * being adverse to manual labor * career retardation * being stuck in a job that allows you to party long into retirement * an excellent position with a generous salary and benefits * an employer pays for your living expenses * something big to celebrate * important parties coming up associated with work * any business that provides gathering places for people to meet, such as resorts, restaurants, bars, cafes, clubs, and theaters * all sporting arenas and events, amusement parks, and more localized community affairs * making income from weddings, holidays, reunions, and celebrations * mindless enjoyment provided by the entertainment industries * gambling and gaming * overenthusiasm about the scope of your success

# Spiritual Growth:

taking heavy spiritual responsibility lightly * feeling great pleasure in being alive * seeing the cosmic joke in everything * you face adversity with laughter and hope for the future * celebrations that renew your spirit * claiming your right to joy and happiness * you have nothing to complain about once you tap into the bottomless divine source * a humanitarian who loves to help others * being revitalized by a vacation or a night of partying * the more celebration-oriented elements of organized religion ❊ the performance of sacred music and dance ❊ the observation of traditional holidays ❊ a spiritual practice you love that grows all your lifetime through ❊ girlfriends who do Tarot, astrology, runes, and other divinatory readings together ❊ word-of-mouth recommendations for intuitive counselors ❊ giving or receiving readings at cafe or storefront settings ❊ psychic fairs or private parties with practitioners as the entertainment ❊ a group of friends who enjoy working together spiritually in a social setting ❊ being grateful for the blessings you have earned in this lifetime ❊ attracting like-minded people who share your beliefs ❊ achieving a wider range of emotional expression ❊ experiencing an increase in intuitive abilities ❊ helping others feel better about the truth behind the drama of their material lives ❊ light and humorous spiritual information that uplifts the soul ❊ avoiding the destructive aspects of alcohol, sex, and drugs ❊ opting for nice or natural vices ❊ intimacy as a gateway to spiritual growth through a tantric relationship

## Four of Cups

The four of cups speaks of a period of distraction from your environment as your thoughts are riveted on emotional issues that obsess you. During this time, it is difficult to concentrate on the details of daily life because you are overwhelmed by powerful feelings that separate you from normal activities and the people around you.

## Romance:

you are not interested in dating * waiting for the right moment to move forward with him * having another chance at love * knowing where you stand in an existing relationship * feeling bored with a man * attached to thoughts of a certain person day and night * a preoccupation with his attitude toward you * being haunted by the memory of a past lover * offering stability to another * being certain of your role in his life * having trouble letting go of one who is always on your mind * do not verbally react in any way to what he says * enchantment or disenchantment with another * being ready to settle down for a life of socializing at home with your mate * two people who do not want to be apart * not discussing him with your friends and family * he does not want to appear vulnerable * he may only be thinking about you too * having trouble figuring him out * someone is emotionally unavailable * a relationship as a total distraction from reality * slow withdrawal from a union that has stagnated * healing from sexual betrayal * analyzing what went wrong with a connection that is not quite over * remaining in love with someone who does not know you exist * replaying your encounters with him from the moment you wake up until you fall asleep at night * severing a tie that is not fruitful or growthful for you * holding out from getting involved until you meet a quality individual ✶ a relationship has lost its overall appeal ✶ a long-distance romance helps develop telepathic communication between a couple

## Work & Business:

trying to get a larger vision of a project ✶ wondering where your next opportunity is coming from ✶ achieving right livelihood ✶ a serene and secure employment arrangement ✶ money issues are constantly on your mind ✶ waiting for the right offer ✶ daydreaming about more interesting career options ✶ seriously considering leaving your current job as soon as possible ✶ stepping back from a deal before completion ✶ giving yourself time before you arrive at a professional decision ✶ analyzing the situation fully before you respond ✶ do not reject an offer immediately ✶ studying the scope of a project in great depth ✶ material benefits are available to your entire family ✶ a solid opportunity for career advancement ✶ feeling stuck in a dissatisfying job ✶ having trouble seeing hope in the future ✶ not caring anymore about tedious and petty office politics ✶ you do not like your coworkers personally ✶ looking for something new that could be financially rewarding and emotionally fulfilling ✶ playing a waiting game until you receive constructive feedback ✶ hoping to find a job that is enjoyable and has a future ✶ being unsure of your professional direction ✶ figuring out your next step in negotiations ✶ an offer may appear exciting but may not be right for you ✶ making alternative plans ✶ having trouble concentrating on your work

## Spiritual Growth:

establishing clear emotional boundaries with others ✶ a reflective time as a growthful time ✶ during crisis moments, listen to soothing messages from the universal force of the good * a basic readiness to begin an intuitive arts practice * balancing out relationships from the past by looking toward the future * moving into a psychic state once your personality is stabilized * taking quality time for your own development * psychological blocks are removed * drawing spiritual energy to yourself through the process of detachment * gleaning information from the higher spheres through meditation and channeling * your immediate environment supports and accelerates your personal growth * being completely secure in the realm of your own beliefs * working to achieve inner peace and contentment * a calm spiritual state of alertness * assessing your religious values * living up to moral principles * not letting relationships distract you on the path toward enlightenment * being absorbed with intricate philosophies that delineate all that exists in the universe * a stable emotional life would improve your physical condition

### Five of Cups

The five of cups appears to prepare you for potential romantic disappointment where your expectations of love and pleasure are not quite fulfilled. The lesson behind this letdown is to stop making emotional demands on others and respect their true feelings, even if you are unhappy with the conditions that result in reality.

### Romance:

you are worried that he will toss you aside * meeting the challenge of authentic intimacy * showing affection may be difficult for him * the failure of an idealized dream with a man * he may not care anymore ✳ he may still be recovering from a breakup ✳ someone who is painfully alone but will not reveal it ✳ being acutely sensitive to his moods ✳ he may not be as nice or pure as you think ✳ a connection may never become more than a friendship ✳ nobody is going to be completely perfect ✳ if the love is gone, let him go ✳ filling yourself with hope after a tormented affair ✳ being honest and exposing your own mistakes ✳ taking the blame for interpersonal problems ✳ stop looking at the turmoil of the past ✳ seize a real opportunity for growth by releasing what is not working ✳ start loving yourself and stop choosing losers as partners ✳ having a cynical or distorted view of love ✳ a couple who maintains humor during upsetting times ✳ he feels guilty about hurting you ✳ having difficulty achieving happiness and personal satisfaction with men ✳ your shared dreams may be hard to actualize unless he lightens up about his problems ✳ he may not be over you yet ✳ passive behavior by a man is like a slap in the face ✳ if he does not call or show up, forget him immediately ✳ you may have subconsciously wounded him by what you said ✳ the date is canceled ✳ the vow is broken ✳ the engagement is off ✳ a troubled relationship is falling apart

## Work & Business:

a time when nothing seems to be coming together ✳ sinking under the weight of responsibilities unfulfilled ✳ a loss of capital ✳ a stock value or rating drops ✳ regretting an investment ✳ a business is not paying off as you had expected ✳ possible delays on payments or job news ✳ not the greatest indicator of success ✳ leaving your current position ✳ a job loss or demotion is probable ✳ your dreams of success may be too high ✳ you could encounter private humiliation at work ✳ recovering a portion of your losses ✳ an affair gone bad with a colleague whom you see every day ✳ look to the future, let go of the past ✳ if you do not utilize talents, you could lose them ✳ feeling bored and dissatisfied with your field of occupation ✳ having trouble raising money for a project ✳ someone may not come through as promised ✳ trusting a partner with your money and getting ripped off ✳ lacking interest in your present job ✳ not receiving the title or position you want ✳ you are confused about investing in someone who has a record of previous failures

## Spiritual Growth:

bad relationships and their spiritual significance ✳ losing someone as a vehicle moving you along your path ✳ a broken heart prevents you from developing your sense of lovingness ✳ a life in avoidance of intimacy ✳ celibate nuns and monks ✳ stop worrying about the past and enjoy the present ✳ a warning against missing out on pleasure by denying your sensual birthright of tastes fulfilled ✳ joining a religious group in the aftermath of a disastrous affair ✳ having a sense that reality is meaningless ✳ feeling existential nothingness ✳ renunciation based on experiencing the unkindness of others ✳ your spiritual teachers let you down emotionally ✳ realizing someone is a lost soul and you cannot save him ✳ transcending your neuroses ✳ on the highest level, unconditional love that never questions or fails ✳ getting control over moody behavior ✳ breaking codependency issues by letting him go ✳ feeling left out of a religious group ✳ a mortifying loneliness of soul ✳ reclaiming your serenity after an ordeal that twisted your peace of mind ✳ acceptance of the reality of your current material situation ✳ due to soul imbalance or karmic interference, you would be better off alone than with him

## Six of Cups

This cup symbolizes well-being expressed through properly balanced emotional channels. The six of cups radiates trust and sincerity between people, and brings soul renewal and a return to a more innocent time when happiness seemed simple to achieve.

### *Romance:*

youthful memories of love * what the relationship was like when it was new * once he starts up with you again, it will keep going * someone who is childlike, lighthearted, optimistic, and playful * getting joyful energy back into a partnership * mutually opening up to each other * a good sign that he will turn out for the better * he will ask you out again * he is easy to get along with * you can safely move forward with him * he is coming back into your life * instant familiarity with someone * a friendship is rekindled * seeing him for the second time only * he hopes you will want him eventually * believing you can fall in love again * if the guy is pure, you could have a nice sex life * cuddling and kissing boosts antibodies and virus-killing T cells * you could stay with him for the rest of your life * a major implication of marriage potential between two people based on feeling good together * some sort of reconciliation * restructuring your lifestyle to have more time for fun * someone you already know steps forward * reunion with a childhood boyfriend * a retired couple finally enjoys long days relaxing * when he ends his current relationship, he will want you

### *Work & Business:*

fulfilling a lifelong dream * new and exciting opportunities * honest and open-minded people make better employees in the long run ✳ major rewards come in that improve every area of your life ✳ getting back to interests you enjoyed when younger ✳ a hobby turns into a lucrative business venture ✳ dropping out of one profession to live your ultimate employment dream ✳ being completely committed to seeing a project through to a satisfying conclusion ✳ two people who are comfortable doing business together ✳ reestablishing an existing operation in a better location ✳ an old investment suddenly increases in value ✳ creativity inspired by happy conditions ✳ your partner perfectly balances your temperament ✳ a childhood connection comes through for you financially or gives you an excellent lead ✳ starting a business with a friend ✳ occupations that cater to the youth culture ✳ the anti-aging bonanza ✳ buying into health programs that promise a revitalization of the body ✳ industries that promote clean lifestyle habits and natural diets ✳ working at spas and resorts ✳ a career in sports, exercise, massage, or yoga ✳ getting an influx of funds to expand an existing business ✳ restarting a bankrupt operation under a new name ✳ optimistic news about something potentially successful ✳ taking a much needed vacation ✳ your employer is incredibly kind and generous

## Spiritual Growth:

positive changes result from seeking happiness in your life ✳ you are completely free to love as a whole person ✳ radiating good feelings to everyone ✳ returning to your childhood beliefs ✳ giving of yourself to humanity for the cause of peace on Earth ✳ achieving a balanced healing power ✳ all the clean energy you put out comes back as cosmic rewards ✳ practicing forgiveness every single day ✳ a good upbringing with conscious parents assists in early spiritual unfoldment ✳ passing out reaffirming messages every chance you get ✳ an old soul who has been on this planet many times before ✳ trying to achieve a harmonious state with another ✳ avoiding fighting with others ✳ letting go of critical behavior ✳ the greatest thing is to love and be loved in return ✳ your evolution moves forward when you stop blaming others ✳ having someone who openly and eagerly embraces and supports your spiritual development ✳ attracting all that is right and good to your life ✳ extreme contentment with your place in the world ✳ feeling like your own self again ✳ emotional regression into a childlike state during therapy or recovery ✳ letting go of destructive habits that are preventing a peaceful existence ✳ trusting in high-level friends who respect your beliefs ✳ expressing love through all your actions ✳ the natural world as a powerful healing force ✳ a humanitarian who fights bias, hatred, and prejudice and tries to mend rifts between war-like factions

## Seven of Cups

Traditionally, this cup describes a powerful imagination fueled by visions, dreams, and fantasies. You should keep your options open and examine the entire field before you focus on what can be realistically developed. The seven of cups brings emotional expansion and creative inspiration and often finds you madly in love with another.

## Romance:

knowing how amazing sex could be with the right person ✳ an emphasis on experimentation in bed ✳ unbridled sensuality ✳ experiencing inaccurate delusions about his interest in you ✳ he knows he could have it all with you ✳ finally meeting someone you have admired from afar * wondering if he shares your intense feelings * a man who understands all the things you are * missing somebody who was never there * irrational mood swings can destroy great physical chemistry * communicating your desires to him * fantasizing that you are a part of his life * having a false sense of self-importance in the consciousness of a powerful, wealthy, or famous man * your fears may be unfounded * throwing an emotional tantrum over imaginary crimes you blame on him * glorious memories of carefree, decadent days * your passion is building toward delirium * you may be afraid of letting go in love * your highest, deepest dream of a man comes true * an inner resistance toward that which feels good * he is petrified that you might reject him * wondering if he is real or not * the departmentalized sex drive of the bisexual person * the labyrinthian libido of the pervert * having premonitions of a man before he enters your life * narrowing down your dating field to one man * receiving information about him through the enigmatic language of dreams

## Work & Business:

watch out for those who promise big things * a partner has many ideas to incorporate into a project * having the freedom to be totally creative through your job * bad financial advice could lead to rapid expansion or sudden loss * to land the career of your wildest dreams * visions of future accomplishments are waiting on your doorstep * income earned by the products of your active imagination * too many opportunities can be confusing * outside influences only serve to strengthen a deal direction * after a divorce, you need to refocus on bringing in abundance through new contacts and projects * hopeful pursuit of a lifetime fantasy * to want more than you can afford

❈ living beyond your means ❈ pretending to be wealthy ❈ buying luxury items on credit ❈ the stupidity of spending large amounts on useless status items ❈ the glamour, fashion, and jewelry industries ❈ having a talent for acting, writing, or directing films ❈ the field of cartoon animation and its subsequent merchandising bonanza ❈ making money off of fantasy worlds ❈ expanding your career horizons by thinking big ❈ creative work that is highly original and often eccentric

## *S*piritual *G*rowth:

a time when all dreams come true ❈ the psychological conditions behind mystical delusions ❈ unexplained psychic phenomena ❈ channeling imaginary beings from outer planes of consciousness ❈ living out a fantasy by adopting the name and costume of a spiritual being ❈ the personification of universal force through the creation of deities and spiritual icons ❈ angels, elves, sprites, fairies, and water spirits ❈ having clairvoyant sensitivity toward ghosts and apparitions ❈ the pathology of believing in ETs and UFOs ❈ astral sex with dream lovers ❈ delusions of grandeur concerning your past life associations with major religious figures ❈ those who insist they are current incarnations of prominent characters from recorded history ❈ acting out of deep devotion rather than self-interest in your romantic life ❈ exploring many diverse spiritual studies with an open mind ❈ being gullible and buying into the illusion of a corrupt, self-appointed guru ❈ reflective images of Jesus and Mary as seen by thousands in ordinary places ❈ your intuition opens up but is not completely reliable yet ❈ prophecy ❈ recalling the people, cultures, and dramatic situations of a past life ❈ unseen worlds of intelligence ❈ choosing the pathway that offers the greatest potential for soul development in this lifetime ❈ using creative visualization to manifest exactly what you need ❈ a highly inspired religious disciple ❈ approaching a problem by viewing the big picture * completing preparations to fulfill your destiny * getting a mental glimpse of the future

## Eight of Cups

The eight of cups is a card of serious devotion to achieving a treasured spiritual or emotional goal through total dedication and commitment. You are finally ready to direct yourself toward that which deeply satisfies you and helps you mature psychologically.

## Romance:

being ready for a relationship with a worthy partner * his presence is with you everywhere you go * you cannot shake thoughts of a guy * you may not tell anyone about him * he may be offering something real * you want to be taken seriously love-wise * his attraction to you is bringing up old intimacy issues for him * he does not plan to let you go * after he heals, he will offer himself to you * a lifelong relationship with a deep guy * growing out of fantasy substitutes and looking for someone substantial * choosing a man who will always be there for you emotionally * a romantic partner could become your marriage partner * a slowly developing union based on devotion to a higher power and a sober mentality * you must see him one last time * hoping that he will be moved to make a genuine effort * returning to what is true and solid * he comes back from a trip with an increased commitment * you both share a secret desire * a solitary quest to find a soulful partner * journeying in search of true love * whoever appears as a response to prayer is your righteous mate * send him healing light to give guidance about which way to go

## Work and Business:

making a decision to leave your job ❊ desiring work that motivates you on a deeper level ❊ focusing on finding real solutions to financial problems ❊ fulfilling serious career dreams ❊ being totally obsessed with making money ❊ honest, trusted workers who stay with their jobs for life ❊ your employer values you ❊ staying cool and keeping your head during negotiations ❊ smooth teamwork amongst coworkers ❊ doing what you really want to do ❊ satisfaction guaranteed ❊ having no more enthusiasm for your current position ❊ you have gone as far as you can go ❊ a new intellectual challenge accompanies a career change ❊ seriously considering an entirely new field of endeavor ❊ not giving up the pursuit of a job or a person ❊ leaving a status quo, income-producing job ❊ seeking out work that lets you explore a variety of options ❊ putting great care into every action you take regarding your goal ❊ having to finish an enormous amount in a very short time

## Spiritual Growth:

what once was fantasy could become reality ❊ a solitary spiritual quest ❊ being of service to others as karmic payback ❊ going through a deep healing process ❊ some resolution occurs and the grief is lifted ❊ the pure of heart have an inborn love of humanity ❊ getting in touch with your internal dialogue ❊ a quiet time spent doing inner work on your own ❊ a profound and moving soul experience ❊ withdrawing from the world in search of a spiritual life ❊ trying to understand the meaning behind your destiny leads to greater wisdom ❊ you may witness some miracles as a result of prayer and well-directed intentions ❊ pushing yourself out of a time of avoiding personal growth issues ❊ feeling disillusioned with a group and moving on alone to discover new types of faiths ❊ you want to be taken seriously for your beliefs ✳ a period of soul balancing ✳ realizing karma must be resolved before you can move forward on your path ✳ having a solemn spiritual side that nobody else sees ✳ initiation into the mysteries ✳ people who devote their entire lives to playing a religious role for their community ✳ studying metaphysical subjects in a private setting ✳ giving up superficial people and activities ✳ following your inner voice by surrendering to the divine

## Nine of Cups

The nine of cups symbolizes long-lasting love and brings deep contentment to a fortunate couple. The happiness that accompanies this cup is plentiful and makes you a productive member of society. Relationships here nurture and accelerate your process of personal growth and emotional fulfillment.

### Romance:

you are the only woman in his heart ✳ he has decided he wants to be happy ✳ maintaining joy is a huge part of marriage ✳ he wants to provide romance in your life ✳ a big love lived fully in your soul ✳ amazing sexual chemistry due to the depth of emotions felt ✳ someone is a potential lifetime mate ✳ he needs to recognize how precious you are ✳ perfecting an already wonderful union ✳ being good to his people ✳ an easy, future-oriented relationship ✳ complete sensual gratification with another ✳ knowing you would sleep only with him forever ✳ he meets all your emotional needs ✳ a substantial love offer from a guy ✳ accepting and appreciating his goodness ✳ wishes fulfilled * all he wants to do is live with you for the rest of his life * a deep friendship is a crucial part of your incredible intimacy with him * he wants to be satisfied by your attentions * he is considering asking you to be his wife * a long-term commitment * he finally feels good about having a relationship with you * making future plans together * a guy that could help you actualize your dreams * there is someone for everyone romantically * you feel complete only with him * an extremely sympathetic partner who tries to understand your feelings * the love of your life * living in a perpetual state of ecstasy due to a lover

## Work & Business:

excellent financial security until you die * getting set up in your career with the future in mind * your investments gain value beyond your wildest dreams * the successful fruition of deals made long ago * you finally get a promotion at the level you deserve * employers or partners know you need to be satisfied financially to stay with them * taking a sabbatical or a well-deserved vacation * rising above dicey monetary circumstances into an arena of major players * knowing for sure that a business idea will work out beautifully * retirement funds are secure * hoarding or stockpiling basic products * the business of art and collectibles * the future value of creative properties, extraordinary furnishings, and highly rare vintages * a good harvest ensures a pleasant year ahead * a position that completely engages you creatively * a happy and secure home for later years * actualizing a comfortable lifestyle you have planned since you began working * the ultimate fulfillment of monetary dreams * you wake up each day looking forward to your job * achieving a self-sufficient lifestyle

## *Spiritual Growth:*

tolerating, accepting, and understanding those who are different from you, if we are to survive as a species * seeing everyone as a potential spiritual teacher * claiming your own personal happiness * securing an emotional base in cooperation with others puts you in a good healing space * you work energetically to help people discover their grounding center * idealistic dreams for humanity as expressed through unlimited love for all creation * maintaining cosmic flexibility by accepting any belief system at face value * being a source of growing peace in the world * the many who are working towards the unfolding of our collective enlightenment at a poignant time of mass social de-evolution * the purity of joyful feelings devoid of limitations by reality * awareness of being a vehicle through which the holy spirit manifests for all eternity * a pledge by a couple to the planet to make the world a better place for future generations * pacifists and the disarmament movement * enjoying the gifts of life * having a great deal of respect for your own moral values * achieving eternal happiness after a lifetime of good deeds

# The Cups

## Ten of Cups

The ten of cups makes you fully aware of the members of your tribe and indicates the involvement of others in a familial arrangement. As your affection is reciprocated by like-minded or biologically connected individuals, you have more success on every level and become part of a larger community. The ten depicts a positive lifestyle that completes your path of learning to love that began with the ace of cups.

## Romance:

finding a secure place for your feelings ✳ considering someone a member of your immediate family ✳ remembering a time when the good life was the ultimate reward ✳ let your relatives win in arguments to keep the peace ✳ a high-quality relationship where the couple includes others in important activities ✳ a cultural tradition that you and your lover enjoy collectively with others ✳ an easy entree into a well-established group ✳ the influence of both of your families is positive ✳ his parents or yours help out with childcare or with improvements to the quality of your living arrangement ✳ dating a guy and being in sync with his children from a previous partner ✳ a couple who creates a perfectly harmonious union together ✳ your greatest dreams culminate with the creation of a lasting marriage that includes children ✳ a large traditional wedding brings joy to everyone invited ✳ being deeply loved and mated ✳ talking about starting a family with a guy ✳ he is totally open to having kids with you ✳ being amongst the half of the population that does not get divorced ✳ an older couple raises their grandchildren with great care ✳ deep contentment with your place in the world ✳ your lifestyle is heaven on Earth ✳ feeling blissfully ecstatic after you accept his romantic proposal * never losing custody of your children * your closest friends are your relatives * creating a new type of family with those who understand you most * being totally sincere with a man * he makes you feel like a complete human being * achieving a fulfilling social life together * a relationship that unfolds naturally without preconceived expectations * he is concerned about the well-being of your people

## Work & Business:

maximum financial security that covers even your grandchildren * a family home passed down through the generations becomes yours * extremely high achievements * taking over a business started by your relatives * sharing expenses with brothers or sisters to care for your parents * moving to a new location positively affects the earning power of you or your husband * owning a neighborhood business that caters to locals * wanting work that is totally fulfilling and helps others improve their quality of life * being self-employed in a home-based operation * providing childcare for kids other than your own * living and working in your hometown * great prosperity and huge accomplishments professionally * you could keep your job until you retire * your coworkers become a substitute family for you * marrying into a business * employment comes through your spouse * renting a larger residence or receiving funds to improve your current one * giving back to the community due to your financial blessings * making a contribution to an organization that helps mothers and children * investing in a business that has been established for generations * employees utilize smooth teamwork to create a positive environment * a communal group goes into commercial production to achieve a self-sufficient lifestyle * finding the best people around to employ you ⁕ happily working for your mother or father ⁕ retiring from work to become a wife and mother ⁕ major connections come through your family

## Spiritual Growth:

a good relationship uplifts your vibration and helps heal the entire planet ⁕ one who is tired of slaving for humanity and wants a traditional family life instead ⁕ the spirit of community service ⁕ your relatives support your beliefs ⁕ having good communication skills with all races of people from all stratum of society ⁕ having unconditional love for everyone ⁕ finding ourselves stuck in this world together, we could do a better job of taking care of each other ⁕ your family gets you through bleak times by showing real concern ⁕ your saving grace comes from those who help and love you ⁕ group soul karma where people incarnate together collectively to work out moral crimes they committed previously ⁕ making a spiritual agreement before birth to do the family thing with a certain man and bring in highly conscious children ⁕ experiencing different lifestyles is growthful and expansive for your soul ⁕ the ultimate goal is the blending of the races ⁕ releasing childhood issues and realizing your parents were not so bad ⁕ your mother and father as huge karmic influences over your destiny ⁕ a ghetto mentality where people who share common religious or cultural backgrounds live in the same geographical area ⁕ trying to find the players who belong on your spiritual team ⁕ following the belief system of your ancestors ⁕ a clan who supports a childbearing woman until her baby comes to term ⁕ communities cooperate to raise funds for one of their own ⁕ support group members who have relatives with similar problems ⁕ giving birth as a profoundly cosmic and life-changing experience

## Page of Cups

The youthful, inexperienced Page of cups is a gentle soul who responds emotionally to everything and everyone in his life. Though primarily a passive creature, he gives of himself in all situations without hesitation. The Page is immature in his view of personal relationships and appears shy and sensitive because he is afraid to show his feelings.

### Romance:

his children or your children may be a big part of your union * someone who is needy and insecure * he may be an emotional adolescent * he has to decide whether to stay a boy or become a real man * having a tendency to be dominated by your partner * he may have only been with little girls, never a woman * he is unsure what to do about you * he may be scared of your equal power and intelligence * he may not think you want him * realizing that you are safe and loved * to feel needed by him * supersensitivity to criticism from your mate * he craves attention and affection * he will be hurt if you neglect him * a guy who is sentimental and may write poetry or songs dedicated to you * he can be jealous due to his insecurity * a loving, attentive companion * he has a tendency to be moody * he may be naive about games played by the opposite sex * someone who becomes attached to you like a mascot * it is a sign of emotional weakness if he never takes action * you need to be more confident around him * losing your ability to trust another * old traumatic baggage overshadows his current reality * you need stronger self-esteem * try to take risks in love * he is easily influenced by those in his environment * a young admirer * a nice person with good intentions * you may have to

make the first move with him ∗ surrendering the child in yourself to another ∗ shared sensuality builds trust ∗ he may desperately fear that you will reject him ∗ men who are sexually
and emotionally open and vulnerable

## *Work & Business:*

being a pushover who cannot say no to any requests for
financial aid ∗ being replaced by younger workers ∗ losing your
edge at work ∗ you may be too insecure about your abilities ∗
someone who is not materialistic at heart ∗ working with a person who is a minor ∗ it is hard to be aggressive with your
employers ∗ selling yourself out by taking a job beneath you ∗
bringing one of your children into your business ∗ much confusion over how to proceed with a project ∗ someone may be too
inexperienced to handle responsibility ∗ any industry that
caters to children ∗ a teacher, daycare worker, or full-time
mother ∗ worrying over lack of funds ∗ enjoying the social
aspects of your job ∗ someone at work appreciates all your selfless efforts ∗ being supportive of young people just starting
their careers ∗ a devoted, considerate, and loyal employee ∗
unpaid volunteer and intern positions ∗ having trouble developing your ambitions ∗ you may stay at a low-level job forever
if that is the best you can do ∗ the most junior assistant role in
an operation ∗ the contribution of baby boomers to the economy and its effect ∗ the artistic dreamer lost in his imagination
who creates unique work ∗ say yes to all social invitations from
your colleagues

## *Spiritual Growth:*

healing your inner child in recovery ∗ you may be subconsciously acting out a childhood role with a spiritual teacher ∗

gathering psychic impressions * expressing the gentle side of your personality without fear * joining a cult-like group with a father figure as leader * being attracted to new and enlightening people and experiences * a devoted and trustworthy disciple * listening to the beliefs of others without judgement or prejudice * personal growth comes from expanding your social circle more boldly * you need to learn to ask for help from others * being afraid of the unknown has a negative effect on soul development * the compassionate heart * intuitive ability opening up * being highly impressionable when it comes to psychic readings * someone who is spiritually immature * sensitivity to hidden undercurrents in human behavior * innate receptivity to the higher planes * a helpful, cheerful assistant or devotee of a religious leader * dead-on impulses lead you to the right people and places for knowledge and information * a child or younger person with whom you forge a deep bond * the work of healing damaged children * a pregnancy that is meant to be * inspirational messages erase your skepticism * you need guidance to become highly developed spiritually * you cannot follow your path alone * surrendering to a greater heavenly power * helping others by nurturing their more sensitive emotional natures

# The Cups

## Queen of Cups

The Queen of cups easily adjusts her personality to master all people and situations. She commands her immediate social arena and is comfortable adapting to an ever-changing environment. She is ruled by her intuitive nature and openly offers support and friendship to everyone regardless of existential differences.

## Romance:

being nebulous about your feelings for a guy * exposing your vulnerability to him * being good-hearted and compassionate toward him * he brings out your feminine qualities * being gullible when he tells you his fantasies * trying to seduce him * achieving safety with a guy who loves you for yourself * there could be another woman he socializes with * you have no agenda with him * he will help soften your personality * contact him only when you feel it in your gut * call to him spiritually when he needs your help * say one nice thing after another to him * not projecting a future together * trying to stay in reality about him * make sure he gets your phone number * he knows he has a friend in you * definitely invite him over for dinner * be casual when testing the waters of his feelings * tell him that he has been on your mind * opening up emotionally to him * if a relationship is meant to be, you should not have to do anything * having so much love to give to the right man * being incredibly patient and compassionate while he grows up * he is active, you are passive * love and caring as a normal state of being * you are a calming influence in his life * classic courtship should be effortless on your end * making sure he has a good time * he sees you lose it in public * forgiving a past partner who hurt you * being the mistress or secret lover of an unavailable man * you are unsure about a commitment * a warning against getting involved with dangerous men * he expects you to fully participate in his social life

## Work & Business:

being unfocused about your career * having trouble deciding which way to go * trying to make work fun * an easy living * loss of identity on the job * attracting excellent employees * building a diverse group to tackle an important project * drawing on your soft power professionally * a casual attitude toward financial responsibilities * being content with a daily routine * getting along well with coworkers * an elegant and classy boss makes your life easy * a woman who relates well to customers or an audience as her energy draws people in * any business that relates to creative products or the intuitive arts * standing up for your rights at work * a good connection comes through a female in your life * socializing with coworkers at a special event * being a space cadet with money * spending beyond your means * creating a good work environment * waiting to hear from someone * a good friend helps you financially or pays your way for something special * excellent salespeople * the restaurant, recreational, or entertainment fields as career options * everyone you have ever known comes through on a project * an artist * a charity worker, volunteer, or selfless activist who promotes a positive cause

## Spiritual Growth:

an extremely tolerant person * not taking life too seriously * the most generous woman in the world * the more you give away, the greater the spiritual rewards * trusting in the power of love and inner faith to deliver the truth * a channeler, mystic, psychic, medium, clairvoyant, Tarot card reader, or astrologer * yielding to the will of God * keep asking the universe for what you want * a dreamer or visionary being * your instincts are right on * knowing something will happen ahead of time * finding comfort and security in your beliefs * adopting the rules and following a pathway as a devotee * your inner prayer helps you keep it together in the material world * female deities, saints, and spiritual leaders * passively receiving the word of God * practicing unconditional love and faith * having a compassionate heart of gold * a sympathetic humanitarian always able to understand and accept the shortcomings of others * releasing the past through forgiveness * watching out for so-called spiritual types who beg for money from poor people * healing self-destructive tendencies and letting go of negative habits * offering physical assistance to another * not forcing issues because the correct outcome will occur naturally * witnessing the drama of your destiny unfold * becoming less defensive by opening up to new experiences in your life

## Knight of Cups

By tradition, the Knight of cups is the offer, invitation, or proposal that alters the outcome of the reading. His personality and opinions constantly change so it is hard to believe him or feel secure emotionally with him. This is the flakiest knight in the deck due to his romantic unreliability, poor memory, or excessive partying.

## Romance:

he could just be an illusion passing through your life * believing the words of unworthy guys ✳ he may not be thinking about you at all ✳ someone could show up but nothing may develop from the encounter ✳ the attraction may not turn into a relationship ✳ he may pretend he is romantic initially ✳ a man who does not know himself ✳ a sexually precocious cycle ✳ going with the flow ✳ making it a party for him ✳ he could be content just to flirt with you ✳ a major sign of a marriage proposal ✳ he may not be serious about having children ✳ being attracted to an uncentered person ✳ he may still be running around ✳ he is far from settling down with one woman ✳ a flirty guy who leads you on and then runs away ✳ be careful about codependency issues with him ✳ he wants a connection to you but is unsure about what that means ✳ he would never pressure you into a commitment ✳ the Seinfeld-ization of the American male psyche regarding relationships ✳ a guy who is offering you nothing ✳ he may be lazy and does not even want to try for you ✳ he is in a period where his mind is cloudy ✳ the foreplay was great, but then he disappeared ✳ an unbalanced guy who drags you into a scandal or an emotional ménage à trois ✳ if he asks you out, only consider it a casual date ✳ flakes, drifters, druggies, and drinkers ✳ his sexual development may be stuck at an adolescent level ✳ his flirtations are inappropriate and irresponsible ✳ an untrustworthy guy who never comes through ✳ promiscuity as a reaction to his own insecurities or feelings of inadequacy with women ✳ he could be mentally unstable and playing games with you for his own twisted amusement

## Work & Business:

the blind leading the blind financially ✳ a man who drops huge figures and brags about his wealth ✳ a deadbeat person who is unreliable ✳ a half-baked proposal ✳ someone who fakes their references ✳ an offer for employment that may never happen * feeling unsure about which way to go * being indecisive about accepting a new position * having trouble living your dreams in reality * not taking your job seriously * borrowing money you never intend to repay * a very enjoyable temporary job * an opportunity for mixing business with pleasure * a liar who is a big talker and name-dropper * taking distance from a project to figure out which way to go * a self-destructive man who ruins his financial security due to sex, drugs, or alcohol abuse issues * having too much fun and avoiding responsibilities * a con man who is a total loser and has nothing in reality * waiting for an offer to be made to you * any business that caters to drinking, dancing, and loud entertainment

## Spiritual Growth:

making offerings to the divine source * spiritual practices that utilize trance, dance, mind-expanding natural substances, and music in ceremonies where the entire congregation participates * the shaman who ingests certain psychotropic drugs for visionary or healing work * to lose yourself emotionally in your spiritual studies * learning to set up boundaries with others * ignoring those who try to push their beliefs on you * making yourself the most important person in your life * you cannot help someone who needs to bottom out * a person may get well but never get better * to extend money and services to a charitable cause * sacrificing material rewards to accomplish important spiritual work * submitting to a higher power to overcome weaknesses and addictions * something prohibits you from making rational decisions * a downward moral spiral * to go really low before you find God * the use of intoxicants to reach a state of extreme intuition * never take your health for granted * avoid excessive appetites and behaviors

## King of Cups

The King of cups is a man of intense but controlled emotions. He takes command of every situation and manipulates others in power struggles. This card represents the business world with a special emphasis on long-distance commerce and international markets.

## *Romance:*

he wants what he wants * he is a master who could play you out romantically * he has not said anything yet * a guy who loves you from afar * someone is testing you to see if you like him * he may be attracted to you, but he sure is putting you through it * he is enchanted by you but does not show it * his feelings about commitment are getting stronger * he enjoys the power you have * he is completely turned on by you * in his heart, he knows it is you * he may seem peaceful, but he is not pliable * he may be watery, but he is smart too * he is deeply affected by you * a guy who is interested but reserved * an obsessive guy could be hard to get rid of * a man who is devoted in his mind yet has trouble actively pursuing you * he has had a spiritual awakening and wants to describe it to you * powerful emotions are scary for him * he will not discuss his feelings with anyone * an inflexible man who loves you, but cannot say the words * he clams up over your direct approach to life * he is like emotional Teflon * a guy who is far away from you physically or is otherwise unreachable * a jealous and possessive man * a mysterious yet charming person * a man is distracting you from work

# Work & Business:

a person who lives for work to the exclusion of all else * do not verbalize your intentions * someone with a powerful reputation * a business owner, top executive, or global player * a killer investor on an international scale * importers and exporters * foreign markets * manufacturing or purchasing goods abroad * someone who hides their wealth successfully from others * excellent money management * never reveal, always conceal * keeping financial information to yourself * your boss is aware of your performance * long-distance phone calls are needed to seal a deal * intuitive business decisions * an offer to form a partnership with a major person * someone you have to speak with is inaccessible * a manipulative operator who builds a fortune * a dangerous competitor with money and contacts at his disposal * a man who seeks revenge against those who ripped him off * the perfect political operative * you may have to travel overseas for work * a tough employer * an important message is not getting through to you

# Spiritual Growth:

any business associated with spirituality and types of faith * foreign markets for religions established domestically * building a global network of devotees * traveling to another land for a retreat, workshop, or to meet a master being * a hypnotizer or mesmerizer * the world soul * practicing peaceful detachment * outer reflections of internal manifestations * an introspective time * letting go of the instinctual impulse to project your emotions onto others * a major male clairvoyant * a foreign-born spiritual teacher * a person who holds together a group of seekers with similar beliefs * a religious leader who uses humiliation to control and enslave his followers * a self-styled guru who utilizes brainwashing techniques to secure his power base * being internally prepared for any crisis of faith * when you have relationship riches and pure spiritual values, you do not need material distractions

## THE WANDS

### Ace of Wands

The ace of wands is a signal to move forward to new ideas, challenges, people, and creative ventures. You start over with renewed confidence and take immediate action on that which captures your attention. The ace helps you make a fresh start as you experience a rush of impulsive energy and excitement that expands your field of reference.

*Romance:*
    sexual intercourse * the male erection * a rush to the bedroom * taking the initiative to approach another * major erotic chemistry between two people * he has plans to seduce you on the first date * being forced into a physical relationship * he definitely has a hard on for you * feeling superhorny * someone who is hard to resist * deep desire that fills you with anticipation * falling in lust * having complete confidence in your partner * being an active and aggressive lover * grabbing someone you just met * starting over in love * he helps you overcome fears of intimacy * forcing him to meet your demands * being totally honest with your man * a new romance revitalizes and refreshes you * spiritual growth comes through your physical connection with him * entering a passionate phase in an existing relationship * a guy who plans exciting events and occasions to make you happy * feeling overwhelmed when you first meet him as though you were hit over the head * finding the energy to get rid of a dull person who is not your sexual equal * feeling secure about your erotic skills * a couple who

changes their lifestyle to lead a more vital and dynamic life together * going after someone with all you've got * finding yourself in the throes of ecstatic desire the instant you see him * getting ready to have great sex * may indicate pregnancy, birth, or the arrival of a child without warning

## *Work & Business:*

a project moves forward * you expand your field of opera-tion in the world * changing your profession * a new location for your place of business * beginning a recent job with a pos-itive attitude * choosing a career which you are passionate about * leaving a position on impulse * following your bliss through your work * dropping out of the rat race to live more simply * pure ambition * any business that involves sex, risk, sports, travel, or adventure * taking a sudden trip for business purposes * being turned on by someone at work * a one-night stand with a man you meet through your job * changing your work schedule or profession for spiritual survival * an employ-er or adversary meets your demands * taking the initiative to increase your income through new activities * beginning a proj-ect that exposes you to ideas and systems that are unfamiliar * pursuing your greatest material goals * child support as a result of an unplanned pregnancy * a job lead comes from out of the blue * a sudden rush of creative inspiration that should be actively developed * doing work you truly love * invention and innovation * visionary artwork unlike anything seen before * promoting a cause as an activist * exploring interests that you currently know nothing about

*S*piritual *G*rowth:
   eternal truths carry you to another level in your evolution ✳
being excited about a new course of spiritual study or a charis-
matic teacher ✳ feeling reborn ✳ having a major awakening of
consciousness ✳ looking forward to a positive future ✳
untouched territories of metaphysical knowledge ✳ picking up
telepathic energy from one you have just met ✳ a healthy sex
life revitalizes your soul ✳ following your wildest dreams on a
path free from past karmic involvement ✳ preparing for what is
yet to come ✳ opportunities for personal growth come to you
through universal force ✳ a guardian angel hitting you with a
club to move you on to greater wisdom and experience ✳ an
abundance of purely positive energy ✳ spiritual rebirth ✳ the
process of soul purification begins ✳ the presence of the holy
spirit ✳ the primal spark of the life force ✳ tantric sexual practice involving the worship of the male phallus ✳ starting a crusade to promote a humanitarian cause ✳ a new beginning for
those with substance abuse problems ✳ changing environments to
increase vitality ✳ comets, meteors, and volcanoes as powerful
explosive sources that begin and end certain cycles of creation

## Two of Wands

The two of wands is a time for taking action and establishing your power of will to accomplish major creative and passionate goals. By energetically gaining control over your life and becoming responsible for your own conduct, you are free to independently pursue your interests without the assistance of others.

### Romance:

you are totally ready to meet someone new * you have to make all the initial moves with him * being pushy and forcing yourself into his life * the first face-to-face meeting with him will lead to another * a recent acquaintance invites you to a sudden rendezvous * looking for someone who works outside of your profession * being easily turned on by an attractive, happening man * he is very sexually responsive and has a normal, healthy, and athletic libido * a quick hop into bed * you want him right now * he will make an arrangement to see you soon * he likes how you both appear as a couple to the world * transmitting messages of mutual attraction and desire * he is ready for a relationship * if you get a chance, grab him and hold on tight * having to maintain control over your passionate impulses * he is motivated to go forward with you * he has fallen in love with your ideas, energy, and enthusiasm * some action is exactly what you need * as wonderful as he is, you may not hear what you want * it may be hard to keep him away from you * he has the capacity to protect and take care of you * you are extremely sexually compatible with him * he may be wondering where you are and who you are with * he has definitely thought about having intercourse with you * fresh energy enlivens an existing union ✳ not giving up on him due to his problems ✳ forcing him to make a decision ✳ willfully trying to trap a man ✳ becoming totally involved in his personal and professional life

## Work & Business:

becoming master of your domain ✳ taking control over your financial affairs ✳ reaching a goal depends on your actions alone ✳ you are deeply motivated to conquer the world ✳ not expecting support from colleagues for your projects ✳ intensely inspired business transactions ✳ taking full command of your creative output ✳ passionate involvement in your work ✳ reaching solid ground materially ✳ securing your assets against loss ✳ being the one who initiates negotiations or brings up the subject of a deal ✳ you need to invest in peddling a project by yourself ✳ you must do all the legwork if you want something done right ✳ every moment in life is an opportunity for creative expansion ✳ make a low offer ✳ you need to energetically market your products, services, or self ✳ constant activity is mandatory for increasing sales ✳ sales reps who travel to see clients ✳ the importance of publicity and promotion for the success of a venture ✳ figuring out what you want to do next ✳ taking the ball and running with it ✳ you have to actively confront someone at work ✳ looking ahead to the future with great excitement ✳ you are right on track with your plans ✳ looking for financial results from impulse investments ✳ you can bring in the money you need ✳ lowering costs and increasing profits ✳ a new professional life begins with good connections ✳ staking out virgin business territory ✳ a changing of the guard at the top level of an organization ✳ your only objective with your creative work is to please yourself ✳ establishing your career identity in the world ✳ overseas markets ✳ being noticed for your enthusiastic job performance * having control over your source of artistic inspiration * being recognized for your ambition and extraordinary self-confidence

## Spiritual Growth:

your recovery is moving in the right direction * maintaining a strong equilibrium * taking care of yourself on every level * vigorous action in the name of all that is decent * accelerating the arrival of your soul mate by adopting a positive attitude * a change in consciousness is underway * someone who lives and breathes religion every minute * having a powerful identity in your spiritual world * a cosmic crusader who spreads the word * soliciting money and handing out literature in public for a religious group * those who sell theological products and prayers for a profit * money earned from healing work done out in the community * believing what you want regardless of those around you * the collective energy grid of the global village * the scope and impact of the major religions of the world * a fire is being lit to ignite a new spiritual path * by expressing your passionate nature, you touch people's feelings * defending your faith despite opposition * having the strength and courage to leave your job, friends, and family and begin a whole new life * actualizing creative ideas discovered during a spiritual epiphany

# The Wands

## Three of Wands

The driving force powered by the two of wands reaches a fuller expression with the three of wands. You show your creative work to the public and find an audience inspired by your passion and commitment. Your artistic endeavors stand on their own as major symbols of your deepest aspirations and highest objectives.

*Romance:*

you come alive in his world * he is seriously considering a spiritual partnership with you * he will say more next time you see him * easy communication of love and caring * wanting to do the right thing * getting out and about socially * having warm feelings for a lively guy * an affair may begin without warning * respecting him by not hurting him * discussing sharing a life together * making dates for future events * putting all your energy into a relationship * always being honest and trustworthy with him * he offers you pleasure and passion * he will fight to win your heart * tell him over and over how you feel * he responds with equal desire * meeting someone new while attending a film, play, concert, or art gallery opening * making an effort to socialize in his sphere of activity * being romantically interested in more than one person * feeling comfortable with your current partner * going through a phase of casual dating * getting back on the single girl menu * making an effort to meet new men * introducing yourself to someone attractive * wooing another with an open and eager heart * telling him you love him for the first time

## Work & Business:

pushing a project to the next stage of development * having lots of irons in the fire * you need to have a discussion with your partners or coworkers * presenting your plan to a potential investor * great opportunities come your way * good creative material that is commercially salable * having to hit the road for business * taking fairly safe risks * searching every avenue for employment * positive expansion through your profession * discussing possible marketing plans during an energetic meeting * getting your work into a public display * architectural installations * being open to new pathways for artistic expression * finding an audience for a creative product * a book is published, a gallery show is scheduled, a record hits the stores, or a film is on the screen * museums * all musical and theatrical performances * fashion, style, and the decorative arts * you get the word out through vigorous promotional activity * happy enterprises run by satisfied owners

## Spiritual Growth:

having a clear vision * being a direct channel to the divine source * you welcome everyone equally with open arms * bright, positive devotees who draw others into their belief system * having the unconditional energy to actively support the development of those around you * taking a bold stance publicly to defend your spirituality * expressing your ideas during a confrontation with a narrow-minded dogmatist * the creative spirit produces artwork that goes out into the world * books, tapes, art, and film that document the works of great spiritual thinkers and leaders * the cottage industry of craftspeople who cater to the new age market * collective social events that showcase relics of religious significance * tangible evidence of the existence of unknown forces * weird communications from the land of disembodiment that utilize electricity to send messages * visual manifestations of supernatural beings * the search for other voices in the universe * people gathering to discuss teachings of a particular spiritual philosopher * art, music, and dance as healing therapies * the use of objects of beauty and value on altars and in ritual

## Four of Wands

This balanced wand symbolizes passionate contentment in a happy and satisfactory lifestyle arrangement. You are pleased with the structure of your daily activities, and your self-confident social exchanges give you a sense of well-being and the feeling of belonging.

### Romance:

a guy welcomes you into his life * a regular, fulfilling sexual relationship * he is coming home sooner than you think * two people who relax and have fun together * a serious romance is developing * having tunnel vision due to your interest in only one man * admitting that you care about him * learning how to stop trying to control a guy * a loving, peaceful residence as a strong foundation in love * discussing moving in with him or buying a home together * enjoying the good life with a healthy man * never taking your partner for granted * he likes to waste time hanging out with you * feeling good together is the key to the relationship * knowing what you offer him is substantial * he invites you to his home * he visits you on a routine basis * you make friends more easily as a couple * you need to calm down over him * your shared house is a gathering place for others * hoping he is refreshed and ready to play * a happy dream comes true as a close confidante turns into a lover * a fulfilling social life with good people you both enjoy * you adore the community or neighborhood where you reside

## Work & Business:

solid retirement funds * staying cool and centered in financial negotiations * cottage industries begun in a residential structure * telecommuting as an option * a home-based business * opening up your living space for people to gather who share professional interests * setting up headquarters for an organization in a spare room * holding regular meetings to discuss community issues * any business that warmly welcomes customers * a job that requires constant courtesy and greeting the public * a new and improved work environment * being genuinely happy with your coworkers * starting up a venture with close friends * an opportunity to purchase real estate * adapting residential space for commercial use * an expanded domestic life requires room to grow * finding the right business partner for an important project * your creative gifts could generate income to help you purchase a home * any business that deals with the development of real estate * gentle, noninvasive, and noncompetitive sports as a potential career option * getting a fresh perspective on your employment picture * being extremely content at your current job * moving on to better monetary circumstances * receiving encouragement upon the completion of a project * your work is accepted by a committee * deciding to move back to the town where you grew up * refinancing your home * finding a perfect new place during a major change of residence

*S*piritual *G*rowth:

being at peace with your true self ❋ realizing that you are perfect and not doing anything wrong ❋ an innocent person who only cares for others ❋ the creation of a serene home environment is an important step in your spiritual development ❋ learning how to deflect negative energy ❋ possessing an unwaivering faith ❋ trusting your own religious perspective ❋ strong development in your level of interpersonal caring ❋ inner longings of the heart which desire the ultimate relationship with a man ❋ architectural structures, sacred monuments, and tombs dedicated to a religious or political leader ❋ a church or group that welcomes all ❋ 12-step meetings where you are automatically accepted by those gathered ❋ holding services in your living space ❋ establishing community-based locations or branches of national organizations that serve the grassroots population ❋ the ultimate transformation is accepting the truths spoken by your inner voice ❋ the writings of a spiritual thinker find a place for publication ❋ making a decision to get clear ❋ arriving at a place of spiritual contentment you have created for yourself ❋ neighbors unite to assist the needy in their community ❋ domestic harmony improves physical health ❋ a quiet time of healing at home ❋ spending a vacation just hanging around relaxing ❋ participating in group sports as a positive experience ❋ finding a spot on Earth attuned to your energy ❋ acting as a peacemaker who offers neutral guidance to opposing groups ❋ practicing compromise and cooperation while working with a group that aids humanity

## Five of Wands

The five of wands inspires you to take action on an issue that passionately moves your spirit. This card brings challenges into your life and forces you to make a commitment to finding solutions to the problems that prevent your personal healing. The five of wands also symbolizes competition and an ego-based struggle between two strong-willed individuals.

*Romance:*
he turns you on more than anyone before * giving yourself permission to feel anger when hurt * realizing you have not yet had a successful sexual relationship * false rules of the dating scene * little antagonistic games associated with courtship * making him jealous intentionally in order to get his attention * it is difficult to have calm moments of intimacy with him * couples who fight and then have make-up sex * your partner is competitive with you * he may be jealous of your past accomplishments * a passionate encounter that is explosive * expressing hate and resentment by projecting it at him * relationships should not be based on rivalry * finding it difficult to show your feelings in a temperate manner * being excited about moving to a new environment together * he is trying to fight a fierce desire for you * you have got to have him now * you are thrilled to have an opportunity to express your love to him * when he leaves his current partner, his greatest wish is to finally be with you * going through a crucible-testing process in your love life * hot physical chemistry between a couple * sexual obsession * he does not listen to your feelings * you get involved in social causes together * taking major risks in romance * a difficult guy

who is suspicious of your interest in him ◦ purely defensive behavior hides his true attraction ◦ he still wants to sleep with you, even if he denies it ◦ a spontaneous and fiery love affair ◦ having lived through the drama of a contrary man ◦ dying with sexual excitement over someone

## Work & Business:

protecting your turf ◦ fighting with competitors ◦ struggling to get a project off the ground ◦ your inner passion for your work takes you far ◦ someone who has courage and conviction for what they do ◦ rallying others to support a cause ◦ getting excited about a new career opportunity ◦ you would do anything to land a particular job ◦ laboring hard to draw attention to your talents ◦ doing what you love professionally ◦ you could have a huge fight to get what you want ◦ antagonistic colleagues challenge your ideas ◦ inner rage used as a creative force ◦ making time for personal business on a busy schedule ◦ powerful concepts you feel compelled to bring to reality ◦ humanitarian messages are communicated through your work ◦ your career makes a difference in the lives of others ◦ all charitable and activist efforts bring rewards ◦ volatile investments and holdings ◦ any business that deals with extremely competitive sports and pushing the body to the limit ◦ staking out new territory to expand your business ◦ not being intimidated by angry or pushy people you have to deal with professionally ◦ passionate creative artists who are deeply inspired to produce huge amounts of artwork ◦ arguing with your employer on behalf of your rights ◦ battling an intense and annoying rival ◦ having a bad attitude about getting a job

## *S*piritual *G*rowth:

universal anger directed at earthly injustice * being hostile toward a belief system that differs from your own * religious wars * championing a cause or charity * being a warrior for human rights or the protection of the environment * protesters engaged in an open battle against status quo forces * rising up against personal strife during a spiritual awakening * someone whose actions help spread the influence and message of their ideology * a religious leader who uses methods of intimidation to enslave followers * realizing the problems of self-absorbed people are not your responsibility * healing your tendency to resort to negative feelings as a defense mechanism * degrading yourself by associating with the wrong people * religious nuts who plot to hurt innocent, liberal people due to their archaic codes of behavior * the eternal battle of good against evil as expressed through great spiritual tales * enhancing the part of your personality that makes you feel alive * being challenged to choose a more balanced lifestyle * anger has a damaging effect on the physical body * working toward lifting the collective consciousness of humanity * struggling to heal our poisoned planet Earth * becoming spiritually responsible for your actions and words * hating things in others that you really hate in yourself * the overall healing power of regular exercise * arguments with others lower immunity and kill off your sense of well-being

# The Wands

## Six of Wands

The six of wands is a triumphant card earned through the experience of the five of wands. The risks you took are worth the victory that is now rightfully yours. The opposing forces that drained your energy are no longer an obstacle to achieving your highest goals in love or the financial arena.

## Romance:

couples who radiate goodwill toward others * a happy relationship that is actually good for you * attracting the right person next time around * a completely satisfying sex life * you will eventually win the heart of the one you cherish * both of you share the same ideals and values * someone who appreciates you for yourself * an honorable gentleman steps forward to claim you * he assists with all aspects of your life * a passionate guy who is sexually obsessed with you * he knows how to please you * two people recognize the best qualities in each other * getting what you want from an infatuated man * he could come back and rekindle the fire * he is not through with your energy yet * getting physical with him at the right time, in the right place * he always responds when asked how he feels * he will open the door wide for you * being included in all his plans for the future * old sorrows melt away and a new soft vulnerability emerges * he will definitely tell you he loves you * staying together through minor rough periods * winning his heart after a long struggle * finding happiness in a long-standing balanced relationship * finally discovering the man of your dreams * attaining passionate harmony with your one true soul mate * having impossibly high romantic ideals * both of you are sexually sophisticated and uninhibited ❋ ignoring jealous or negative comments from others regarding the man you adore

## Work & Business:

actualizing your creative potential ❋ lifetime goals achieved ❋ arduous financial battles won ❋ doing whatever it takes to make things happen ❋ not running from confrontations at work ❋ standing your ground over controversial issues ❋ receiving well-deserved praise for your efforts ❋ help is on the way just when you need it most ❋ someone new enters the picture to further the success of your plan ❋ getting the job you want ❋ finding employment for friends with your current company ❋ added responsibilities at work through a new position, job title, or hard-earned promotion ❋ doing freelance projects for an employer leads to steady work from them ❋ someone suggests a novel and viable business concept that you run away with ❋ completing a course of study at the top of your class ❋ a strong creative partnership helps you believe in your own abilities ❋ being able to see the forest from the trees ❋ winning a long, tough fight with adversaries at work ❋ a colleague who is a thorn in your side is fired or quits ❋ career goals attained through independent efforts ❋ your employment schedule fits in perfectly with your personal life ❋ juggling work, family, and school successfully ❋ risky investments pay off ❋ putting yourself in financial jeopardy and it works ❋ having extreme self-confidence in your creative talents ❋ being rewarded for your commitment to a career goal

## Spiritual Growth:

having hands that heal through the therapeutic touch of massage, acupressure, or energy field manipulation ❋ full recovery

# The Wands

after a difficult time ⁂ feeling really great physically, mentally, and spiritually ⁂ to earn freedom from the material in your current life ⁂ wanting to be a better person ⁂ winning a battle for a cause close to your heart ⁂ being passionately committed to a religion ⁂ creative energy surrounds you and feeds your spirit ⁂ having a highly charged aura ⁂ victory over deep-seated psychological issues ⁂ desiring a physical bond with a kindred soul ⁂ your inspiration comes from your universal beliefs ⁂ having a huge release of feelings triggered by a miraculous event ⁂ recreating scenarios from your cosmic history through many reincarnations ⁂ getting ready to move to a higher level of spiritual development ⁂ believing in your own ability to reach the right audience at the right time with your creative work ⁂ the creation of a healthy relationship excites you and provides you with excess love to give away ⁂ experiencing instantaneous compatibility with someone makes your energy soar ⁂ sharing spiritual beliefs with your partner brings steady fire to the union ⁂ appreciating the deity that shines brightly in your lover

## Seven of Wands

There is a tendency with the seven of wands to decrease your efforts toward a particular creative goal. You need to actively pursue opportunities and maintain an interest in the subject matter of the reading, even if you must force yourself to complete the constructive achievements represented by this card.

### Romance:

hesitating about putting energy into a guy * he could be in way over his head * hoping to build a honest and secure relationship * not letting old insecurities resurface * anticipating a sexual encounter but the timing is off * being wrapped up in concern about a weak and floundering affair * he could not handle you the first time * a guy from before is building up the confidence to contact you again * both of you must try harder for a successful partnership * he could take some time to heat up * deciding if you want him or not * you may not fully understand his way of doing things * he needs to be more caring before you reveal your ardent feelings * wondering if a steamy encounter will repeat with the same intensity * making an extra effort to keep the physical connection vibrant * building up your confidence as a social creature * forcing yourself to go out with a guy who is not worth the time and energy * meeting his demands halfway * putting in time to accompany him to events * he may be unsure whether to make a move * a period of not caring about anyone at all * giving up on looking for the right person * using all your creativity and resources to maintain an excellent sexual life with him * having hot and cold feelings for each other

## Work & Business:

attempting to get others interested in your projects * overcoming financial adversity * pushing yourself to go out and get a job * analyzing career goals * establishing strictly delegated responsibility boundaries to complete a team effort * becoming more secure professionally in your field of interest * gaining recognition for your work does not come easily * hanging in there when nothing seems to be coming through * you need to spend more time working * being creative in unusual ways * feeling like a shield while coworkers fight * trying harder to woo clients and customers * setting yourself up creatively in new ways * becoming self-employed in an independent operation * doing every task yourself * good things will come, but there could be a struggle * forcing yourself to stay interested career-wise * not meeting your potential because you are not getting the support you need from others * finding it difficult to go at it alone * you should not lose track of work responsibilities * trying hard for the common good of the project * you realize goals in your own way by your own schedule * pushing through your plans helps you deflect obstacles * a weak creative link slows down production * fighting to stay on top of a deal * do not procrastinate about taking action * stick to your original ideas * keep paying attention to all details * not letting others distract you from career pursuits * a slowly developing interest in a new professional field * staying positive about getting a job even though the odds are against you * not wanting to complete a course of study * bailing out on a promised loan * not caring what people think about your work situation

## Spiritual Growth:

a stream of karmic lessons for you to process * having patience with the timing of your own unfoldment * developing a heightened personal awareness * finding it difficult to fulfill your creative dreams * needing a boost of spiritual inspiration * owning your own energy, owning your own information * defending your right to your individual beliefs * taking big leaps forward in consciousness * feeling soul liberation after a long, tedious inner struggle * being at liberty to pursue creative and religious freedom * exploring a belief system that has few followers or is heretical * disciples who break from a religious leader to form a rival sect * someone who touches you at a new spiritual level * your family and friends may not see how personal growth work is improving your life * releasing negative messages received in childhood that stunted the maturation of your soul * being physically drained by the needy people around you * struggling with a moral dilemma that zaps your strength * avoiding angry, toxic people accelerates your healing process * not caring what anyone thinks about your spiritual commitments * finding it hard to continue along your path without the assistance and inspirational support of other entities * not losing hope during tough times * utilizing high-level principles to maintain your integrity during uncool displays of bad behavior by those closest to you

## Eight of Wands

The eight of wands is a card of urgency as unexpected events suddenly move you closer toward your preferred destination. This is an exciting and highly stimulating time when everything is happening way too fast for spiritual reflection. This wand brings quick results—within moments, hours, or days—as the future unfolds with a spontaneous intensity.

### Romance:

all the passionate ecstasy of a new love affair ✳ after having sex with him, you can think of nothing else ✳ romantic impulsiveness without any planning ✳ he drops by unannounced without hesitation ✳ he has heavy-duty desire for you ✳ he is turned on by the exchange with you ✳ immediate mutual attraction, even over the telephone or Internet ✳ meeting a fiery, lively guy who gives you great sensations ✳ full-body, instant lust ✳ he comes on like a mad dog ✳ a recent acquaintance changes your life overnight ✳ the chemical release that accompanies unbearable physical chemistry ✳ he is moving as fast as he can ✳ he is anxious when he cannot see you ✳ both of you are dying to spend more time together ✳ when you see him, you blush, get heart palpitations, and sweaty palms ✳ an uninhibited man who is wildly sexually compulsive ✳ knowing what it takes to get him horny ✳ your words were exactly what he needed to hear ✳ he may not be as smart as you but he is amazing in bed ✳ phone sex ✳ running a nervous internal dialogue reliving all moments spent with him ✳ having a massive crush on someone who drives you crazy with desire ✳ you could become bored with a new guy real quick ✳ if he is not ready for a relationship,

treat him like the little boy he is ✳ you cannot wait to see him
again ✳ you move in or marry him too soon ✳ being together is
a magical time of heightened sensitivity ✳ to your surprise, you
have fallen in love ✳ he appears out of nowhere and changes
your life forever

## Work & Business:

a fire needs to be lit to get a project cooking ✳ moving at
lightning speed to implement a business plan ✳ the check
arrives early ✳ the processing of important paperwork happens
quickly ✳ stock and futures prices fluctuate rapidly ✳ taking
immediate advantage of rising market values ✳ the churning of
capital stock ✳ the economic picture changes suddenly ✳ the
public panics and the markets are affected ✳ Internet stock
trading ✳ e-mails, faxes, phones, and pagers, and getting instant
responses to messages left on same ✳ employment opportunities disappear in minutes if you hesitate to take action ✳ major
financial realizations going down ✳ being thrilled and excited
by your job ✳ an unprecedented promotional acceleration, like
going from mail clerk to company president ✳ receiving a swift
communication about the future of a creative project ✳ clear
perceptions arrive as a rush of inspiration ✳ brainstorming for
new concepts and ways to expand a current plan ✳ having to
complete work in very little time ✳ you need more creative
insight to fulfill a job properly ✳ forces are moving in your favor
financially ✳ fast movement toward your ultimate goals ✳ an
opportunity to prove yourself is quickly approaching ✳ a spontaneous, rushed trip necessary for business ✳ making many
brief stops on a much longer journey ✳ panicking due to the
overwhelming choices of ways to go

*S*piritual *G*rowth:

the details of your destiny suddenly fit together ❋ otherworldly guidance assists you in all areas of your life ❋ your spirit soars ❋ the presence of a master heals you instantly ❋ suddenly opening up to new pathways of learning ❋ the early, heady days of metaphysical discovery ❋ quick spiritual healing from the laying on of hands ❋ having an ecstatic omniscient feeling ❋ reacting biologically to a miraculous experience ❋ being full of energy and optimism about the future ❋ the most enthusiastic of students ❋ you can accomplish anything if you get to it immediately ❋ being led to the right person at the right time ❋ your outer-world purpose unfolds as soon as your specialized skills are needed ❋ understanding your spiritual assignment in a bolt of clarity ❋ having a buzzing energy field ❋ you may have to calm others, find your center, and stay grounded in a time of crisis ❋ panic attacks where complexes flood the ego ❋ the debilitating anxiety of the neurotic personality ❋ feeling physical sensations, such as tingling, during psychic or mediumistic sessions ❋ any and all transmissions from the divine source as perceived through the science of language ❋ witnessing the power of synchronicity in everyday life ❋ information that you feel compelled to record comes automatically to you ❋ writing a creative piece in a short amount of time after a long gestation period ❋ astral navigation through a higher level of existence ❋ intense spiritual inspiration fills your soul with superhuman energy ❋ an increase in the vital force of the body

## Nine of Wands

This solid wand finds you in a position of security where your passionate nature reaches a level of permanence. The force of the nine of wands helps you create a base where your intense desires find a new source of power. By placing yourself on top of matters, you make attacks from the outside world impossible.

## Romance:

a guy who has been in love with you for ages * feeling protected by a secure relationship * he intends to take control of the situation * new territory conquered as a couple * he decides to try a bolder approach with you * time cannot weaken your passionate bond * he wants to satisfy you sexually * a couple who has to overcome negative societal pressures * he is not insecure about expressing deep feelings * having to wait awhile before you see the one you love * he has his own interests and you have yours * you could have rivals, but they will not affect your union with him * a love affair may take time to solidify * being sexually confident with men * always maintaining your creative work and spiritual beliefs, even if he does not support you there * you are very protective of your lover

## Work & Business:

you are a financial survivor * taking risks and winning each time * a fearless struggle to achieve a goal * being in a strong position at your current job * complete success through a lengthy period of intense labor * feeling confident about business arrangements * surrounding yourself with the best people as employees ✳ hiring the most expensive subcontractors for a construction job ✳ using the best-quality ingredients when manufacturing a product ✳ making business promises and keeping them✳ staying on top of a complicated negotiation ✳ securing a broad investment base for yourself ✳ creating order and solid cooperation among coworkers ✳ when faced with making financial decisions, you will know what to do ✳ you are more than equal to your competition ✳ business is moving in the general direction that you want ✳ you are raring to go on a potentially major endeavor ✳ projecting a sense of confidence on the job ✳ you will never lose rank in your profession ✳ the many branches of sports-related businesses ✳ hard work has never deterred you before ✳ helping your subordinates with infallible support ✳ the possible delay of an achievement ✳ waiting to take action when your position peaks ✳ stalling to prevent premature efforts or the failure of your plans ✳ your self-confidence leads you closer to lifetime goals ✳ success comes through a sense of purpose, developed abilities, and a desire for security

## *S*piritual *G*rowth:

maintaining your beliefs no matter what others say ✳ building up a strong foundation of character ✳ utilizing the power of will to change your life ✳ feeling ready for something, but knowing you must wait ✳ getting rid of people who try to control you ✳ building up the human spirit through your works and days ✳ developing a forceful resistance toward temptations that would undermine your ethical enlightenment ✳ avoiding victimization in any religious associations ✳ gaining community support for plans that will assist those in need ✳ surrendering to a divine power speeds physical and emotional recovery ✳ rising up to battle evil in all and any manifestations ✳ making your own choices about whom to confide your deepest dreams and ideals ❋ achieving a higher ground spiritually ❋ thinking for yourself and not following any gurus ❋ exploring your own individuality ❋ witnessing the spiritual significance behind your life ❋ establishing a foundation with others that benefits future generations ❋ coming from a place of unconditional love that grows better all the time ❋ having firm religious ideas ❋ a zealot, missionary, or harmless fanatic ❋ a true believer

## Ten of Wands

The ten of wands shows you doing anything you can to make something work by taking on a heavy load of responsibilities. Though you are overwhelmed, you pull things together with a huge amount of energy and activities. You gain creatively through the important commitments brought into your life with this card.

## Romance:

romantic maturation ❋ being ready for a permanent relationship ❋ a deep and lasting passion for another ❋ mutual trust and caring on every level ❋ feeling accountable to another for your actions ❋ his emotional baggage may be a burden for you ❋ he thinks you are too dependent on him ❋ he is preoccupied with problems that do not concern you ❋ if he chooses you, he will be behind you one hundred percent ❋ your heart is full of ardent feelings for him ❋ getting ready to dump someone who is dragging you down ❋ taking on his daily responsibilities gives you little free time ❋ not complaining when he is too busy for you ❋ he does care deeply but may suppress his desire ❋ he may want to be with you all the time ❋ the burden of raising children comes to you through a guy * he wants a committed relationship with you * having overwhelming feelings for a man * knowing he will make you accountable for his career, family, and social life * feeling oppressed by the intensity of his passion for you * hoping to share a future with him * having to achieve equal responsibility for chores around the house * if single, throwing yourself into mindless activities as a substitute for love * being ready to take the marriage vow

## Work & Business:

having a lot of pressure on you at work * success comes through perseverance * a major contract comes in, giving you plenty to do * living under a code of conduct on the job that is restrictive * learning how to delegate responsibilities to others * letting employees take over some of your tasks to lighten your load * your diplomatic skills are tested * someone who is a total workaholic * if self-employed, you do everything yourself * taking care of parents or children as a consideration in your choice of employment * talents passed on to the next generation * your children inherit your creative abilities * wearing many hats professionally * the awesome task of setting up an entire business * discovering you have more to accomplish than you originally thought * old burdens return and demand your attention * possessing so much talent that it overwhelms you * taking responsibility for past actions with a previous employer * something big is definitely happening * feeling accountable for the welfare of others * mentoring younger people in your spare time * you have so much to do and have to keep going

## Spiritual Growth:

being locked into issues of family guilt * spending all free moments pursuing spiritual knowledge * the burdens of earthly existence * owing karmic debts to your dependents in this lifetime * your vital energy is being drawn away by others * being fully aware of how family life can interfere with personal growth work * feeling ready to leave your body but personal responsibilities keep you here * taking a spiritual path to the limit through total immersion into a formal course of study or in apprenticeship with a master * collective creative expression without a stage or audience where everyone participates equally in art, song, or dance * a grueling initiation right to enter a religious sect * a figurehead who ministers to those with grave problems * the healing power of confession * trying to instill good moral values in your children * feeling spiritually responsible for many people * an oppressive arrangement with a group that suffocates your soul * not signing up for an easy path in this incarnation * fully implementing a time-consuming health program

# The Wands

## Page of Wands

The person symbolized by the Page of wands is always cheerful and ready for action. He is eager to follow any opportunity that offers excitement and involves highly energetic people. The Page of wands easily makes commitments to any group or creative project that captures his passionate nature.

### Romance:

you may not take him seriously * someone who is eating his heart out * he is happy just to be near you * he likes to hang out with you * his maturity develops from being with you * waiting to see who shows real interest * he is eager to grow as a lover * being in love makes you feel younger * you may be friends first * someone who could be your spiritual equal * two people who remain cordial while separated * his dream is to share romantic moments * mutual attraction with a younger man * having inspiring sex with a lively guy * a goodhearted yet naive person * a guy without ex-wives and children * someone who has been rejected badly by another * a trustworthy mate who always tells you the truth * he brings constant joy and excitement to your days and nights * he adores every inch of you * he is always ready to make you happy * he inspires you creatively * having to tag along as he makes the social rounds * falling in love with someone because of his ideals or moral principles * making him your main concern in life * being easily aroused by each other * fully enjoying his superlative companionship

## Work & Business:

sticking with your goals * staying on course * developing your own creativity * having an innate sense of obligation to your job * you may only get the second-place position * finishing one project before beginning another * someone who gives you a connection but nothing more * you need to hang out and meet more people professionally * encouraging others at work * making a huge effort * being the biggest fan of your company * getting others engaged in your work * you have to rally people to gain support financially * feeling loyal to your firm * desperately wanting to keep your job * energy and excitement bring a new level of interest to your career * you need to stand up for your rights at work * beginning at the bottom of the ladder * being grateful for the opportunity to learn a new business from the ground up * any industry that caters to young people at play * looking for money to purchase enjoyable gifts and games for your children * you will do whatever it takes to land a job * being faithful to your employer * an excellent team player * an intern, volunteer, or junior assistant * becoming the central force of a project that would fall apart without you * waiting to hear about an offer of employment

## Spiritual Growth:

finding a group of people who support you readily * loyal and devoted followers * your entire life revolves around your spiritual beliefs * one who is eager to pursue enlightening knowledge * feeling happy, hopeful, and more alive due to inner work * a true believer in the healing process * a hardworking disciple of a religious cause or sect * staying on the higher path no matter how big the distractions * gladly recreating the religious holidays and ceremonies you experienced as a child * learning to be confident in your own spiritual authority ❋ deep devotion can transform the most ordinary person into a superman ❋ taking a religious vow to join an order ❋ making a commitment to be faithful to someone as a major soul development ❋ a gullible student who could easily be used by a controlling leader ❋ seeking out instruction on interests you wish to explore ❋ being inspired by the lofty ideals of universal truths ❋ moving ahead on new spiritual paths without hesitation ❋ caring for each other makes a huge difference in the world

## Queen of Wands

The Queen of wands is a passionate and socially aggressive woman who supports the causes and people in whom she believes. She inspires everyone to apply their talents brilliantly and channels her intensely feminine physical and creative energy into her own projects as well.

### *R*omance:

you draw men to you by your forceful self-confidence ❋ trusting your own perspective on interpersonal issues ❋ a guy who wants admiration—not sex—from women ❋ you have to help show him what satisfies you ❋ having who you want when you want them ❋ he already knows he needs you in his life ❋ you connect him socially to others ❋ being turned on by a new love interest ❋ not tolerating being considered second to another woman ❋ having intense physical reactions when you see some guy ❋ being a drama queen to draw attention to yourself ❋ intentionally flirting with other men to make him jealous ❋ your mature sexuality may intimidate him ❋ your being dynamic and outgoing can be hard on him ❋ you could be his first real

woman * he sees you as someone he can trust and rely on *
being the woman behind the man * he has a real respect for
your feelings * a bitchy, competitive woman who is a thorn in
your side * he could be attracted to another woman * a female
figure may be trying to seduce him behind your back * his past
wives or girlfriends continue to make demands on him * you
should not believe what you hear from the women in his life *
playing the romantic role he demands of you * being completely expressive and fulfilled in a secure long-term relationship *
taking time to improve your physical appearance * getting into
your femininity as a woman * you should think before you
speak with him * never letting any man turn you into a helpless
victim * taking control of your own life after dating an oppressive guy

## Work & Business:

a potential employer is impressed with your looks and manners * pulling out all the stops for an interview * convincing
someone to hire you by showing an enthusiastic interest in the
position * a generous but demanding woman who has seniority
over you * a female friend who is trying to help you make
money * using everything you have to become a bigger success
* you need to socialize more for business purposes * pushing
for your own rights on the job * if you forcefully demand a
raise, you will receive it * a promotion requires an entirely new
wardrobe * your outgoing personality is crucial to your career
rise * working in marketing or sales * any business that deals
with style, glamour, fashion, cosmetics, and the enhancement
of physical beauty * actresses and models * artists in any medium, especially film and printed matter * a woman who is
extremely inspired creatively * your expansive personality
draws others to your work * you receive publicity for your writ-

ing, acting, directing, or crafting projects ✴ being a hostess, waitress, or professional greeter ✴ sex-industry workers ✴ social directors in charge of gifts, parties, and invitation lists ✴ being outspoken about a controversial cause or helping a struggling group of people ✴ a tough and often difficult woman who has extensive knowledge in your field of interest

## Spiritual Growth:

creating the life you want for yourself ✴ fighting fearlessly for what you believe ✴ having spiritual strength and understanding ✴ a woman who is an inspiration to others ✴ touching people deeply through good deeds and words ✴ taking control of your own destiny ✴ gaining more freedom ✴ valuing your own spiritual authority ✴ how women connect men to god ✴ acting out sexually as a rebellion toward childhood religious training ✴ goddess worship ✴ female deities ✴ sacred sexuality and sensuality ✴ the female body as an object of worship ✴ feeling like the embodiment of a religious archetype, icon, or heroine ✴ the cosmic dilemma of being a feminine soul trapped in a masculine body and vice versa ✴ being sensitive to the needs of others ✴ learning hard moral lessons from the world of superficial obsession with fake and contrived physical images ✴ wearing the costume associated with a particular religious group ✴ motivational lecturers ✴ publicly speaking on your spiritual specialty ✴ using your image or name to promote a humanitarian cause ✴ performance or entertainment that has spiritual themes or raises the consciousness of the audience ✴ deciding to get with the program ✴ taking better care of your appearance lifts your spirits ✴ a support group helps you meet personal health goals ✴ strong mental stability ✴ excellent intuitive faculties

## Knight of Wands

Traditionally, the Knight of wands indicates travel, a change of residence, or leaving behind a person or situation that no longer interests you. The Knight disdains commitment and rarely takes responsibility for his romantic actions. He avoids any serious interpersonal challenges or connections by perpetuating a constant state of motion and excitement.

*Romance:*
you are instantly attracted to a new guy * he has ambivalent feelings about the relationship * he does not realize that he cannot escape himself * he has an extreme sense of sexual freedom * someone you meet while traveling * a person who is passing through your town * a hot guy charges into your life from out of the blue * running into a man who has always turned you on * an overnight romance in a strange environment * he wants to sleep with you on the first date * he asks you to take a trip with him * he shows up where you live or work * a man who flees when attracted to someone * running away from what is truly heartfelt * he is not ready for a commitment * he feels guilty about avoiding you * he may be afraid of what he wants * a man who is not marriage material * he is cowardly about expressing his feelings * wondering whether he can handle your magnitude * he has passionate potential but is too young and scared * your sensuality may overwhelm him * a guy who runs hot and cold * a cocky, flighty man who never has a steady girlfriend * he may not want you, but he may want to be like you * he is only studying you to morph your personality into his lost one * if he turns away from something special,

he definitely has a problem * leaving behind one man suddenly and moving on to someone new * impulsive, short-lived, passionate affairs

## Work & Business:

someone who is briefly in town for business * traveling for work * a small window of opportunity to meet an important connection * attending an out-of-town convention * an employee shows up to retrieve his belongings and walks out forever * completing work on a plan so you can present it in committee * someone offers you a project that begins immediately * trying to avoid confrontations with adversaries * a salesperson who is always on the move * travel is crucial to finalize an agreement * a long commute leaves you frazzled * going on tour with a play or musical act * you want more independence professionally * a brief trip is fun and exciting even if for business purposes * hanging loose and working part-time jobs * you need to feel physically free in your occupational routine * having difficulty actualizing creative work * turning away from inborn talents * escaping serious financial difficulties without a scar * your business changes location.

## Spiritual Growth:

you need to go off on your own and do inner work * a morally unreliable person * you have to release yourself from a lifestyle that suffocates your soul * a move to a new residence could greatly improve your sense of well-being * you change your spiritual direction quickly * not pledging allegiance to any one religion or any brand of dogma * avoiding people who challenge your faith * having a mission in the world makes you feel important * a complete avoidance of morals and proper behavior ✳ floating for awhile without a permanent base in favor of spiritual development ✳ can be a denial of peace of mind and inner happiness ✳ a restless soul on Earth and in the heavens ✳ having trouble handling your own awareness ✳ struggling to temper certain sexual energy ✳ having a type of tantric sex with casual partners ✳ avoiding confronting issues of personal growth ✳ freaking out when strange precognitive events occur ✳ not gaining complete consciousness about your own beliefs ✳ a core of resistance toward accepting any religious or metaphysical concepts ✳ one who travels to spread the word, but may not practice what he preaches ✳ having superficial knowledge of a subject due to lack of study time ✳ a charlatan who is a spokesperson with no real ethical or spiritual core ✳ going off alone to lead a better life in a completely different location

### King of Wands

The fiery King of wands supports your creative efforts but will never become deeply engaged in your personal life. He often represents a spiritually or romantically unavailable man who is committed elsewhere but could become a trustworthy friend for life.

### Romance:

he will be totally honest with you ✳ he will not always be there to help you ✳ having to share him with other women ✳ all the good ones are taken ✳ he will remain a friend if you choose to stay in touch ✳ he has only positive intentions ✳ he is fair and faithful in his own way ✳ a man concerned with doing the right thing ❋ he is basically a nice, upbeat person ❋ a healthy guy who is not lazy or debauched ❋ he may deal with you differently than what others say ❋ having a nice physical connection with someone who is not free ❋ he is a great guy, but not great for you ❋ he looks to you but cannot get out of his current commitment ❋ giving him the benefit of the doubt ❋ he sees himself as a married man ❋ he is a real ally who could help you create a whole new life ❋ falling in love with his spirit ❋ being drawn to a guy through his creative work ❋ he is caring and respectful of your feelings ❋ he is giving you the wrong message of being interested ❋ a man who is used to getting attention from women ❋ a flirtatious voyeur who cannot get close ❋ a grounded man of proper moral behavior ❋ having to trust someone new ❋ a spiritual or platonic connection with a man brings clear energy into your life ❋ if he is your partner, you have found a monogamous, affectionate, and wonderful man who should be making you completely happy

## *W*ork & *B*usiness:

an honest boss ❋ an overseer not directly involved with a project ❋ a socially expressive partner ❋ someone who will give you an excellent reference ❋ a man assists you in your rise to fame ❋ a very creative person who backs many ventures financially ❋ someone who is responsible for the welfare of many people ❋ your employer loves your interesting ideas ❋ a close friend at work who is always nice to you ❋ coming up with fun, innovative business plans ❋ a good-natured manager who has the respect and admiration of his workers ❋ someone well-established in business brings you into the fold ❋ a person gives you money to help you finance expansion plans ❋ someone who watches out for you at work ❋ a guy agrees to buy your creative product ❋ a definite signing of a business document or legal agreement * a major male figure such as your lawyer, mentor, or boss * dealing with trustworthy people who bring projects in on time and budget * the men in power who have the final word * a righteous man influences your career direction for the better * an excellent partner who is prominent in the world

## Spiritual Growth:

a man who makes casual judgements about your beliefs * an inspiring man of virtue * a religious leader who is truthful and does his job of helping others * maintaining your own spiritual integrity * being honest as a force of personal liberation * accurate intuitive readings that capture the one and only truth * a teacher who motivates your soul development * seeing the spirit in a guy rather than the reality of his uncool personality * everybody should be free to live their own lives * a guru who uses his position to flirt with female followers * a guy who talks the talk to get women to admire him * controlling your own destiny helps you pull in what you need * celibate types who get close to all women but sleep with none * being in denial of physical pleasure for religious purposes * you are attracted to the soul of one who practices spiritual work alone * avoiding messy love affairs to stay focused on your devotions * a meeting of the minds on a higher level of telepathy

## THE TRUMPS

### The Fool  -○

The Fool represents chance, risk, and surprise as important elements influencing the subject matter of the reading. As the first of 22 trumps, the Fool heralds the beginning of a brand-new life on a spiritual path. By taking the first step of your journey as the innocent Fool, your destiny unfolds through the consciousness-raising experiences that will be complete with the Universe card.

## Romance:

meeting someone new when you least expect it ✻ having a childlike belief that a rocky relationship will work itself out ✻ lacking rules about how a romance should develop ✻ he takes risks to call you ✻ a guy behaves like an idiot ✻ an ordinary coincidental encounter launches an affair ✻ a lover suddenly falls off the face of the earth ✻ never assume anything with him ✻ he could pop up in a casual way ✻ acting nonchalant around him to cool him out ✻ running into someone from your past who asks you out immediately ✻ the beauty of love is its randomness ✻ wait until you run into him for best results ✻ a sign that someone new will appear ✻ he may not have a clue or a plan ✻ a couple who always enjoys themselves when together ✻ he may be too young, stupid, or unconscious for you ✻ you want freedom from commitments at this time ✻ you are unexpectedly invited to a fun event that you should attend ✻ a couple who laugh together at the humor of their idiosyncratic behavior ✻ taking a chance with a man who is your worst nightmare ✻ he drops by your place of work unannounced to see you for romantic purposes * a deadbeat guy who makes attempts with women that go nowhere * you stupidly express your feelings to a guy who does not know you exist * he may lack ambition and an interest in money * he laughs in your face when you open up to him emotionally * having sex with someone you do not really know * letting a relationship develop spontaneously * not formulating a future with him * his behavior is making you insane * being crazy in love with a man * leaving your partner to run off with a guy who is a free spirit * gamblers, con men, wanderers, madmen, and risk takers * emerging unscathed from a dangerous romance * ignoring the worst aspects of his behavior * he says things just to listen to his own voice

## Work & Business:

a general lack of interest in ownership * not having a typical consumer-oriented mentality * being adrift financially and maybe potentially homeless * plunging ahead with a wild business idea that puts your capital at risk * borrowing money from others for personal investments * you try a new approach knowing you probably will not succeed * pay attention to all details * the first step in a career that will take you far * all jobs and money matters that involve risk taking * speculative real estate deals * the stock and futures markets * an unexpected opportunity arrives * a surprise windfall * you receive an inheritance you knew nothing about * launching an entirely new career * a recent venture is dicey because the results are unknown * talking up big money dreams that never seem to happen * you are on the verge of major changes at work * a clean sweep of the old guard ushers in a better era of leadership * poor management of finances * throwing away good money on useless items * going out on a limb in a risky, offbeat business * a whole new ball game professionally * being a gypsy moving from job to job without a future * opening up to new avenues of potential income * you would welcome change at work * trusting your instincts * breaking free from the memory of past failures * you need to be more practical with your spending habits * initiating deals but not following through

## *S*piritual *G*rowth:
thinking life is a game of monopoly * the eternal soul that has always existed * divine principles that run the universe * not caring what others think as a primary spiritual law * the nature and origin of the soul * the insanity of destructive religious leaders * always in the void of becoming * epidemic madness in the world * regressing to childlike behavior when you cannot deal with psychic pressure * an idealistic hero who works for the good of the planet * taking hallucinogenic journeys without any particular plan * having strong cosmic protection around you * humor and lightness of spirit * giving up the dogmatic religious training of your childhood * a theological chameleon * initiation into a new pathway to God * physical rejuvenation * being in the dream-world stage of metaphysical development where you have imaginary friends * the hippie philosophy of existence * not being afraid of dangerous conditions * not seeing death as something to fear * having an unconscious ignorance about natural law * not worrying about what you cannot control * a wanderer who lacks roots and is not concerned with survival * feeling like you are from another planet * the bliss of not dealing with material problems and burdens * the spiritual iconoclast * a lunatic filled with the holy spirit * self-styled saviors and false prophets * a phase of development where people think you are crazy due to your beliefs * a big birth of consciousness for an ordinary person * idealism is your middle

name * the world is your home * you adapt easily to different cultures, customs, and religions * overlooking superficial differences * not having strings attached to any person or place * being colorblind toward racial variety * taking life as one big cosmic joke * destiny springs from the ashes of fate * guidance comes through people and opportunities that fall in your lap * being eternally curious about metaphysical truths * inborn divine treasures inherited from our human ancestry * listening to too many empty spiritual thinkers * undergoing an actual change in body cells * being free to follow a path of enlightenment in your current incarnation * a prophet, visionary, or ecstatic * the deeper symbolism of everyday events

### The Magician, Magus, or Juggler  — |

The Magician always has a secret agenda and works behind the scenes to procure what he wants. The truth is well hidden behind his mask of detachment, though underneath the surface he is plotting away. He shifts his point of view rapidly so nobody can discover his true intentions and interfere with his private plans.

*Romance:*
   how men and women treat love as a game * being awestruck by a heavy-duty dude * a guy who lies about everything * not talking about a new man * he could have ambivalent feelings toward you * the kind of guy who keeps you guessing * a relationship that builds a foundation on quiet strength * being attracted to a stimulating but difficult man * it is hard work to develop a heart connection with him * he is keeping his emo-

tions under wraps * there is some mystery or deception about him * his scheme is to get you to fall hard for him * a master of understatement * he may not be able to sustain a real romance * true love is not the result of some well-laid plan * edgy sex * he is smart in the way he handles you * he wants it his way * keeping him a secret insures the development of a powerful intimacy * he may be playing a role with you * a guy following you around and bothering you * his flirtatious fantasy games caught your attention * he is eliminating the obstacles that keep you apart * he did not tell the other woman anything * he wants you because you are unavailable * he likes to control women * a flake, druggie, or pervert * he may have a secret life you know nothing about * he plays you through emotional dominance * protecting yourself so he does not slam your feelings * he is talking his way out of a current partnership * he has his mind on you but he is still stuck in crap * he will return later and explain everything * he is holding back with you * a strong-willed man who makes a bold and dramatic move * he may not trust women * his mercurial personality is a problem * being choosy about the men you date * his friends give him reports about you * he is definitely checking you out behind your back

## Work & Business:

tricking investors to gain financially * powerful people around you exploit you * an extremely manipulative boss * a guy sees the income potential of your idea * a spy in the ranks who reports on the behavior of others * sneaky and scary rivals * major business decisions made from sudden realizations * your plan needs to be precise and private * using your genius for logic to find solutions * you can make things happen for yourself * someone is helping or hindering you behind the scenes without your knowledge * being used by others for your information and then dumped from a project ❋ incredible concepts you feel compelled to make real ❋ a con artist who lies about easy money deals ❋ respecting confidential issues ❋ a partner may be pulling a fast one on you ❋ displays of power and control through money or social status in the spotlight ❋ secret investments, bank accounts, and safe deposit boxes ❋ hearing exactly what you need to hear ❋ pursuing employment takes a huge amount of effort ❋ creepy guys who test you sexually on the job ❋ a married man who plays romantic games with women at work ❋ a guy who uses you for inside information or sends you out as a spy ❋ computer hackers ❋ checking people out through the Internet ❋ secret tape recordings ❋ all forms of surveillance ❋ a perfectionist who is hard on himself ❋ going to a trusted ally for help with money problems ❋ cheaper imports have a huge impact industry-wide ❋ imposing quotas makes other countries retaliate and leads to greater hardships in the future ❋ not letting anyone interfere with your plans ❋ dealing with fierce competition in the marketplace

## *Spiritual Growth:*

keeping your physical presence low key during retreat time ❋ trying to enhance your power by manipulating appearances ❋ sorcerers ❋ wicca ❋ witchcraft ❋ magicians and the secrets behind their magic tricks and illusions ❋ thinking you can control forces of nature ❋ gaining mastery over your environment ❋ having an ability to create change in others ❋ being tested as an initiation right to a group ❋ alchemically producing catharses in people ❋ an ancient mystery comes into the light ❋ having a high level of self-confidence ❋ feeling optimistic about the future ❋ healing yourself without reliance on a guide ❋ being connected to an ascending divine master ❋ how the state of the mind controls the physical body ❋ healers who utilize the laying on of hands ❋ the manipulation of energy fields ❋ deep tissue massage ❋ physical therapists ❋ yogic mastery ❋ aura cleansing and chaktra alignment work ❋ dynamite psychic readers ❋ esoteric metaphysical books and belief systems ❋ a strong willpower keeps the system vital ❋ alternative medical care ❋ mastery over your emotional nature ❋ opening your crown chaktra through the healing of others ❋ changing the course of events by the power of thought ❋ the wisdom of keeping private counsel ❋ being aware of your own psychological process ❋ inhibition of your feelings is your greatest freedom ❋ a major escape artist ❋ a guy who seems spiritually aware may really be a mess ❋ shamanistic abilities ❋ utilizing an omnipotent perspective over life ❋ tapping into the universal healing force and bringing it down to the planet ❋ having a deep knowledge of the mysteries ❋ delineating cosmic force as it manifests on the earth plane

## The Priestess, High Priestess, Juno, or the Female Pope
*- II*

The Priestess card represents having faith in the power of your own intuition and inner knowledge to gain valuable insights from your infallible instincts. To be at peace with yourself, you must tell the truth and trust the validity of your completely personal vision. You attain a lifestyle within which you actualize your divine nature and follow your destiny to the farthest reaches of your mental and spiritual faculties.

### Romance:

you have more life experience than him ∗ you keep who you sleep with to yourself ∗ a very happening relationship is when the telepathy is right on ∗ he may use you as a free source of talking therapy ∗ he feels your energy constantly ∗ there is a core of your being that will never be his ∗ your romantic wishes appear in the secret and symbolic language of dreams ∗ conscious parenting and having a deep soul connection to your children ∗ he feels he has to walk a tight ship with you ∗ say anything that will encourage him on a spiritual level ∗ he is mysteriously drawn to you ∗ he needs to hear your voice and insight ∗ you are more intelligent than the men around you ∗ he knows you are psychic ∗ you can know many men without acting out sexually ∗ call him to you ethereally and reassure him everything will be okay ∗ you have the power to design a relationship as you go ∗ he is concerned that you are more powerful than him ∗ he knows you can read his mind ∗ you feel him inside of your body ∗ having an illuminating moment about the type of men you are attracting ∗ he could take you off-track from your inner work ∗ you are ignoring a man who is in love with you because you are too self-centered ※ you do not want to worry about someone else ※ you may not legally marry in this lifetime ※ a woman who may be too powerful to have unconscious, status quo-type children ※ love as a mystical experience ※ to see beyond the barriers of time with him ※ he enjoys your spiritual insights ※ he feels indebted to you for pulling him through ※ a past boyfriend in a distant corner of your memory ※ he could be dreaming about you ※ there is an unspoken psychic bond between you and him ※ an intuitive reading alerts you to the arrival of a man ※ meeting someone who shares your values and beliefs ※ having a deep awareness of past lives you shared together

## Work & Business:

receiving premonitions on how to proceed with financial matters ※ business ideas come to you in dreams and visions ※ your spirituality may be an issue at your job ※ a powerful woman who knows what is going on behind the scenes ※ using intuitive information for financial planning ※ you live by your own rules in terms of your career ※ secrecy may be necessary for the success of a project ※ stay open and you will be led effortlessly to the right position ※ an employer knows who you really are ※ using everything you know to get ahead professionally ※ someone whose inborn talents are of enormous value ※ go with your gut feeling when making decisions ※ your instincts are usually right ※ you are an excellent judge of people and this is a career asset ※ channeling a project from a place of great inspiration ※ past life abilities and societal roles return in a new, more modern format ※ trusting yourself to relax and let your right brain do the work ※ secret jobs or hobbies you hide from coworkers ※ keeping your personal life private from your colleagues ※ not discussing controversial issues with others * concealing financial information for protective purposes * a woman who is at the top of her field * someone with more knowledge in their area than anyone else * do not act immediately * solutions come to you during quiet times of reflection * a woman with a gigantic public reputation * launching a one-woman crusade against civilization * any business that relates to healing and psychic work * earning income as a Tarot card, palm, or rune reader, astrologer, psychic, medium, channeler, numerologist, priestess, therapist, herbalist, or body worker * social or political work that champions women and children * lobbying for issues that advance the human race * a career focused on innovation and invention * visionary artists and poets, and professional dreamers * creative work that draws on past forms within the medium * people are hungry for the services you provide * a teacher who imparts her acute knowledge of a highly developed skill to others * the inner mechanisms of an operation * a strict and demanding educational program helps you make great leaps forward

## Spiritual Growth:

seeking out the truth in everyday situations * walking a mystical path * leading a principle-centered life * being aligned with the god force * becoming aware of the truth behind the illusion of reality * someone who is a force of evolution in how they affect others * contributing to the changing consciousness of the world * accepting the spiritual confirmations that come through intuitively * precognitive dreams * recognition of a past life in a matriarchal period when women ran the show * the worship of goddess energy * having an ability to see auras and chaktras * temples, schools, and institutions of sacred knowledge * information coming to you from the subconscious * astonishingly accurate predictions that reveal the future * the universe is populated by all sorts of unseen intelligence * being attuned to a higher wavelength * being a source of metaphysical information * a miracle worker whose prayers are answered * you pass on to others all you have learned spiritually through personal crises * calling people to you psychically * you show great understanding for the feelings and experiences of others * one who facilitates the healing of humanity * being liberated from the material to discover your true destiny * applying ancient information for the spiritual benefit of the entire planet * an ability to read the Akashic records that contain the collective history of the universe * biblical prophets and religious visionaries * all occupations that utilize the sacred intuitive sciences for healing purposes

## The Empress  — \|\|

The Empress symbolizes the mature, adult female who is enlightened and inspired and whose emotions are rich in love and aliveness. She possesses great resources of strength that she draws upon to nurture those around her. Her potent physical energy makes her sensually receptive to tasting the gifts of life and enjoying the beauty of the world we share.

## Romance:

the establishment of domestic harmony with another * teach him by example to relax and have fun * he is looking for his ideal woman * your family values are important to you * you are his renewal * being open to receiving his love or his sperm * you may be an icon to him already * feeling worthy of a man who respects your feelings * he loves you for who you are * you can be yourself around him * practicing unconditional love with an immature guy * being the flower accepting the bee in courtship * you are ready to appreciate true intimacy * he realizes you are a woman, not just another little girl * a caring person who does not undermine your essential dignity * he needs to see what a gem you are * enjoying your femininity * you are conscious about being a lady * restoring his faith in women after he has been badly burned * you are pretty close to his ideal woman * he is definitely enamored with you * he has never been with anyone like you before * practice forgiveness with him every moment * you know who you are and what you have to give * you enjoy the protective feeling he provides * when the right man comes along you do not have to do anything * he is craving affection and attention from you * when he is needy, he seeks out women he can trust * you become his lover, mother, and guide for life * examining why you choose men who have been neglected by other women * he may have a mother-fixation complex * a guy who acts or thinks like a woman * transvestites and transsexuals * a man born with feminine physical characteristics * his self-image could be subconsciously female * he may be gay * you have the power to make a relationship really great * being the muse behind all his ideas and creative projects * he makes you feel maternal instincts * pregnancy * motherhood and the raising of children * a strong possibility of a marriage * becoming more domesticated and involved with nourishing the family unit * enjoying sensuality on a new level with him * he opens you up sexually for the first time * you are the woman of his dreams and his personal goddess

# Work & Business:

doing certain work because of your deep love of people *
others look to you for ideas and inspiration * a woman who has
excellent financial advice * investments bear fruit * a great lady
and a grand thinker * supporting the business of your husband
* being the main breadwinner in the family * alimony and child
support issues in the case of divorce * talents inherited through
the maternal line * an indication of wealth * a woman with
matriarchal energy brings joy to those around her * feeling
grownup and ready to take on material responsibilities * a
project will blossom and be more successful than you think *
kill enemies with kindness and they disappear * remaining calm
* making decisions that are harmonious with coworkers *
women move into leadership roles as the patriarchy loses its
grasp over society * becoming a highly inspired creative force
in the world * any business relating to pregnancy, childbirth,
and motherhood * working with the fruits of the earth as a
nutritionist, farmer, florist, or chef * a job that places you in
nature or around animals * catering to the broad market of
women and their particular needs * health food stores, organi-
cally grown products or holistic lifestyles become potential
professional areas for you * being a teacher or daycare
provider * surrogate motherhood as income-producing * the
process of legal adoption * foster care * a mentor oversees the
development of your talent

# Spiritual Growth:

having a child as a peak spiritual experience * working hard
to improve your appearance * having a healthy body image and
enjoying food * do not forget to nurture yourself too * all
actions come from the heart when you give to others * your life
force returns after an absence * to see yourself in everyone

else * the data on how to lead a truly fulfilled life * having compassion toward those in need * the fertility of the womb of Mother Earth is at risk * creative work that helps others evolve to a higher level * a card of receptivity to pregnancy due to a soul agreement between the mother and child * soft, opulent healing energy * inner and outer beauty come from telling the truth * the principles behind the natural laws of the universe * trust as a divine agreement * being content with your own inner treasures * if you cultivate the best in yourself, all else follows * inner joy comes from loving others and having faith in God * the spiritual teaching and healing network within a community * being pregnant with a really deep partner * the essence of who you are * being a good listener and friend * waiting for a higher kind of love * dreaming big dreams for your family * providing moral guidance for your children * spiritual centers run by women * fertility cults * goddess worship * female deities * using your sensuality as a positive healing force

## *The Emperor*

The Emperor is the adult male whose expertise is organization. He serves every situation by analyzing the necessary requirements, procuring them, and placing his prizes within a system he has designed himself. Psychologically, this trump represents reaching maturity and taking responsibility for other people in a family or community arrangement.

## *Romance:*

a righteous dude * a well-respected man * the male counterpart of yourself * a relationship with an older, more established man * he needs to grow up, get a life, and plan his future * he has to pull himself together to be with you * a traditional courtship where the man pursues the woman * someone is getting ready to make a major move * a person who was previously unsure finally comes through * a guy who calls and does not play phone games * feeling safe and secure with your partner * he likes to do things in a classical way * he is an archetype who could be the one if the timing is right * he knows you are going to be his wife * an honorable mate * a serious suitor * a marriage proposal * he could be the father of your children * a guy who takes responsibility for whom he sleeps with * there are men out there doing the work on themselves * let him be the man and make decisions for both of you * choosing a grounded partner whom you secretly wish was a little more exciting * he is analyzing how to work out the details of a relationship * a guy who likes to take you out and feed you * he will pay for the children * a man who knows who he is * he wants to finish business transactions and come to you complete * his main impulse is to protect you from others * he will grow up and come around * a very masculine man * the whole relationship rests on the question of his maturity * a monogamous mate who has a deep desire for a solid, workable union * establishing order in the home * a long-term, rock-solid marriage * having an affair with a married man * dating someone who is a father figure to you * taking care of the welfare of an entire family

## Work & Business:

the head of an organization who has employees beneath him * work will be there for you * wearing many hats at once * getting your kingdom together * a big-time person offers you a contract * having productive pursuits * someone in a prominent position in big business or government * top-ranking management and executives and other stellar corporate entities * those directly above you in the hierarchy * a deal comes down * a man who teaches you how to be powerful in the world * successful authority figures who coach others with their business knowledge * responding to the real needs of the marketplace * a huge promotion puts you on top * not being pushed around at work * being the bigger person during disputes * a man who increases your social, political, or financial weight in the world * government benefit programs * you need to master a challenging situation * getting your act together money-wise * a business that has many branches or locations * multinational corporations * attaining a leadership position socially * those who work with the creation of policy and adoption of laws * honest and dependable workers * becoming a successful entrepreneur * financing your own home * your long-term investments increase in value over time

*S*piritual *G*rowth:

having clear intentions when dealing with others * a magnanimous soul * the philosophy of the rational mind * someone of equal experience you admire and rely on for the truth * contributing to the welfare of your community * becoming involved with groups that give local aid during crisis times * taking care of the family of man * mastering each situation by being totally present each moment * knowing exactly what you are doing spiritually * being your own religious authority * compassionate and knowledgeable heroes for the new age * by respecting our mutual integrity, we form complex, quality intimate relationships * making it through the journey of life as a whole person * your karma ripens to the point where you meet your complementary male archetype * highly developed souls communicate harmoniously * spiritual tests of loyalty, honesty, and faithfulness

## The Hierophant, Jupiter, Priest, or the Pope √

The Hierophant card revolves around learning a great deal of information on an esoteric level. This can relate to work or personal interests, but spiritually, this trump refers to an understanding of divine law. You utilize a deeper philosophy to observe the world by comprehending the symbolism of everyday events as your destiny unfolds.

*R*omance:

he touches you at a spiritual level * you admire his morality and the way he treats others * a guy who worships the ground you walk on * you are teachers for each other * you need to be philosophical about love at this time * courtly love * a chaste courtship * his intuition is right on * he recognized your soul connection immediately * you share the same religious beliefs * relationship choices based on loving wisdom * the moment he saw you, he knew you were it * you need to know the truth about his feelings * a commitment, but not necessarily in a legal sense * friendships with men can evolve into the best romances * he will go for what is sacred * he is aligning with his higher self * he is finding God and developing a conscience * the psychology of love * a mate shift to a conscious guy who shares your values and beliefs * a relationship as a spiritual awakening * he has noble thoughts about romance * your greatest desire is to rise above karmic entanglements * studying metaphysics, philosophy, or ancient texts together * one or both of you attend school and this influences your connection * you are his channel to the divine source * you have a lot of inside information for him * a soul-to-soul bond transcends age, race, and gender * a really good person who is new tunes into you * a guy who thinks he is being spiritual because he does not sleep with you * a platonic friendship you wish could become more * having to coach him on how to satisfy you * falling in love with his beautiful soul * having an eternal karmic bond with another * a man who is philanthropic and concerned with conditions in his community

## Work & Business:
every level and form of education with an emphasis on higher learning * an authority figure interprets the code of behavior * heart over head professional choices * someone who knows everything about their field of interest * your soul must

somehow be engaged in your work * a great teacher or mentor who has a lifetime of experience and knowledge * someone who is a major influence on all who follow him * gaining the tricks of your trade * the power behind the thrones of the most important players * getting financial backing from a wealthy individual or a family trust or foundation * worrying about the impact of your business on the health of the planet * maintaining your personal integrity when faced with material choices * having success promoting worthy causes * a career in healing that benefits the upliftment of humanity * an older person hands his practice and clients over to you upon retirement * attending college or university as a full-time student * going for an advanced degree or highly specialized training * getting involved with educational associations * becoming a teacher, trainer, or professor * taking or giving workshops * directing social welfare programs * joining clubs and groups affiliated with your work * going to a convention or conference for educational purposes * having a political conscience * getting involved with philanthropy, charity, and community activism for the safety and protection of others * religions that serve as investment bankers, bartering their dogmatic beliefs for the currency of the common person * the business of supporting a spiritual group with food and housing * the marketing of formal theologies * your creative material comes from a deep space * religious architecture, sacred writings, and priceless art objects commissioned to catch the eye of god * past-life abilities being reintegrated into this incarnation * bookstores, archives, and collections of arcane information in any field of interest

## Spiritual Growth:

pure thought from the one true source * a blessed union of souls sanctioned by heavenly grace * organized religions and their hierarchy of leadership ✷ sacred ceremonies, holidays, and other calendar-oriented rituals ✷ to believe in God ✷ to seek divine counsel ✷ making contact with a higher source ✷ approaching others on a nonphysical level ✷ having only the best intent with other people ✷ seeing everyone as a potential teacher ✷ universal force compels us to understand ourselves ✷ prayer creates direct effect and profound results ✷ totally devoting yourself to spirit ✷ service to others as true liberation ✷ the eternal cycle of teaching the principles and inner workings of a mystery to the select few ✷ Kabbalah ✷ understanding the laws of synchronicity ✷ transcendent relationships ✷ otherworldly friends ✷ spiritual symbols, languages, and concepts ✷ an empathetic soul doctor who works miracles for those in need ✷ helping others recognize and cultivate their true selves ✷ selflessly laboring for the evolution of mankind ✷ if you are good to others, you will be fine ✷ a major spiritual teacher who is with you on a soul level ✷ many truths emerge through dreams, visions, and earthly coincidence ✷ a sincere, evolved person with a great deal of insight ✷ organized religion as a system of moral lessons to help you discover your reason for living ✷ a couple called together to do collective healing work ✷ not projecting your neuroses on others ✷ tapping into the millenniums of now-forgotten arts, sciences, and languages ✷ increasing your understanding of abstract philosophical principles ✷ any religious or spiritual figurehead who is the leader of their organization ✷ dead thinkers whose works guide and inspire you ✷ all spiritual teachers, study groups, foundations, institutions, healing centers, schools, bookstores, libraries, and community groups ✷ choosing your own code of belief freely as you move forward in your evolution

## *The Lovers or Love*  √ı

The Lovers symbolizes romantic attraction, falling in love, courtship, and the choice of a lifetime partner based on intense mutual feelings. This is a very passionate card which indicates that your purest desire is to be with someone whose dreams and ideals match your own.

*R*omance:

someone will show up soon, if they have not already * deciding which fabulous man to choose * taking your friendship with him to the next level * the blossoming of a compatible union * if you and he ever get physically involved, it could be explosive * in affairs of the heart, never let the icing substitute for the cake * true love never dies * to feel his presence all around you * when you meet someone special, you will certainly know it * getting ready for the love of your life * you experience shortness of breath and a racing pulse when you look into his eyes * hoping to marry your equal partner * he knows you are his next girlfriend * instant recognition the minute you see each other * he stares at you with a look of sucking on a milkshake through a straw * all the emotional fulfillment of two meant to be together * you decide jointly how to proceed with the relationship * acting and feeling married to him although you are single * you are the same person * being infatuated with someone forever * one or both of you could be married to others * you are best friends and great lovers * a serious marriage proposal * preparations for a major wedding * making a lifelong commitment to each other * having a union that improves with the years * going into business with your romantic partner * being attracted to your total opposite personality * feeling struck by lightning when you meet him ＊ experiencing a closer rapport with him than with anyone else ＊ having intense intimacy and a total desire for a permanent relationship

## Work & Business:

a harmonious business partnership ＊ choosing between two equally great jobs ＊ receiving benefits through the employment arrangements of your husband ＊ making a major decision whether to legally marry or not ＊ wondering if you should stay with your current job or move on ＊ long-term business associates ＊ you could work for your employers until you retire ＊ complete immersion in the work you love ＊ a mom-and-pop operation thrives and expands to new locations ＊ buying into a franchise ＊ making an instantaneous decision to purchase a property you fall in love with at first sight ＊ a couple as a totally united team in the marketplace ＊ lifetime job security if you want with your current company ＊ groups form in the name of a common goal ＊ someone at work is extremely attracted to you ＊ sexual harassment on the job ＊ marrying a man you meet professionally ＊ a perfect partner who has qualities you do not have, and vice versa ＊ any business that profits from engagements and weddings ＊ buying high ticket items on impulse ＊ your man needs you to make it financially ＊ being with a guy as a social or monetary upgrade

## Spiritual Growth:

a relationship that challenges you to grow emotionally ＊ when soul mates have identical physical appearances ＊ earthly marriages based on soul union ＊ sexual pleasure was meant to be sacred, never decadent ＊ heart problems healed when you develop lovingness in your personality ＊ a partnership that honors the independence of both people * falling in love puts you through an amazing spiritual initiation * the pure of heart have the most elevated sense of purpose * a holy union preordained in the heavenly spheres * the dance of the soul mates * the instant recognition between twin flames * an eternal companion * having a romantic, mental affair with a deity * a nun or monk who sublimates personal feelings for the detached adoration of the creator * sexual healing through a high-level liaison with a generous man * a relationship where the telepathy is intense * your right to love and be loved in return * practicing spiritual teamwork because we are in this earthly drama together * sharing spiritual beliefs with your partner * wanting him with all your heart and soul * showing compassion for all living things * a union that is blessed by God * attraction to someone you recall from an exquisite past life together * you share intensely poignant karma from long ago * love as a heavy drug unequaled pharmaceutically * wanting to be with him every chance you get * having a physiological connection to your mate

## The Chariot  √ıl

The Chariot indicates that there is nothing you can do to hurry the outcome of a situation. As a passenger, you are required to sit back and let the vehicle of life guide you as quickly as possible toward your goals. The Chariot teaches the value of perfect timing when fate is out of your hands and nothing seems to be happening. You must wait, watch, and witness your own development without any anxiety concerning the future until the opportunity arrives to take action.

### Romance:

a cosmic relationship that is preordained by destiny * he could make rapid progress if he chooses * when the right day comes, he will pursue you * love is on the way * someone new is around the corner * he invites you on a trip and makes arrangements so your journey is effortless * you will see him again very soon * people do not change until they are ready to grow * he was what you needed at the moment * a pleasant, but relatively brief, encounter * your feelings for him came and went quickly * you pull away from someone just passing through your life * see him as often as you can * if you go off with him, you will go far * your experience with him is preparing you for the next man * having a healthy emotional detachment from him * meeting the man of your dreams while walking down the street * you will travel with him * you could have to commute to where he lives * going through the motions of a dead marriage * he creates a whole new world for you * leaving guys behind as a romantic pattern * a troubling relationship could suddenly become easy * discovering the lessons learned

with him and then moving on * his only purpose is to help you
heal your self-esteem * you never meet a guy on your own timing * feeling ready for a relationship, but there is no man
around * trusting that God makes better romantic choices than
you * not having to do anything during courtship except say yes
* someone who connects you to your destiny * he is another
variation of the male archetypes that attract you * there are no
real obstacles if you choose to be together * a union that is
meant to be * fate places your soul mate directly in your path
* you cannot rush him into making decisions * gathering information about him * in retrospect, all past relationships make
sense

## Work & Business:

your work has everything to do with where you are going *
wondering if the deal is real or another false alarm * do not
worry about what you cannot control with coworkers * being
on the fast track toward promotion * your career path unfolds
at the right time with the right business * new connections are
an asset to long-term goals * getting a job is a matter of destiny
* you are right on schedule with a major project * having a general feeling that everything will resolve itself * you may not be
settled into permanent employment at this time * proving yourself to others * your boss assures you of a raise or a new job
title * you can blow a deal by being too hasty * your strategy is
to move in the right direction * you may have to give up a certain lifestyle to get somewhere in the world * all obstacles to
your plans should be taken lightly * keep your eyes on the prize
* remember the bigger picture financially * do not lose sight of
your ultimate creative purpose * moving quickly through negotiations * expanding an existing business * moving an operation
to a new location * your ambitions have brought you a certain

level of success * not having expectations but finding value in being part of the process * you glide through all responsibilities with great efficiency * timing is critical and could make or break a deal * being absolutely certain about your game plan * wanting more than anything to be a success in your field * making good use of the skills you already possess * staying neutral so you emerge victorious in any struggle * transportation to your job as an issue * commuting every day by bus, train, or plane * financing the purchase of a new car * slowly and steadily building a formidable power base of connections * having to take a business trip

## Spiritual Growth:

letting nature run its course * traveling to a special holy site or headquarters of a spiritual teacher * letting go of the past * instant karma coming back at you * evolving at a rapid rate * awareness of the laws of coincidence * dangerous natural disasters are out of our control * never say never, just say, I do not want this * destiny always moves you to a place for soul development * feeling content with your life, self, and path * you are compelled to attend a spiritual gathering * being drawn to a belief without knowing why * what will be, will be * always remember, God is driving the bus * fate dictates your future direction * the best thing about the problems of others is that they are not yours * everything happens because of precise universal timing * the movement of our lives is preordained by the physical placement of the planets at birth * realizing how a romantic affair with a guy saved you in the best way on many levels * there is nothing to do but surrender to the journey * your inner voice will tell you when to change residence and specifically where to go * your car manifests symptoms of illness instead of your physical body and deflects the damage away from you ✳ being guided to travel to a power center on earth to experience a revelation or bear witness to a miraculous event ✳ enjoying the wonder of your spiritual evolution from a calm meditative state ✳ you cannot rush the expansion of consciousness through pharmaceutical sources ✳ soul maturation can take a whole lifetime to occur ✳ nothing good happens quickly

## *Justice* √\|\|

When Justice appears in a spread, it can signal a pending legal matter awaiting a final verdict. Your past activities have created a problematic state where all debts must be paid and all ancient misunderstandings resolved. It is time to balance your behavior and become more loving, selfless, and honest in your thoughts and deeds.

## *Romance:*

being drawn back together with someone from a previous lifetime ✳ already having a long, intimate history with another ✳ an opportunity to get it right with him this time ✳ giving him money to get rid of him ✳ he may have trouble handling your power ✳ he wonders if he can ever be at your level ✳ a brief encounter of a purely karmic nature ✳ he plays by the rules ✳ he does not want to blow it with you ✳ trying to get out of a marriage ✳ separation and divorce and being a united front when announcing the same ✳ if single, a sign of getting legally married ✳ he is waiting until he settles with his current partner so she does not bother you ✳ the choice of a mate is in your hands ✳ he has to physically maneuver someone out of his life

* he may be having legal problems * a guy creates a healthy sense of balance for you * the gift of freedom in equal partnerships * you pick your husband when the right one appears * learning to trust in what he says * recreating childhood traumas through your current relationship * hoping for honesty and integrity in your marriage * he gives you an ultimatum to marry him immediately

## Work & Business:

reward time if you have paid your dues * forming or ending a legal partnership * be sure to get it in writing * being bound by a contract * signing a deal * negotiating a legal document * somebody needs to honor an agreement * you may have to compromise * it is time to get what you deserve * being arrested or busted and wasting good money fighting the case * going straight after a lifetime of crime * all activities considered unlawful by the rules of society * settling misdeeds with the government * trying to get away with anything illegal without getting caught * the financial system makes it difficult for the individual to get ahead * corruption in government services places an extra burden on the taxpayer * be prepared to pay your own way * a business partner who is your equal * following a strict behavioral code at work * someone could get caught for doing the wrong thing * upholding what is fair and right helps you move ahead karmically in your career * making a major statement by taking a bold professional step forward * a settlement is reached in favor of a woman * courts, lawyers, lawsuits, and taking legal action * debt or tax problems need to be resolved * working in the political arena * running for office * initiating new laws for the public good * lobbying * helping draft new social and political policies * becoming involved with issues facing your community * risking arrest by protesting for what you believe * tempting fate with authorities * fighting with a business rival and hoping to win * receiving an inheritance or monetary windfall

## Spiritual Growth:

treating others badly returns as physical or mental imbalance * making your own needs a priority * establishing strong boundaries with others * integrating an active outer world with a rich inner life * feeling that everywhere you go, you have been before * living above earthly laws * karmic manifestations of negative behavior * the soul keeps returning to the body to learn more lessons * forgiving those who hurt you in the past * grave moral crimes committed to insure personal power * the recognition of past-life careers and abilities * you cannot get away with improper actions * the universe will place people before you, and you can deal with them or not * you have to do what you have to do * being a spiritual person is not easy * a great social, religious, or political leader returns to the earth plane * the eternal code of unwritten law * living by the right rules for conscious moral behavior * your fate is nothing like your karma * the ethical responsibility of making predictions for others * fulfilling prebirth agreements to work toward humanitarian goals * reincarnation is so often reenactment * someone from ancient times comes back into your life to settle a score * becoming a better person by hiding your ego * the purpose of any incarnation is to achieve spiritual equilibrium

## The Hermit    IX

The Hermit lives apart from the world and searches for the truth on his own terms. He depends on himself completely and often shuns the mainstream of society. This trump symbolizes a solitary period in deep reflection when you quietly search your soul to understand the wisdom and value behind the drama of your life.

*Romance:*

lonely ways are inner ways that develop true character * looking for someone who is on the path * being dead serious about a guy * holding back your emotions * you get the news that he has become single * it may not be an appropriate period for a relationship * your journey toward love is yet to unwind * a platonic friendship * it is okay to go through a celibate phase * abstaining from sex until you know him better or find a worthy partner * he is not ready to fulfill his passion for you * he will be alone when you see him next * an introverted man who prefers solitude to being with a woman * you need to check him out truthfully * he has to follow his own way * he needs to discover who is right for him * a man who is sexually unresponsive to you but is not gay * he can live without romantic companionship * a developmental stage of not being attached to others emotionally * sometimes it seems like he has no feelings * your relationship suffers from too much physical separation * he is entitled to private time alone * he is scared that you will leave him * to be on your own for awhile * an introverted monastic lifestyle without pleasure or sensuality * take the focus off of him so the right person can come in * make sure your life flourishes regardless of him * developing

your inner treasures instead of playing dating games * by culti-
vating your real nature, you attract someone deserving of your
attention * wanting more independence in your marriage * staying pure of heart as you wait for your soul mate to appear *
somebody has to tell the truth * you are probably not pregnant

## *Work & Business:*

you can do no wrong in a business deal * working from your
home * a job that isolates you from the rest of the world * it is
lonely at the top * going through a secluded period during
unemployment * seeking out the truth in a rough negotiation *
self-reliant problem solving * having a wise and experienced
elder at your disposal * thinking over money matters seriously
without distractions * figuring out the best way to go * you need
to make a detailed investigation independent of the system *
research planning * dealing with controversy head-on * establishing a clear work environment with positive and friendly
workers * keeping information to yourself * looking out for
number one * you are ready to discover your outer-world path
* becoming your own person professionally * you need to go
out and see what is happening in the marketplace * self-
employment * subcontracted work * retirement * being laid off
* receiving unemployment or disability payments * having to
force yourself to look for a job * recovery from a work-related
injury * convalescence to heal stress and drug-related problems
* company-wide vacations * spas, resorts, rehabilitation centers, spiritual retreat compounds, wildlife sanctuaries, or
wilderness adventures as business possibilities * having an ability to shut out the world and focus on business * trying to take
care of yourself financially * running an operation totally on
your own * an office, studio, or separate room where you can
work undisturbed * moving to a more secluded environment
during a major lifestyle transition

## *S*piritual *G*rowth:

male and female gender characteristics integrated in one person * celibate beings * having an inhibited experience with interpersonal exchange * someone who is out of their body a lot * androgynous disembodied entities * actively searching for answers * going off alone * assessing your past and planning your future * inner peace must be attained at all costs * being spiritually responsible * the soul has ears if you call to someone through the ethers * creation on a mental level and applied through the healing principles * giving heavy thought to the meaning of soul purpose * coming from a place of rational consciousness * taking the high road through prayer and meditation * know thyself * spiritual people often find themselves alone * retreating into yourself for a period * joining a dull cult to escape material responsibilities * finding your own relationship with God * not letting anybody tell you what to believe * the best solutions can be found within you * the religion of the individual * trying to be honest with everyone in your life * going for correct behavior * leading an evolved, principle-centered existence * giving up things and people you enjoy as required by a religious order * psychic development as a personal process * utilizing meditation as a tool for going within * searching your soul and the new age books for clues * receiving guidance from the infinite spirit * setting realistic goals for yourself based on absolute values * getting closer to God in a forest or on a mountain or island * joining a sacred scholarly enterprise * having your own philosophy to carry with you * relying on your own judgement * a light worker who tirelessly struggles to uplift the collective unconscious

## The Wheel of Fortune  X

This fortuitous turning point implies a lucky cycle that brings in prosperity and personal happiness. The Wheel creates opportunities for expansion and finds you winning on many levels. Your success is far greater than you imagine, so prepare for all the positive and growthful developments that accompany this card.

### Romance:

finding the perfect person for yourself ❊ you cannot believe the twists of fate that brought him to you ❊ something amazing with someone special ❊ trying to imagine where you would be without him ❊ you do not know what is happening, but it sure feels good ❊ he is one in a million ❊ you will get everything you want when the time is right ❊ a great chance to travel with him ❊ if you are his destiny, he will not blow you off ❊ you made a big impression on him ❊ it could be a roller-coaster emotional life with him ❊ if people do not measure up, let them go ❊ having the best time in your life ❊ the relationship is unfolding at its own speed ❊ you are grateful for all the fun he provides ❊ your next man will be more beneficial in general ❊ he is still going through the motions of an existing commitment ❊ he could have financial ideas for you ❊ a wealthy guy who likes to play ❊ he has no troublesome ex-wives or children ❊ a marriage of monetary convenience ❊ a couple whose energy has already peaked ❊ mind-blowing sex above and beyond anything you have experienced before ❊ he may have a plan to work with you ❊ something is going down that will move the relationship forward ❊ he is good for you, even if he is only a piece of your complete romantic puzzle ❊ a marriage partner beyond your wildest dreams ❊ he makes your life effortless

## Work & Business:

you need to go out and make some big money ∗ the alloca-
tion of capital from less to more productive uses ∗ tremendous
opportunities for advancement ∗ to make a fortune ∗ to hit the
lottery ∗ watching your investments grow ∗ success comes
together after a long effort ∗ being connected to a large financial resource ∗ a huge career change involves more earnings
and power ∗ a substantial job offer ∗ a high bid on a home or
property you have for sale ∗ the vicious economic cycle of borrowing and incurring higher interest payments ∗ paying in, taking out ∗ legacies, gifts, and inheritances ∗ business success and
expansion ∗ making a big splash with a project ∗ to be financially blessed ∗ a sudden promotion occurs after a period of
waiting ∗ a deal finally materializes ∗ you sell an intellectual
property for a goodly sum ∗ prosperity and an enhanced social
standing ∗ your time has come to buy a residence ∗ you are at
the height of your career ∗ achieving freedom from material
concerns ∗ not knowing when something will happen ∗ marketing a product on a grand scale ∗ you will not believe where you
are going ∗ fame and fortune come to you

## Spiritual Growth:

feeling positive about your life ∗ recovery from a difficult
period ∗ receiving money to spend on personal growth work ∗
you always avoid experiences that would set back your development ∗ life is too short to waste time suffering ∗ finding the
right knowledge at the right time ∗ harvesting spiritual rewards
∗ cosmic people pop up to guide you forward along your path ∗
feeling blessed and protected ∗ attracting exactly what you
need ∗ comprehending your change in consciousness ∗ utilizing
all mysteries as springboards to mastery ∗ having awe in the
face of eternity ∗ an accelerated evolutionary state ∗ feeling

excited about all the good things to come ✽ the greatest wealth is living in the truth ✽ having an excellent life due to past good deeds ✽ being aware of the universal force that pushes you higher and higher ✽ your karma dictates the future circumstances of your soul ✽ events are happening beyond your control ✽ our collective movement forward as a species ✽ making great spiritual leaps as the galaxy speeds up ✽ the destiny you dream of finally unfolds ✽ you begin to see the lighter side of fate ✽ to be here now, and happening ✽ astrology as a sacred and highly valued science that explains every movement of every atom throughout the cosmos ✽ your natal horoscope ✽ major transiting astrological aspects ✽ all calendar-based divination systems

## Strength, Force, or Fortitude   Ⴈ

Strength builds courageous character in those ready to clean up physical and mental imbalance in their personalities. This trump signifies a battle between opposing sides of your conscience and gives the self-discipline necessary to remove the negative attitudes and lifestyle habits that reinforce your animalistic tendencies and give you a false sense of power.

*R*omance:

when you meet him, you undergo an immediate healing ✽ he will get his courage up ✽ let him in, but keep up your guard ✽ when he is ready for action, he will check in ✽ a man who is gutsy and sincere ✽ he will regenerate emotionally if he takes a chance with you ✽ a relationship that is very much alive ✽ lifting the caliber of your lovers * passion deeply felt for another * a growthful challenge ahead with your next boyfriend * you want to do what is proper and right * he is an adventure who tests your limits * having total self-confidence in love * he is clearing out his messy love life * he is busy getting ready for you * a healthy body means better self-esteem with the opposite sex * he is extremely athletic in bed * he can definitely keep it going * you need to get active about him * he is a nice, respectable person * a couple who needs to transcend any competitive feelings * get rid of him if he criticizes you mercilessly * being yourself in a relationship and it feels great * he opens a door to you that never closes * an instantaneous healing of a hurt caused by a misinterpretation of defensive behavior * taking a major chance in love

## Work & Business:

success comes from hard work * it could be a risk not to do a project * solid financial plans move forward * an excellent time to make an investment * you need to put energy into overcoming career obstacles * being on the verge of a major change * coming to grips with your burgeoning debt * you will win in the long run * everything is in your favor * your loan is approved * you have the winning edge in a deal * you are talented enough to handle the most important tasks * discovering what you need to learn from a tough situation * you should just go in and ask for the raise or job * your inner strength pulls you through a messy crisis * taking on rivals at work * competitors force you to be more efficient and turn out a better product * an impressive ability to take on professional challenges * only the strong survive in the marketplace * achieving success after a difficult confrontation * having confidence in your own abilities * after receiving your share of the profits, you arrive at a new level of power and influence * getting your body into shape improves self-esteem and job performance * any business involving physical training, sporting goods, or the marketing of sports to a mass audience * getting the contract you have patiently waited for * an energetic worker who has the stamina needed to endure the stress of large assignments * feeling secure in your job and worthy of your financial benefits * building up funds to leave the rat race completely for a more self-sufficient lifestyle

## Spiritual Growth:

having a strong immune system that resists disease * regaining your physical equilibrium after a rough period * healing is guaranteed * by cleaning up your habits, you will save your life * beating the odds against a gigantic challenge * kicking drugs, sugar, or alcohol * battling the urges of your lower, animalistic instincts * overcoming subconscious defensive behavioral mechanisms * relying on your inner strength to fight your battles * getting rid of laziness and thoughtlessness in your character * removing insecurity and a sense of worthlessness from your being * someone new inspires you to purify your intentions and moderate your appetites * liberating yourself of negative karmic blocks in your personality * preparing for earth changes or natural disasters * the ultimate power is that of our self-healing planet where catastrophic events regenerate the delicate environmental balance * having a positive attitude toward your right to personal expression * having the strength to overcome darkness in your heart and soul * forgiving those who wounded you in the past * having the courage to examine painful issues * a higher level of perception helps you let go of your personal history * making a commitment to work with others for a better future * evolution is based on avoiding danger and physical survival * a better attitude improves every area of your life * learning to balance the spiritual with the material * faith moves mountains * raising your vibration is crucial to maintaining your health * an interest in personal growth increases your vitality * renunciation to the core of your being * evolutionary changes encourage soul healing * the struggle between truly holy people and corrupt charlatans

## The Hanged Man  XII

The Hanged Man infers a total commitment that requires you to give up old ways of thinking and living. You must sacrifice the past so new activities and interests can thrive and move you closer to your goals. The devotion characterized by this trump challenges you constantly and forever changes the direction of your destiny.

### Romance:

you may need to take a break from each other * doing some soul-searching about a certain person * seeing more of the truth about him * being ready to go all the way into or out of a relationship * trying to get rid of him * learning to let go of those not at your spiritual level * being free when the right person comes along * keeping clear of losers and users * may indicate a lonely period without a boyfriend * rebuilding an existing partnership on a higher level through insightful warmth * it could be very different next time with him * he needs to evolve and get himself ready for you * he wants to begin a new romance after he ends a dying one * someone in the process of leaving a marriage * separation or divorce * he wants to get rid of everyone and just be with you * making emotional decisions free from behavioral or cultural patterns * reconciliation depends on him changing his way of thinking, acting, and being * making a total commitment to see the relationship through to the end * surrender to him or give him up * going out with him forces you to sacrifice things you enjoy * if you choose him, your life will be entirely different * he is ditching her really fast * moving away from a stagnant lifestyle you share with a man * loving each other out of a sense of duty or loyalty * practicing unconditional love and forgiveness with him * learning the value of compromise in a relationship * there can only be one star in the family * waiting for someone who shares your deepest beliefs * a nonconformist partnership that exists beyond social mores

## Work & Business:

full or no participation in a business plan * selling a property or operation that is not profitable * your hours are decreased * you go from full-time to part-time employment * a loss of responsibility or seniority at your job * somebody you work with is leaving * a new opportunity unlike anything you have ever had before * you will do whatever it takes to make something happen * waiting for a decision that affects your job future * total devotion to your career to the exclusion of normal activities * hoping others understand your ideas and are enthusiastically supportive * cutting somebody off financially * paying someone to get rid of them * firing or retiring an employee * you see a situation differently than your coworkers * removing nonproductive workers * selling nonperforming investments * getting out of the stock market for good * giving up on a project due to delays * a business moves to a new location * you liquidate an existing operation * filing for bankrupt-

cy to avoid paying creditors * nondisclosure clauses in contracts * you will never work in a certain town or with a specific company again * leaving your position and coworkers forever * within a month of walking away from your job, you forget
it completely * to engage in creative work at a level of surrender * a time of professional transition between two totally different types of businesses * adopting and applying new ways of
thinking about your career

## Spiritual Growth:

giving up bad habits and attitudes * changing your lifestyle
for health purposes * controlling your appetites on a deeper
level * releasing the negative part of your psyche * overcoming
debilitating personal problems * sacrificing this lifetime for
something better, later * authenticity of spirit * saving yourself
* evolving due to actual cellular shifting and reforming * rising
above the usual concerns * finding it hard to transcend your
personal ego * a lofty revelation received during total surrender * the important choices you make today influence your
development for centuries to come * completely letting go of
material * undergoing an ordeal of pure evolutionary change *
a self-reliant attitude helps you see more clearly * accelerated
gains in consciousness * seeing the joke behind the social
power of biological ties * aligning with a deeper level of existence * uplifting your vibration is good for the planet * clear
moments of peaceful detachment from reality * simplifying
your life to focus on long-term truths * helping people get
through spiritual transitions * the higher meaning of natural
and unnatural disasters * deflecting negative energy * a feeling
of crucifixion * realizing losses are due to karmic paybacks
owed to others from previous days and times * going within to
complete your inner work * becoming a better person * living

up to spiritual principles * surrendering to who or what is best for you * practicing unconditional love as a rule * being the embodiment of divine law * self-service is an outgrowth of your desire to uplift humanity * being in tune with the themes of your incarnation * extremely holy and righteous spiritual beings

## Death  XⅢ

Death brings a total healing transformation that stimulates personal growth and leads to an entirely new lifestyle. This deep process of renewal requires the destruction of old habits and behavioral patterns that no longer serve your spiritual evolution. A better person, who is mature enough to experience more challenging stages of development, emerges from the outdated physical version of yourself.

### Romance:

someone who is inappropriate for you * old male archetypes are dying fast * wondering if a new location would improve your chances of meeting a guy * emotional flat-liners * friends suddenly become romantic * a completely new life in another relationship * someone who is sexually fried * impotence * asexuality * the walking wounded who will never try at love again * finding it difficult to share your feelings with him * whether he tells you or not, he has gone down over you * you are saved by his awareness that he cannot be truly intimate with another * your behavior toward him has nearly killed him * he will be extremely different toward you the next time you see him * choosing an empty shell of a man because you have nothing left to give * losing the magic in a romance through too much psychological analysis ❋ your living situation changes like night and day ❋ letting a hollow marriage die in the most honorable way ❋ having a major change of heart about someone from the past ❋ if you open up to him sexually, he will have power over you ❋ things come to a head in a messy relationship ❋ he needs to move a woman who is dead weight out of his life ❋ he needs to see that she does not love him ❋ he has fears about letting her go and not being able to keep you ❋ you are devastated by the loss of one you love dearly ❋ renewing your vows in a solid union ❋ feeling dead inside because he is gone ❋ wondering if your joy of life will ever return

## Work & Business:

to give up the ghost on a deal ❋ being pushed to the edge by the competition ❋ a physical death influences your financial or professional status ❋ a dramatic promotion you did not expect ❋ somebody is on their way out ❋ to remove a coworker from your personal social circle ❋ a strong bull market ❋ new work that showcases abilities you have not used yet ❋ mass-marketed messages of death through the mediums of film, television, music, video, games, and performances ❋ abusive and violent sporting events ❋ damaging products and programs aimed at children ❋ the big business of endless war that only destroys life, homes, families, and communities ❋ murder for profit ❋ joining the armed forces for the income only ❋ a new job requires a different image ❋ leaving behind a way of life forever ❋ moving to a new location forces you to change jobs ❋ major shifts of power where you work ❋ inheritance and goods of the dead ❋ wills, legacies, trusts, and family foundations ❋ a drastic career move ❋ dropping out of the corporate world for a more laid-back profession or vice versa ❋ a totally different business plan emerges ❋ a major shift of ambitions ❋ loss of a job ❋ how supporting the military undermines the structure of a private economy and hinders its capacity to produce and flourish * anyone associated with farming who dreams of huge harvests as he or she waits through dormant periods until the next go-around * any business that promotes anti-aging products

## *Spiritual Growth:*

a deep-level healing * physical rejuvenation and renewal * a change in lifestyle dramatically improves your appearance and overall condition * a fresh new you emerges * shedding old skin and becoming more youthful * the strange karma of suicide * being spiritually affected by the death of a loved one * turning within religiously due to an empty feeling * a transformed person comes forth from old decay * weight loss alters your entire perspective * a different sense of style matches your radical personality changes * creating new soul substance for yourself * being liberated for the next cycle of growth and evolution * artifacts and architectural ruins as records of the ancient past * communicating with noncorporeal beings * having disembodied spirit guides * out-of-body experiences * the world of astral travel * glimpses at the immortal nature of the soul * fear of the future * learning not to be afraid of finally dying * shedding beliefs, people, and associations that do not measure up * resurrection of the spirit * being ready to slip out of your mortality * death as the great social equalizer * most of humanity is at an evolutionary standstill * our survival requires radical activism * extinction of the life force on the planet * major endings in your life * emotional release accompanies the dark nights of the soul * how past lives exist in the here and now * becoming detached, centered, and peaceful as in a trance * taking on a new name and identity after a spiritual conversion * preparing yourself for an expected passing over * communicating with the dead * believing that those on the other side can see you * ghosts and incidents of hauntings * ouija boards, mediums, and seances * grief therapy and the cyclical timing of the healing process * to know what it is like to die * near-death experiences * the spiritual transformation of rebirth * learn the lessons or take the leap * letting go of anger resolves many problems * the right-to-die movement

## *Temperance* XIV

Temperance is a guiding and healing force leading you toward a more whole, balanced existence as you blend contradictory forces in your character. There is always a period of waiting implied here, as you develop your creative potential to produce high-quality work that has the power to lift the human spirit.

### *Romance:*

you need to put him on the back burner for now * his sobriety could be an issue * a passage of time spent apart * true love begins as friendship * a slowly unfolding romance * when opposites attract, both personalities are tempered * if you have sex too quickly, you could be sunk * he needs to purify his intentions * choosing a partner based on personal qualities you find important * taking time to know him before jumping in * engaging in a casual discussion to air grievances * a person who has a hard time expressing emotions * it could take him awhile to clear his head * all the insanity must come to a halt * being guided toward the right person * you wish he would try harder with you * he is afraid to lose control of his feelings * staying calm and patient with him ✳ he knows if it is real, he should not rush you ✳ struggling with the abrasive elements of your own behavior toward him ✳ separation as the only solution to the problems between you ✳ falling in love occurs on its own schedule ✳ liberated women often have to wait for the man to make the first move ✳ you do not hit it off with him right away ✳ he begins to mellow out and get used to you ✳ a great sense of relief when you finally find the right man ✳ working on a romance that has been spoiled by poor communication and hurtful fighting ✳ relationship on a level of spiritual mastery ✳ you need to take a break from each other ✳ he needs to cool out and relax with you ✳ staying with him and trying to resolve issues ✳ he will wait forever until you fall in love with him ✳ not wanting to partake of the chaos in his life ✳ making quiet time for yourself ✳ you cannot handle his mood swings ✳ taking a pause before you can see him again ✳ bad past experiences with other men fade from your consciousness ✳ you end up with someone you have known for a long time

## Work & Business:

having to wait out delays so your plans can be successful ✳ a slow-moving project finally gets the green light ✳ finding a job that utilizes all your previous experience ✳ the business picture becomes very clear ✳ not a time for gambling or taking risks ✳ holding back and observing before jumping in ✳ seriously trying to discover what is right for you ✳ being guided to the perfect position ✳ a compromise may be necessary ✳ seeking employment just to get out of the house ✳ an undertaking is on the back burner, but not by your choice ✳ successfully completing creative work ✳ your goals may be overly ambitious in light of your reality ✳ becoming more tolerant of others at work ✳ not letting money problems get to you ✳ taking slow periods in stride * skills and talents acquired over the years * go slowly and check out every detail * nothing is going to happen overnight * a long apprenticeship, internship, or training period * if it seems too good to be true, it might be * grace under pressure in a challenging situation * have an alternate plan * a casual work atmosphere helps cool you out * putting the brakes on an expenditure * looking for ways to give away money * stay patiently focused so a project has ample time to develop * someone who is absent-minded when deep in their work * it can take awhile to discover your true genius

## Spiritual Growth:

physical, emotional, and psychological healing * rest is beneficial for renewal * the soul is imbalanced because of an unhealthy body and mind * living in a suspended state of thought * enlightening details emerge when you slow down * becoming quiet to hear the wisdom of your inner voice * having extremes of your personality in check * being guided toward a particular brand of healing * stop avoiding issues and being in denial * illuminating and uplifting the world vision * an adjustment period during a major awakening * intuitive information that is grounded in reality * being grateful to be alive after an ordeal * wondering if you will make it through whole * adopting a positive lifestyle to increase your energy * examine the situation fully before making a commitment to a spiritual group * showing more mercy, kindness, and forgiveness * by helping other people, you get healed * attracting those who are going through the same cycle of inner work as you * having angelic assistance * being in touch with a hierarchy of archangels or other beings * your core creative ideas are channeled * being guided to the moment * feeling fear and confusion about healing emotional blocks from childhood * deflecting psychic vampirism ✳ achieving a sense of tranquillity and harmony with others in your life ✳ moderation in all things ✳ sending uplifting thoughts to those in trouble ✳ undergoing soul purification ✳ intuitive or visionary artwork ✳ bad memories fading into the past ✳ learning to live more in the present ✳ being at one with the seasonal and astronomical cycles

## The Devil

This trump is the most misunderstood Tarot card in the deck. The Devil represents evil in all its worldly manifestations. The terrible things associated with this card come from the bad choices you make that lock you into negative behavioral patterns. The lesson here is to learn to discriminate between lies and truth, if only in your own heart, and see material tests as temptations that the evolved soul always avoids.

### Romance:

a guy always says the opposite of what he feels ✳ having a fixation on a dangerously unhealthy guy could set you back ✳ he may have been brutalized by other women ✳ he may be worse than you think ✳ why ruin your chance at happiness by staying with a tortured soul who cannot love ✳ having a compulsive need to be emotionally abused by a disinterested man ✳ re-creating the shock of distorted male behavior through your obsessions with unavailable men ✳ a deeper understanding of your despair over a man who could be your match but is too unconscious ✳ if he behaves strangely and is too much of a mystery, forget him ✳ all your friends wonder what you are doing with him * being enslaved to a horrible person * not realizing he is a sexual pervert * his libido may have many fantasy outlets * he may not be able to have a normal relationship * he does sick chicks * get rid of bogus men who do not love you * moving forward too soon with the wrong person * you immediately tell him too many intimate details * no suitable choices exist for you at this time * if he is a drug addict, degenerate, or a debauched sociopath, get rid of him * a combative relationship you should run away from * breaking through your own doubts * being attracted to a person who is beneath you spiritually * trying to trap someone * keeping an unspeakable passion to yourself * suffering due to a man as a total self-delusion * he could ruin you * faithless and corrupt lovers are your downfall * wanting someone real bad * a lifetime of therapy will not help him * he may not have the strength to heal himself * selling out to a loser or unlovable creep * the information he hears about you is false * you may never get a normal reaction from a guy you like * premature marriage or cohabitation with a man who is not of your caliber * rejecting bogus friends who are jealous or anti-you * let go of arrogant, self-absorbed men * do not have hopes about getting back together with him * tolerating a bad marriage for monetary purposes * depression accompanies loneliness * his true sexual orientation is autoerotic or pornographic * you hear terrible rumors about him * he likes fake women who are submissive * feeling poisoned by insecurity and jealousy because he does not love you * he may have hidden motives for courting you * the labyrinthine sexuality of the physically abused

## Work & Business:

getting ripped off * a sure sign of lying * major financial manipulation underway * deciding you have suffered enough at your job and want to get out * inferiority complexes about your creative abilities * trying to control and dominate others * people who are stealing from you and sucking you dry * a business that exploits or abuses people * putting poor families into slavery in a vicious labor cycle * psychopathic people can be very manipulative with money * finding the back door and getting out * feeling trapped by your current job yet afraid to break away * holding yourself back professionally * not using your inborn talents and losing them * being in deep illusion about a business deal * worrying excessively about the competition * entering into partnership with liars, cheats, and bad people * paranoia about losing money * using fear as a negotiation tactic * selling defective goods or toxic products * military programs are not market efficient * the evil that men do to each other * anything hideous that makes a profit * organized crime * prostitution * gambling * earnings from hurting abused people * financial loss * greed runs rampant * drug money * blood money * a miser who shares nothing with anybody

## Spiritual Growth:

getting away from unholy people * the soul develops through tests that challenge negative behavior * releasing jealousy from your repertoire of emotions * ridding yourself of obsession with physical gratification * your urges and desires are stronger than the reality of the situation * giving up a life based on vanity, greed, and illusion * transforming deep discontent into calm detachment * your immature personality acts defensively and creates imaginary problems * you need to meet a higher level of people socially * ending your association with a group that is not supportive of you * seeing scary motives behind the actions of others * paralyzing fear and depression block your spiritual growth * your energy is being drawn away by human parasites * failing to see how long certain betrayals have gone on * living an illusion within an illusion based on lies * psychosexual wounds, such as circumcision * pain as a motivator * low self-esteem leads to modern forms of self-mutilation * your lifestyle may be detrimental to your spiritual development * the breaking down of your childhood belief system * personal suffering draws you closer to the world of spirit * undergoing testing by the divine powers to prove your worthiness * triumph over torment * the eternal battle between good and evil in the universe * being manipulated by greedy religious people * every and all forms of violence * living a lie in the closet is painful * conquering self-doubt and a negative self-image on the path to wholeness * re-creating psychological trauma from your past * you cannot get away with improper actions * paranoid people are usually guilty of past-life crimes against humanity * someone whose hurt is too deep for you to understand * failing the spiritual tests built into the design of your lifetime * religious fascism and fanaticism * holy wars that kill people in the name of a god * bad relationships and their significance in your growth as an individual * not practicing what you preach * playing with the dark side prevents you from evolving into a better person * worry and anxiety are your constant companions * what inhibits your soul from moving toward the light * rage, revenge, insanity, and other bleak emotions controlling the mind * the total illusion of the material world

# The Trumps

## The Tower or House of God  X V I

The Tower symbolizes liberation from a period of impris-
onment due to the arrival of truth to a very murky situation. The time has come to break through all lies and
hypocrisy and find a new way of life built upon a healthy
and strong foundation. This trump shocks you with exciting or unexpected news that moves you toward a better
future than conditions suggest at the time of the reading.

## Romance:

a troubled relationship finally falls apart * seeing him for
what he really is * you discover horrifying things about his hidden behavior * long-held secrets are revealed * he is still shattered emotionally from the breakup with you * matters
between you reach a crisis point * the last thing he expects is
to hear from you, or vice versa * he wakes up one day and
decides he wants you * romantic miracles happen when you are
not looking * your partner suddenly ends the affair without any
warning * he needs to come clean on his feelings * falling in
love with him messes you up * attracting men who do not
understand you * what you told him shook him up * having
trouble recovering from him * he may never get over you * having preconceived notions about how he should act * a suppos-
edly happy couple announces their divorce * being in transition
toward seeing the light with him * your eventual mate will not
be who you think * after the truth comes out, there may be
nothing left for you * the shocking arrival of a man you never
expected to see again * being emotionally devastated over a
romance gone bad * getting rid of a guy who is all wrong for
you * a major change of circumstances opens your eyes to his

real nature * a chaotic relationship where nobody is in charge * liberating yourself from a controlling man * unforeseen events influence the unfolding of the love affair

## Work & Business:

a new career phase begins due to conditions beyond your control * your plans could be drastically altered in a second * not having set expectations about income * opportunities fall by the wayside if you do not grab them * stop using strategies that are not effective * an offer blows your mind wide open * huge changes loom at work * profits are way above or below your current estimation * the answer is imminent * tricking a competitor through lies * a potential job is so amazing, you cannot believe it * your financial future is unknown * broken business dreams * a deal will turn out differently than you think * being read the riot act by your boss * a partner is not who you think * being deceived about the assets owned by another * acts of God influence your money flow or business activity * buying into a bad investment with a bogus person * kiss your cash goodbye * the chaos theory of management * a major shocker hits concerning a client or employee * losing a job without warning * anticipating a potential catastrophe * a payment does not arrive on time * being left hanging waiting for money * the bubble bursts and you need to take immediate action * you could lose everything in a minute * always expect the unexpected * your company is secretly up for sale * being suddenly fired from your job * massive corporate layoffs are announced * your business is displaced from its current location due to either environmental, astronomical, or human-created disaster * after the smoke clears, there will be better beginnings for you professionally * preparing yourself by learning new skills to survive materially in the future * a gigantic gyration in the market * an extreme day on Wall Street * panic buying or selling of stocks, bonds, and commodities

## Spiritual Growth:

cleaning up personal problems that are damaging your health * your world as you know it falls apart * a nervous breakdown occurs because you are not expressing your true self * a crisis of identity * feeling lost and uncertain after having many simultaneous lifetime transitions * miraculous healing * a lot of exciting activity ahead * an opportunity to create a new reality for yourself * you can get rid of those who hurt you * your limitations are all in your mind * secrets revealed * a shockingly accurate intuitive reading provides you with excellent information * spiritual lessons based on experiencing public humiliation * demolishing the ghosts, ruins, and memories of the past * stress as a result of compromising your nature * holding steady as the world falls apart * the shift from material to spiritual values happens overnight for survival purposes * breaking through the darkness into the light of gospel * collective crises bring us down, yet bring us together * your beliefs scare normal people * an entirely new spiritual system unlike anything seen before * sudden insights clarify a weird situation * if you are in denial, you are in for a wake-up call * having a powerful mind-altering experience * someone is not as good or as holy as you think * seeing through the illusion of a corrupt religious leader * your only job during zero hour is to listen to the messages coming from the universe * your ideals and innocence are shattered by cosmic betrayal * a truly liberating transformation * surprise news forever changes the course of your destiny * your lies are exposed * realizing calamities give you a new lease on life * stop fooling yourself with shallow religions * having an emotional catharsis * bad memories surface in your psyche and register consciously ✻ divine intervention saves the day ✻ every-thing good and bad happens for a reason ✻ battling groups who use hate and intolerance as verbal weapons are not honoring the prin-ciples of their leading founders, thinkers, and writers

## The Star  XVII

The Star symbolizes what you were born to do and high-lights your highest purpose on the planet. With the Star as your guide, you never lose sight of your biggest dreams because you are protected and your future happiness is guaranteed. Your positive attitude about your unique des-tiny leads you along a certain path of experience harmo-nious to the needs of your inner self.

### Romance:

your feelings for him are overwhelming ✻ he is sending you rushes of ecstasy telepathically ✻ maintaining purity in a time of cold, mercenary couplings ✻ sharing a double fantasy ✻ you may be too big a person for him ✻ you are blowing his mind ✻ he wonders if he can handle your magnitude ✻ you may be too much of a woman for him ✻ trusting your initial vibes about a person ✻ having tremendous expectations may be too unreal ✻ being grateful to him for all he has given you ✻ he wants every-thing to be timed perfectly ✻ something wonderful happens romantically ✻ a soul-stirring sexual chemistry ✻ being blinded by love ✻ a relationship changes your life forever ✻ dating a famous or well-known guy ✻ enjoying lots of social activities with him ✻ meeting someone new at a popular public event or high-profile party ✻ you see his picture and know he is the one immediately * an outer-world persona affects the partnership * contending with certain aspects of his successful career * having fantasy romances with movie, sports, or rock stars * your twin flame appears the minute you get your act together * instant attraction * an innate openness to passionate love * accept no substitutes for the mingling of souls in deep affection * someone who is by your side forever * otherworldy intimate connections * astral sex companions * the physical consummation of spiritual infatuation * merging in perfect union with another * public displays of desire * a guy has to be close to your ideal to avoid problems * you recognize the best in each other * wondering where you would be without him * you cannot shake your strong attachment to him * clicking up to men who could make you happy * valuing yourself when choosing a mate * soul mates always win their freedom in the end * falling in love with the man you hope to marry * expressing your mutual adoration openly and frequently * the bond you share extends beyond this lifetime * you lose track of time with him * you never tire of looking at him * there are good days ahead at the end of the road in a relationship * two people born to be together * the entire universe vibrates with joy when true love reigns supreme

## Work & Business:

having much to give the world through your creative work * having a career in the movie business * being an actor, producer, director, or screenwriter * theater, dance, music, and all the dramatic and performing arts * the television and cable industries * receiving exposure in large circulation magazines and journals * being well-known in your field * fame as a career * power-hungry people who grab center stage * being in a powerful or influential position * becoming a role model for younger people in your profession * achieving the ideals and dreams which you aspire to * Los Angeles as a place to live * receiving recognition * the public loves you * using your image for publicity * being a spokesperson for a business or a cause * working with aristocrats or companies with impeccable reputations * attaining greatness in the eyes of the world * being noticed for your leadership potential * you enter the next league professionally * your career path is what you are meant to do * receiving a huge payoff for hard work * plotting how to get into the limelight * you land your ultimate fantasy job * the success that awaits you is amazing * a big show is about to begin with you as the star * a major business transition is complete * being a multitalented person * you reach your highest goals by believing in yourself * having skills and talents way above the normal population * figuring out what the next big thing is * funds are available to finance your projects * immortal cultural heroes and icons who get the attention of a mass audience * you have what it takes to make it * good ideas can be activated and will bring in money * feeling self-important due to a new promotion * the strange world of being a celebrity

## Spiritual Growth:

the universe is populated with all sorts of intelligent beings * making contact with a greater source * being called to a higher state of evolution is pure bliss * healing energy surrounds and protects you always * pursuing an outer-world destiny armed with inner knowledge * the moment in time when all dreams come true * your popularity can be used to help others * anything that makes you hopeful is good for you * those who can really see immediately recognize each other * your life bears an affirming message by your experience and example * spreading the light around * a beautiful person capable of only the best behavior * attracting your soul mate or twin soul * being a clear channel * controlled astral travel to visit people at a spirit level * having a rich inner life * your aura sparkles with energy and excitement * being in balance and harmony with the divine principles that rule the universe * the galactic mind * attaining a superconscious intelligence of stored cosmic truths * unknown famous people appear in your dreams as recognizable archetypes or for your own wish fulfillment * the guiding factor leading us ever upward * the higher planes of earth * the outer reaches of the universe * instigating miracles * precognitive visions come to you while sleeping * astrology as the most ancient science and divination system * getting a reading from an astrological counselor * your planetary transits are powerful at this time * educating and enlightening others through what you have to say * having an innate birthright to amazing soul gifts * affirming your own divinity * building positive light around yourself * destroying negative thought patterns * experiencing an increase in vitality in your entire being * the laws of natural attraction through instantaneous thought * living a parallel life in another world * an interest in alien creatures and space craft from other planets

## *The Moon* XVIII

The Moon is a deeply psychological card of projecting fear in your present life due to past ordeals. These trapped emotions result in negative personality blocks causing pain, anxiety, and vague psychic pressure which must be released from your subconscious mind through therapeutic activities. The Moon has great mystical significance and rules over the collective unconscious in all its manifestations, intuitive-based healing work, and highly inspired creative art.

### *Romance:*

what he is not telling you * the emotional baggage that spoils an otherwise solid union * processing your despair takes you to an amazing place * an intense love affair that must be kept secret * take a reality check to see if he even cares * sleeping with strangers to calm anxieties * feeling insecure due to his unstable nature * things could get funkier with him * he is turning your world upside down * he could be completely in love and terrified * feeling haunted by a romance from the past * behind his actions, there are many doubts and fears * he brings crazy people and chaotic situations into your life * he exposes you to bewildering experiences * your purpose may be to pull him through an emotional black hole * you do not know if he is your boyfriend or not * some mystery remains about him * he is one serious idiot not to be honest with you * an obsessive affair where two lovers never want to be apart * deep, unfathomable emotions * he feels heavily drugged when he is with you * he has a subconscious attraction to you * getting caught up and swept away by emotion * your anticipation could be

deluded * he treats you the way his father treated his mother *
a guy who drags you into the underworld of society * he knows
how to push your psychological buttons * he could be an alco-
holic or drug addict * he may be a lunatic * watch out for major
perversions * a couple whose only common interest is getting
high together * distortions in his personality are beyond your
current understanding * he brings out the worst in you

## Work & Business:

opportunity disguised as loss * a financial fiasco * feeling
helpless in the face of adversity * insane people or compulsive
liars you must deal with through work * having irrational fears
about a new job * being unaware of behind-the-scenes activity
* no details are available to help you understand the situation
* you need to turn things around with your career * you want
precise information but are only hearing rumors * being cheat-
ed out of your money by a con man * your profession may not
be pretty, but it is powerful * feeling uncertain about your
future security * your investments could be less profitable than
you think * subliminal advertising * exploitative marketing
directed at target groups * finding it difficult to make financial
forecasts * working a job in a nonintegrity area * someone does
not have the money they claim to * disruptions plague a project * you are completely in the dark concerning your monetary
picture * deceptive behavior could be necessary to win at negotiations * sabotage could make a deal fall apart * everybody at
work is freaking out due to company restructuring * creative
work that is powerful, controversial, or psychologically disturbing * extraordinary artistic pieces that have a lasting
impression on society * any business that relates to film, pho-
tography, theater, music, television, and acting * sculpting,
painting, and drawing * poetry and literature * the psychiatric

profession * any job that puts you in touch with the mentally ill
* you witness disturbing imagery at work * professional psychics, mystics, and hypnotists * the business of drug and alcohol recovery

## Spiritual Growth:

a sign of mental imbalance * uncontrollable subconscious
fears * obsessive/compulsive disorders * hypochondria *
dementia, senility, or amnesia * fearing the unknown * the dark
night of the soul * ghosts from the past haunt your present *
breaking out of a state of psychic negativity * recognizing and
releasing personal demons and delusions * a cycle of madness
as a spiritual passage * your beliefs omit logical reasoning *
dreaming your way out of despair * channeling disembodied
entities * voodoo * spirit possession * psychic wars and violence * paranoid delusions of grandeur * thinking you are the
reincarnation of a religious icon or famous person * brainwashing * joining a cult * spiritual enslavement * dreams create a language we have trouble understanding * your intuition
is foggy with emotional content * clairvoyant visions may be
real or not * following a conscious path ends substance abuse
* past-life images and memories fade in and out * if you are
clear, a blessed state where you receive a bounty of wisdom *
the mysterious nature of the subconscious mind * drinking and
drugs could be ruining your health and your life * the shadow
self * being in total denial of your actions * ancient hidden
truths brought into the light * animism in the spirit world *
obscure mythologies * prehistoric unrecorded history * recur-
ring nightmares

## The Sun

The Sun is a liberating card of positive growth, personal warmth, and simplicity of purpose. The Sun raises your consciousness, increases your awareness, and helps you become more certain about your direction in life. You claim your right to joy and serenity by taking responsibility for your own happiness and escaping to better conditions.

### Romance:

waiting for someone who makes you feel safe * let him know you are up for everything * companions sharing good times together * mutual sexual satisfaction * he does not play emotional games * you bring the gift of life to each other * a couple who communicates honestly * true compatibility with another * a cherished person who makes you completely happy * enjoying the natural world with your lover * he invites you to take a journey to a warm or more southerly environment * he feels secure with you * a bright and conscious man enters your life as an equal partner * he is the sunlight in your life * a mutual admiration society with two members * you are fascinated by each other * exploring ways of feeling good on a new level * getting the existence you want with another * arriving at a place of friendship with him first * he has a great sense of play * your words helped illuminate the situation * you two will bond once you get him alone * he will do anything he can to please you * a relationship rich in unconditional love * exquisite pleasure that is not decadent * he needs a principled yet idealistic mate * he will heal after he removes himself or another from the premises * you get clear on who he is in your life * when you get together with him, you may not have time for others * forgiving yourself for your romantic blunders * a

**297**

harmonious pairing that is naturally growthful * a man helps mend your broken heart with kindness * trusting your sexual partner * honest and faithful couples * he makes you feel ten pounds lighter * a relationship that is in a weird holding pattern until the summer * you share a wordless understanding with him * you want to be together no matter what the circumstances * he is your reason for living * he is your best friend in the world

## Work & Business:

keep smiling when they put you down at work * all the information becomes available to you * having a clear conscience about how you made your money * the best of times financially * being incredibly happy at work * you have the perfect atmosphere at your place of employment * increased productivity * getting rid of chaotic employees and replacing them with eager workers * wait for all the details before you respond to an offer * feeling creatively inspired because of a fulfilled personal life * monetary conditions improve * success helps you achieve a high-quality lifestyle * retirement to a more southern area of your country * your wealth is secure * you are a generous giver to everyone around you * having strong leadership abilities * people like you and look up to you * a new position is opening that would be perfect for you * being totally enthusiastic about an amazing project * having a eureka moment of brilliant insights * positive, healthy advertising images * investing in clean, alternative energy sources, especially solar power * putting consciousness into a form that common people can understand * preparing for a relaxing retirement lifestyle * work opportunities in the summer or in a warmer climate * jobs on cruise ships, resorts, or in the tropics * in the entertainment business—an indicator of Los Angeles

## *S*piritual *G*rowth:

better times ahead \* going for the clarity \* arriving at a place where you can control and direct your mental energy \* expanding spiritual awareness \* beginning to see the light \* bringing information forth to help others along their paths \* counting your blessings for a safe, peaceful life \* being inspired to give to those less fortunate \* the supreme creative and destructive power of the sun at the center of our galaxy \* discovering a private place where you can recharge your psychic battery \* an opening up in your conscious evolution \* developing the greatest level of spirituality available \* looking on the bright side of things \* seeing potential goodness in every soul \* struggling for contentment in a materially demanding world \* learning how to feel good as a process of personal growth \* the type of communication favored by highly evolved souls \* a burden is lifted once karmic debts are repaid \* happiness comes from following what is right \* safety after a long ordeal \* the healing work on yourself is nearly complete \* light workers who uplift the vibration of the planet \* moderate exposure to sunlight could help ease your depression \* having a zest for living \* feeling excited about the future \* having a total illumination about where to go next \* a peaceful and nonthreatening religious system \* an emphasis on your right to joy and happiness \* the atmosphere of heaven is the rich yellow color of pollen \* the near-death experiences of the chosen ones \* seeing the face of God \* forgiving someone by releasing them into the light \* practicing generosity of spirit \* optimism accelerates your evolution \* purification of unconscious intention

## Judgement

Judgement symbolizes a major decision that you make to get on the right path for personal growth. You emerge from this transitional time ready for the future, with an awareness of lives yet to come. This trump urges you to be more spiritually responsible for your choice of employment, your relationships, and the record of your soul as a moral entity.

*R*omance:

being selective in your preference for a certain kind of mate * the slow but steady process of forming a serious partnership * he touches you at every level of your existence * meeting someone new during a time of personal transition * a challenging courtship with no common meeting place * it is difficult to get together with him * separate time alone brings you both highly valuable insights * feeling sad due to the lack of a suitable, mature man * a couple that rewrites the rules of love * both of you take a giant leap forward in consciousness * leaving damaged men behind forever * letting the will of God dictate the path to your soul mate * a lifelong union that transcends the eternal battle between men and women * when you have finished processing the past, he will find you * honoring his offers to you without judging his gifts * it is your choice, whether you want him or not * deciding whether to enter or end the married state with another * he will never recover from the depth of feeling he had for you * being uncertain about going out with him * realizing you cannot save him * releasing him to God * timing is everything in a relationship * being too analytical about love ruins all the fun and pleasure available to a man and woman ❋ you are fully aware that he is testing your behavior ❋ feeling as though he is criticizing your body or personality ❋ let the universe know he is not the type you want ❋ you catch more flies with honey than vinegar ❋ you finally recognize him as a lost soul ❋ you give him all the information, but he does not grow ❋ a wise person who understands the influences on evolution inherent in any interpersonal relationship ❋ a major turning point that requires a commitment to him ❋ living up to your marriage vows ❋ a divorce settlement is left hanging ❋ once you meet, neither of you look back ❋ you forgive him for his past moral transgressions ❋ a couple who does not hide secrets from each other

## Work & Business:

taking active responsibility for your financial security ❋ finally paying back long-term debts ❋ a major business undertaking of soul importance to you ❋ big decisions about lifestyle changes are going down ❋ retiring after working for the same company forever ❋ being at a major career crossroad ❋ good things come from a challenging situation ❋ leaving a dead-end job behind ❋ finding a new position that puts you in the big leagues ❋ a verdict pending ❋ waiting for a lawsuit to be settled ❋ all the evidence comes in for a fair judgement ❋ stepping into the forefront in your career ❋ entering a more mainstream type of employment ❋ you achieve greater visibility in the business world ❋ a life or death financial decision must be made ❋ you are on the right track ❋ trusting in your own professional plan ❋ you are loaded up with extra tasks to complete ❋ finding a practical application for your spiritual beliefs in your career ❋ making conscious investments ❋ work that upholds clear moral principles ❋ moving on to something greater ❋ going out into society in a bigger way ❋ hidden information needs to be revealed * reviewing the futility of lost opportunities * regretting having wasted good money on useless items * having a serious conviction about the success your talents could generate * closing the door on an old business * making a final decision to retire

## Spiritual Growth:

the spirit is indestructible and eternal * the work of saving souls * when the day of judgement comes, you better be free * the eternal timepiece implanted in the universal order * in your greater wisdom as a disembodied form, you chose the path you are on * becoming aligned with the god force behind all atomic activity * feeling awe in the face of infinity * moral choices made today have immortal repercussions * the most important spiritual lessons are learned in the aftermath of great difficulties * all necessary relationships come from the will of heavenly law * desiring to live a deeper, more inspired life * how limited we are by the parameters of the physical body * we are all naked in the eyes of God * those who clear up karma receive just rewards * helping others go through early conscious development * breaking through illusions, yet clinging to the past * all that matters is leaving good works behind * deciding to split from the material world for the next dimension * letting go of the repression button and releasing a lifetime of emotion * tracing the point of origin of your deep despair * not judging others on superficial qualities * being prepared in spirit for whatever comes next * the cycles of birth, death, and rebirth * everything and anything to do with reincarnation and the recollection of past lives * regeneration to the core of your being * spiritual transformation gives you a new identity in the world * struggling to fulfill your prearranged destiny against all odds * the records that chronicle past ages of the earth and other celestial bodies * not creating any negative energy at all * seeking a role that synchronizes with the evolution of your soul * every action determines the speed of your progress toward personal growth * serving the universe helps balance out dues owed from previous incarnations

## The Universe or World  XX I

The spiritual journey from the Fool to the Universe brings you into alignment with your purpose for being here on the planet. The final trump card helps you actualize your personal evolution to some degree of perfection after a lifetime of growing more aware of great universal truths. The appearance of the Universe in a reading guarantees that you are moving toward an intended arrangement. Your destiny unfolds at its proper pace as you constantly reach for the stars before completing your cycle of activity this time around.

## Romance:

once he gets his act together, it could be too late * the end of an era for an existing union * eventually, you could live with him * ultimately, everything will work out * he lets you participate fully in his world * to be with someone for the rest of your life * you come together at exactly the right time * the cosmos blesses all good relationships * the outer forces of destiny move you both in the same direction * enjoying many similar interests and beliefs * a brand of love that is bigger than the both of you * someone who gives you a place in society * an outer-world team committed to common goals * a successful and enduring match of equals * spiritual union with another at last * taking time to know him * mastering your emotional anxieties about not having a boyfriend * chronic relationship problems disappear * waiting for the right person only * he could have a long way to go until he gets to you * someone who is from a different country or cultural background * the path to love is out of your control * serious partnerships develop slowly * enjoying a long courtship or engagement period * repeating past lifetimes together once more

## Work & Business:

carrying the weight of the world on your shoulders at work * you feel you have a greater purpose than your current job * a very well-connected person * always trying to do the right thing with money * projects that require a long gestation period * the research stage is complete * you want to hit the big time professionally * a business owner who is ultimately responsible for everything * foreign trade and overseas markets * selling rights or products abroad * imports and exports * piracy issues * global politics and events affect productivity * expanding your business internationally * establishing manufacturing operations in foreign places * having a global existence * owning homes in two or more different countries * you may do better financially somewhere other than your native land * you are ready to take responsibility for your unique creative contribution * making a difference in the lives of others as a major goal * wanting to leave something of value * to labor endlessly for the greater good of humanity * to help affect change in the world * the ever-increasing need to work to save the planet * the business of outer space * the fields of astrology and astronomy

*S*piritual *G*rowth:

having a pathological fear of doomsday scenarios ❋ it takes time and patience to achieve a harmonious order in your life ❋ it may be a while before anything big happens ❋ the multisteps in growth and evolution that lead you closer to your reunion with the Creator ❋ being in total alignment with your true self ❋ settling your unfinished cosmic business ❋ all delays lead to improved conditions later ❋ not trying to fight the inevitable ❋ working with like-minded individuals for a renewed future ❋ the harmony of the spheres ❋ your horoscope and its implications ❋ the tradition of apocalyptic messages from prophets and visionaries ❋ a really evolved person can change the world ❋ creating your own reality ❋ you could not avoid your destiny if you tried ❋ speculating on the fate of the universe ❋ one comet too close could end it all ❋ life on Earth is conditioned and unfree ❋ the cosmos applauds your good behavior ❋ the eternal soul that has existed since the beginning of time ❋ a bigger pattern emerges ❋ major planetary teachers, leaders, and healers ❋ the universal brotherhood ❋ the residents of outer space ❋ listening to the voices of the heavens ❋ nothing changes, all remains the same

# CHAPTER SIX
## THREE SAMPLE
## TAROT CARD READINGS

### READING ONE

**Question:** I just met a guy I like, and I gave him my phone number. Will he call me?

### Three Card Spread

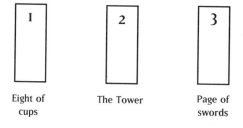

Eight of cups      The Tower      Page of swords

**Conditions brought over from the past:** The eight of cups in this position shows him to be a quiet and remote figure who likes to be taken seriously in all his relationships. He has never had casual or shallow affairs with women in his past, and due to his values of devotion and emotional commitment, this cup card suggests that he has had few long-term unions because of his attitude toward love. He envisions his romantic life as a solitary quest for a partner who feels as deeply as he does about matters of the heart. He has been on a long, hopeful journey to seek out the one true love who could become his lifetime partner.

**Present conditions**: The Tower in this spot indicates that meeting you has turned this man's world upside down. He did not expect to connect with a woman like you, and this encounter has changed him forever. The eight of cups has already established that his love life has been an emotional desert up until now, and he is shocked and surprised to have found you. He is currently undergoing a transformation in the way he views his single status, and he considers you a miracle of sorts, a catalyst for breaking down many of his antiquated concepts of womankind. He sees you as a challenge because his habits are undergoing a drastic reconstructing—a process that began the moment he met you. So it can be said with great certainty that when the dust clears from his mind, he will figure out how special your connection is, especially when he looks back on his solitary past.

**What will happen in the future**: The Page of swords in this placement shows a number of different paths he will take as he pursues his interest in you. He will either call you or arrange a meeting of your mutual friends to create a reason to get together with you. He wants to observe you further and will ask around for information on you in an almost spylike fashion. He may set you up in any number of situations socially to test your behavior and get to know you better, but he may do this in an indirect way so that you are not aware of his interest in you. Your initial conversation really got through to him, and the Tower proves he is all shook up; you are unsettled as well because meeting him has brought you to life and made you feel that there is hope that you could eventually meet a great guy who has serious moral values (eight of cups).

# READING TWO

**Question:** I have been going out with a guy for five years, and he wants to marry me and raise a family together. What should I do?

## Problem/Solution Spread

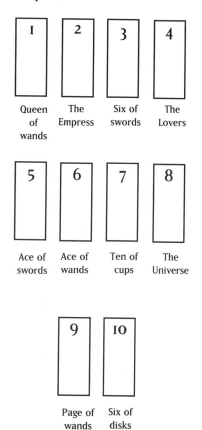

| 1 | 2 | 3 | 4 |
|---|---|---|---|
| Queen of wands | The Empress | Six of swords | The Lovers |

| 5 | 6 | 7 | 8 |
|---|---|---|---|
| Ace of swords | Ace of wands | Ten of cups | The Universe |

| 9 | 10 |
|---|---|
| Page of wands | Six of disks |

**Problem**: The Queen of wands, the Empress, the six of swords, and the Lovers. This combination of cards in the problem position indicates that you are a strong and independent woman who is fully confident in her creative and social abilities (Queen of wands and the Empress). You have established an easy communicative relationship with this man (six of swords), which is probably why your alliance has lasted so long. He adores you just the way you are and is proud to have you as his woman, and he loves to show you off because you enhance his self-image. He considers you the woman of his dreams, and the Empress shows his desire to marry you and create a family together. The Lovers trump is the card of intense mutual attraction and earthly marriage and emphasizes that your physical chemistry is really strong and could grow in intensity in the years ahead. The Lovers card also symbolizes the choice you must make about whether or not to accept his proposal. The six of swords implies that this will be easy for you to do because the two of you are so compatible, and you should feel free to discuss your fears or doubts with him because he is totally open to listening to you.

**Solution**: Ace of swords, ace of wands, ten of cups, and the Universe. This combination of cards tells you that your answer is to say yes with all the power inherent in the aces of sword and wand. You know he truly loves you and wants you to be happy and fulfilled (the Empress), so you can make your decision with all the certainty and solidity of the ace of swords. The ace of wands says that married life will be a new beginning in your union and change the nature of your current arrangement. Your commitment to each other will enhance your mutual passion for life, and both of you will rise to new heights of inspiration and creativity. The ace of wands also suggests that he wants to get you pregnant immediately. The ten of cups shows that you two will have an extremely happy home life and will find great joy in raising children together. This ten also shows that your love for each other is a bond that will not easily be broken, and this should make both of you feel emotionally secure about your impending marriage. You have it all as a couple because you have each other, and his love makes you a complete human being; you are never in doubt about his acceptance of you as you are, with all your faults. The Universe trump only adds to the notion that he was the man you were intended to be with, so you can go ahead and say yes because his is your destiny and your lifetime companion on the road of love.

**Lesson**: Page of wands and the six of disks. The fiery Queen of wands finds it hard to be faithful to one man, but the Page of wands shows monogamy to be the test for you in this union. You should not carry on behind his back, though you may be tempted over the years because you naturally attract attention from the opposite sex. You must remain loyal to him or you could run the risk of losing the happy family life you will estab-lish shortly after your marriage. You must remain true to him and make his happiness your main concern because he wants to do the same for you. The six of disks indicates that you must learn to take from each other only what is fair, merge your financial resources, and give of yourself emotionally without hesitation. You must support each other and push each other to succeed with endless generosity of spirit.

## READING THREE

This reading was given to a female artist who has the Queen of disks as her significator. She was particularly interested in receiving information concerning a recent encounter with a male art-gallery owner who seemed eager to represent her artwork. During their initial meeting, they connected really well, but she sensed he was attracted to her romantically. She wanted the reading to make her more aware of what was going on between them and whether anything would come about professionally from this individual. The subject-combination of the reading was Work & Business and Money & Material Matters.

### The Grand Cross

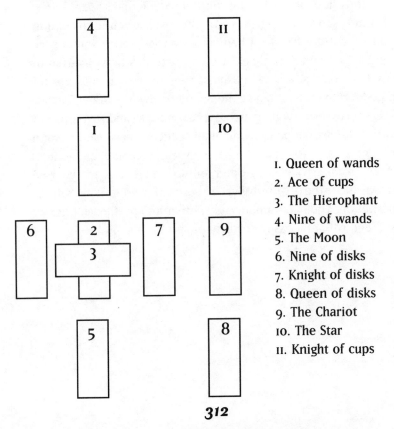

1. Queen of wands
2. Ace of cups
3. The Hierophant
4. Nine of wands
5. The Moon
6. Nine of disks
7. Knight of disks
8. Queen of disks
9. The Chariot
10. The Star
11. Knight of cups

**Your Self Card** is the Queen of wands, who depicts you as a champion of your own interests by coming on strong and exuding confidence whenever you can and wherever you go. As your self card, she shows you feeling courageous about expressing your creative and passionate natures. You are eager to interact with others to advance yourself artistically as you know they could inspire you to become more productive as an artist. This particular gallery owner is just one avenue to investigate for marketing your work. You are smart and enthusiastic; he perceives this and is encouraged by your obvious dedication to accomplishing your career goals.

**Your Present Environment** is the ace of cups, which reaffirms that purely emotional energy was exchanged between you and the gallery owner on a real heart level. You both genuinely and spontaneously liked each other and enjoyed communicating on a similar wavelength. Because you are functioning as the Queen of wands, you are sending out vibrations that naturally invite love into your life. By being more open and receptive toward others, you draw their attention to your sunny charm and countenance. This ace shows that meeting this person has inspired you to become more actively involved in getting your career together, as the time and attention he gave you boosted your self-confidence.

**Your Immediate Obstacle** is the Hierophant, which indicates how much you have already learned from this experience and how crossing the path of this man has been a major lesson for you. You might become involved with him in a business venture, but this trump as your obstacle suggests the difficulty you could have trying to join his group of colleagues. There may be insurmountable problems due to your spiritual philosophy and Queen of wands personality, adding force and honesty to the way you approach people.

**Your Hope and Dream** is the nine of wands, which specifies that your first priority should be keeping yourself on top of matters to protect your dearest dreams and most cherished desires. As the Queen of wands, it is in your best interest to maintain a dominant position and not let anyone or anything threaten your basic security. This wand may bring a slight delay in attaining your greatest ambitions in life due to its placement in the spread, but you must never give up the struggle to establish yourself as an artist.

**Your Difficulty in the Past** is the Moon, which depicts the overwhelming and bewildering feelings you have had about the issue of the reading. You have been uncertain about how to sell your artwork and how to deal with particular people and situations in your quest for success. Perhaps you were shaky emotionally in the past when faced with the task of self-promotion or were under the influence of mood-altering substances that clouded your mind and actions. This period is now coming to a close, and the ordeal has made you stronger, so in the future you will have more wisdom and visual imagery at your disposal to apply to your creative work. The Moon gives you lots of ideas and material that you should share with others who need your knowledge to improve the conditions of their lives (the Hierophant as your obstacle). This trump can also symbolize the years you have spent trying to succeed in a Neptunian industry such as the art world.

**Your Last of the Present** is the nine of disks, which specifies that you are already capable of producing marketable art that could generate a nice income for you if sold through the right agent or gallery. Your talent has reached a point of development where your skills and inspiration are so reliable that you may even take them for granted later on. With the nine of wands held high as your hope and dream, and the Moon behind you in the past, you have many poignant experiences to draw from. Unfortunately, your muddled or failed attempts at selling your work preceded the actual maturation of your artistic abilities, though this position of the nine of disks shows that your genius has been recognized by others to some degree already.

**Your First of the Future** is the Knight of disks, and your **Future Environment** is the Queen of disks. The man in question will come through for you and make things happen for your career. These two disk cards say that you could earn money together for sure. He will be solid, honest, supportive, and serviceable, and you will want to put your life in his hands. The Queen of disks is also your significator and represents you rising to meet the Knight of disks halfway. Your time would be well spent working on common projects should you ultimately decide to take up his material offer. Your relationship with him has brought out the Queen of wands in you, and with the Queen of disks in your future, you can handle the financial realities that accompany selling the pieces you produce. You will have to be practical about your expenditures if you want to pull your career together, and you should showcase your fully developed nine of disks abilities in their best light. The Knight of disks is always helpful to the extreme and makes a wonderful team player. He could become the cornerstone of the foundation of your artistic destiny. You will definitely talk to him or see him again, and both of your cards and his will be laid on the table, so to speak. The final positions of this spread and the Four Card Spread that follows will point out what will happen between you and him in the end.

**Your Outer Influence** is the Chariot, which tells you it is just a matter of time until the puzzle pieces of your life fit together. By and by, everyone and everything around you will help you move as fast as possible toward your proper destination artistically. You should relax and accept any uncomfortable situations you have to endure due to the involvement of other people in your business affairs by realizing that you are experiencing exactly what you need to go through for purposes of your spiritual education.

**Your Hope and Fear** is the Star, which means you will resist certain imminent opportunities that could give you a chance to be noticed or placed in the spotlight, even though up to the time of the reading you have had trouble getting any recognition at all. Part of you wants to shine at center stage, but another part of you holds back due to fear of speaking, leading, teaching, or making a total commitment to a cause through your work as an artist.

**Your Outcome** is the Knight of cups, who indicates a definite offer coming from the Knight of disks, but there will be something questionable about the deal. The Knight of cups, ace of cups, and Queen of wands all affirm that he is attracted to you and is considering making some sort of proposition to you that may be inappropriate. The Star in the hope and fear placement emphasizes your concern about what you might have to do to enhance your career. Unfortunately, the Knight of Cups has an unstable personality that often leads him to extend empty or unsuitable overtures.

## The Four Card Spread

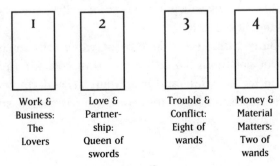

| I | 2 | 3 | 4 |
|---|---|---|---|
| Work & Business: The Lovers | Love & Partner- ship: Queen of swords | Trouble & Conflict: Eight of wands | Money & Material Matters: Two of wands |

**Work & Business** is the Lovers, which reiterates the fact that your connection to the gallery owner could be complex, as there is a genuine affinity between the two of you. This trump falls in the position that is the key to what will happen if you work together. Before you do anything, you must decide if you are going to accept his advances. His turning up as the Knight of disks as well means that his offer of assistance has a lot to do with your appealing to him in more than a business sense.

**Love & Partnership** is the Queen of swords, showing that you are interested in him only intellectually. Though you came on like the Queen of wands, in the end you will act cold and distant, which could lead him to withdraw his interest in you, as he could be more fascinated by the woman in you than the artist in you. This card suggests you saying no to his Knight of cups offer.

**Trouble & Conflict** is the eight of wands, which implies that this matter will be brought up rather quickly between you and settled one way or another equally soon. He urgently wants to express his feelings and will come on a little too strong and fast in terms of what he proposes to you as the Knight of cups. The Chariot and the Star from the Grand Cross Spread demonstrate how attaining recognition is crucial to your career, but you may forgo this chance for success and ultimately decide to reject his invitation forcefully (Queen of swords in the love placement).

**Money & Material Matters** is the two of wands, which depicts your lonely struggle to establish yourself and make some money in your chosen field. You should continue to be pushy and willful in your quest for attention even though you are unenthusiastic about being in the light of the Star that singles you out for your work. This gallery owner is just one of many you will encounter as you take control of your material affairs. In the end, he may be a temporary catalyst whose role is to move you forward in your attempt to gain monetarily through your art. If you accept his terms in the very near future.

## APPENDIX A
### TAROT CARD COMBINATIONS

These Tarot card combinations serve as examples of how to blend the meanings of two or three cards in random mixtures as an exercise to increase your understanding of the associative meanings between the cards.

**Ace of disks and seven of disks:** have patience and let the issue of the reading develop in a slow, proper manner

**Eight of wands and Knight of swords:** shows the need to get things together quickly

**King of swords and King of cups:** both love to play the controlling ruler who withholds information

**The Magician and the Devil:** there is more than meets the eye in an atmosphere thick with peculiar occurrences

**Seven of swords and King of cups:** shows entrepreneurial abilities

**Six of swords and six of wands:** indicates a major breakthrough

**Two of swords and two of disks:** watching and waiting

**The Moon and the Sun:** an eclipse point between the conscious and unconscious minds

**Four of wands and the Hierophant:** contentment on a very high level

**Nine of cups and the Fool:** happiness and emotional security come from an unexpected source

**Three, six, and nine of disks:** finally getting financially compensated for work completed

**Eight of disks, nine of disks, and the Magician:** to practically apply the abilities over which you have gained mastery

**Five and eight of swords:** feeling hung up and vulnerable about communicating with another person

**Ace and three of wands:** you can handle all that is happening

**Five of cups and the Hierophant:** the highest level of romantic love and friendship

**Page of swords and ace of wands:** you have a very powerful guardian angel who uses a club to move you on to new experiences

**Strength and Judgement:** a strong decision based on correct and courageous behavior

**Ace of disks and the Fool:** people and opportunities drop into your life out of nowhere

**The Priestess and the Empress:** connecting with the goddess energy in yourself

**Two and three of disks:** you need to travel in order to complete a project

**Seven and eight of disks:** working diligently and patiently toward perfection of a talent

**Five and seven of swords and seven of wands:** fighting for your independence

**Two of disks and Judgement:** though nothing appears to be happening, major changes are underway

**Ace and King of wands:** a good man who helps you get the ball rolling on a creative project

**Five of disks and the Hierophant:** leading a more spiritual life or adopting a charitable outlook

**Eight of disks and three of cups:** celebration over your ability, creativity, expertise, and industry

**Ace of cups and Wheel of Fortune:** you are jubilant about a love affair and feel lucky and blessed to have found a wonderful person

**Two of swords and five of cups:** the tension that arises from having a relationship that only wastes your energy

**Justice and the Hanged Man:** tests and trials that help you define the purpose of your existence

**Death and the Moon:** you are going through an overwhelmingly difficult time of deep transformation

**Page and King of wands:** you can expect total reliability through the male support system in your life

**The Emperor and the Hierophant:** lots of heavy, influential male energy around you

**Seven of disks and seven of wands:** trying hard to be patient

**Eight of disks and nine of wands:** building up security

**Three and nine of disks:** your skills and talents have been recognized by others

**Ten and Knight of cups:** you sense that a relationship has the potential to grow into a deep, satisfying union but are unsure of the true intentions of the other person

**Eight of cups and the Hierophant:** you need to devote more time to your spirituality

**The Lover and seven of swords:** a romance when, where, and how you want it

**Nine of swords and Strength:** painful lessons that empower you

**Eight of cups and five of wands:** something captures you passionately, heart and soul

**Ace and Page of cups:** being gentle and nice

**King of disks and the Emperor:** those who are concerned about your welfare and help you out unselfishly and practically

**The Hanged Man and the Star:** being in the spotlight as a result of your beliefs

**Ace of cups and ace of swords:** open heart, open mind

**Two of cups and Page of swords:** good news about love makes you happy

**Five of cups and the Universe:** though you are on the right path spiritually, you have emotional disappointments

**Six of disks and three of cups:** sharing pleasure and your riches with others

**The Hermit and Temperance:** the need to spend time alone to work out the rough edges of your personality

**The Lovers and Justice:** working out a marriage agreement, breaking your vows, or divorce

# APPENDIX B
## TAROT CARDS WITH SIMILAR MEANINGS

This section of the book classifies the 78 cards of the Tarot deck by like feeling, activity, meaning, person, place, and thing. This section helps increase your understanding of the total impact of a card in a reading and shows how, ultimately, the cards are all a part of each other.

**Cards of self-defense:** eight and King of swords * King of cups * five, seven, and nine of wands * the Magician

**Cards of self-reliance:** five, seven, and King of swords * King of cups * two of wands * the Hermit and Strength

**Cards of thinking for yourself:** ace, two, five, seven, and Page through King of swords * the Magician, the Priestess, Justice, the Hanged Man, the Devil, and Judgement

**Cards of choice:** ace, four, and five of swords * the Lovers, Justice, the Hanged Man, the Devil, and Judgement

**Cards of independence:** ace, three, four, five, six, and seven of swords * eight of cups * seven of wands * the Hermit and the Hanged Man

**Cards of intelligence:** all the sword court cards and the six and ten of swords * the Magician, the Priestess, the Hierophant, the Hermit, the Star, the Sun, and the Universe

**Cards of authority:** six, seven, Page, Queen, and King of swords * ten and Page of disks * the Priestess, the Emperor, the Hierophant, Justice, the Hanged Man, the Star, Judgement, and the Universe

**Cards of teachers:** King of swords, disks, and wands * the Priestess, the Empress, the Emperor, the Hierophant, and the Hanged Man

**Cards of students:** ace and eight of disks * eight of cups * all the Pages

**Cards of leaders:** ace, seven, Queen, and Knight of swords * King of disks * King of cups * five and seven of wands * the Magician, the Priestess, the Empress, the Emperor, the Hierophant, the Hermit, the Hanged Man, and the Star

**Cards of quiet, solitude, and introspection:** two, four, and eight of swords * Knight of disks * eight and King of cups * the Magician, the Priestess, the Hermit, the Hanged Man, Death, and Judgement

**Cards of coming into clarity:** ace, six, and eight of swords * six of cups * the Hanged Man, Death, the Devil, the Tower, the Star, the Sun, and Judgement

**Cards of inspiration:** ace and six of swords * six, seven, and eight of cups * ace, three, and eight of wands * the Priestess, the Empress, the Star, and the Sun

**Cards of beauty:** ace, two, three, six, nine, ten, and Page of cups * Temperance, the Star, the Sun, the Moon, and the Universe

**Cards of visualization:** ace, two, and Page of swords * four, seven, and eight of cups * the Magician, the Priestess, the Star, and the Moon

**Cards of intuition:** two, four, and Page of swords * Knight of disks * eight, Page, and Queen of cups * eight of wands * the Fool, the Magician, the Hierophant, the Hermit, the Hanged Man, Temperance, the Star, the Moon, and the Sun

**Cards of faith:** two and five of swords * the Fool, the Priestess, the Hermit, Strength, the Wheel of Fortune, and the Universe

**Cards of spiritual devotion:** two and four of swords * Knight of disks * eight, Page, and Queen of cups * Page of wands * the Fool, the Magician, the Priestess, the Hierophant, the Hermit, the Hanged Man, Temperance, the Sun, and the Universe

**Cards of guidance:** two, eight, and Page of swords * the Fool, the Magician, the Priestess, the Hierophant, the Chariot, the Wheel of Fortune, the Tower, the Star, and the Universe

**Cards of purification:** all the aces * six of cups * six and nine of wands * the Hermit, Strength, the Hanged Man, Death, Temperance, the Devil, the Tower, and the Moon

# Appendix B — Tarot Cards
## with Similar Meaning

**Cards of rebirth:** ace and eight of wands * the Fool and the entire force and function of the other 21 trump cards

**Cards of past life ability:** ten of swords * ace of disks * the Priestess, the Hierophant, Justice, the Wheel of Fortune, Judgement, and the Universe

**Cards of balance and equilibrium:** two of swords * two of disks * the Empress, the Emperor, Justice, the Hermit, Strength, the Hanged Man, the Star, and Judgement

**Cards of harmony:** all sixes * ace, two, three, six, nine, and ten of cups * the Lovers, Justice, the Wheel of Fortune, Temperance, the Star, the Sun, and the Universe

**Cards of renewal:** Knight of disks * six and nine of cups * ace, two and eight of wands * the Lovers, Death, the Tower, Temperance, the Star, and the Sun

**Cards of physical well-being:** nine, Queen, and Knight of disks * three, six, and nine of cups * four, six, and nine of wands * Strength, Temperance, and the Sun

**Cards of generosity:** ace, two, six, nine, ten, and all disk court cards * six and Queen of cups * the Empress, the Emperor, and the Wheel of Fortune

**Cards of celebration:** ace, two, three, six, nine, ten, Queen, and Knight of cups * four and six of wands * the Wheel of Fortune

**Cards of ecstasy:** ace, three, seven, and ten of cups * ace and eight of wands * the Fool, the Lovers, the Tower (in its most positive sense), the Star, and the Sun

**Cards of friendship:** two, three, four, five, Page, and Queen of cups * four and Page of wands * the Lovers and the Sun

**Cards of devotion:** six, Page, Queen, Knight, and King of disks * eight and Page of cups * Page and King of wands * the Lovers, the Hanged Man, Temperance, and the Sun

**Cards of happiness:** ace, two, three, six, nine, and ten of cups * four and six of wands * the Fool, the Chariot, the Wheel of Fortune, the Star, and the Sun

**Cards of deep caring:** three of swords * nine, Queen, Knight, and King of disks * ace, two, three, six, eight, nine, ten, Page, Queen, and King of cups * all wand cards * the Empress, the Emperor, the Lovers, the Hierophant, Strength, the Sun, and the Star

**Cards of true love:** ace, two, six, nine, and ten of cups * six of wands * the Hierophant, the Lovers, the Star, the Sun, and the Universe

**Cards of passionate love:** ace, two, three, four, five, six, eight, nine, ten, Page, Queen, Knight, and King of wands * two, three, nine, and ten of cups * the Lovers, Strength, the Star, and the Sun

**Cards of spiritual love:** ace, two, three, eight, nine, ten, and Page of cups * three and eight of wands * the Magician, the Priestess, the Hierophant, the Lovers, the Hermit, the Hanged Man, Temperance, the Star, the Moon, and the Sun

**Cards of challenging love relationships:** three, five, nine, ten, Queen, Knight, and King of swords * five of disks * four, five, Knight, and King of cups * five, seven, ten, and Knight of wands * the Devil and the Moon

**Cards of truth:** ace, two, three, four, seven, nine, Queen, and King of swords * Page and Knight of disks * ace, two, three, four, five, six, nine, Page, and King of wands * the Fool, the Magician, the Priestess, the Hierophant, Justice, the Hermit, Strength, the Hanged Man, Death, the Tower, the Star, the Sun, Judgement, and the Universe

**Cards of honest and faithful people:** ace, two, six, and King of swords * three, four, six, nine, ten, Page, Queen, Knight, and King of disks * ace, two, four, six, eight, nine, ten, and Page of cups * two, three, four, six, nine, Page, and King of wands * the Empress, the Emperor, the Hermit, the Hierophant, Strength, the Hanged Man, the Star, and the Sun

**Cards of activism:** ace, three, five, seven, and Page of swords * five of disks * eight of cups * ace, two, three, five, and seven of wands * the Fool, the Hierophant, the Hanged Man, the Star, and the Universe

# Appendix B — Tarot Cards
## with Similar Meaning

**Cards of liberation:** ace, six, seven, eight, ten, and Page of swords * ace, two, three, and six of wands * the Fool, Justice, the Wheel of Fortune, Strength, the Hanged Man, Death, the Tower, Judgement, and the Universe

**Cards of great force:** ace of swords and all sword court cards * all tens * ace, two, eight, nine, and Knight of wands * the Magician, the Chariot, the Wheel of Fortune, Strength, Death, the Tower, the Sun, Judgement, and the Universe

**Cards of intense activity:** ace, six, ten, Page, and Knight of swords * three, seven, and eight of disks and all disk court cards * seven of cups * all wands, especially the ace, five, seven, eight, ten, and Knight

**Cards of skill development:** all 14 disk cards * ace, two, three, six, seven, and nine of wands * the Emperor, Temperance, the Star, and the Universe

**Cards of completion of work:** ten of swords, three, eight, and ten of disks and all disk court cards * three six, and nine of wands * the Emperor, Justice, Temperance, Strength, Judgement, and the Universe

**Cards of financial success:** ace, three, four, six, nine, ten, Queen, and King of disks * three, six, nine, and ten of cups * the Emperor, the Wheel of Fortune, the Star, the Sun, and the Universe

**Cards of security:** three, four, six, nine, ten, and Page through King of disks * seven, nine, ten, and King of wands * the Empress, the Emperor the Chariot, the Wheel of Fortune, the Sun, and the Star

**Cards of risk taking:** two, five, seven, Page, and Knight of swords * ace, two, five, six, seven, eight, and Knight of wands * the Fool, the Magician, and the Wheel of Fortune

**Cards of surprise:** ace of disks * ace and eight of wands * the Fool, Death, and the Tower

**Cards of endurance:** three, four, seven, eight, nine, and ten of disks and all disk court cards * four, six, eight, ten, and King of cups * four, six, nine, and ten of wands * the Empress, the Emperor, Strength, Temperance, Judgement, and the Universe

**Cards of patience:** all aces * two, four, and eight of swords *

three, four, seven, and eight of disks ＊ eight of cups ＊ nine of wands ＊ the Chariot, Temperance, and the Universe

**Cards of dormancy:** eight of swords ＊ ace, two, and seven of disks ＊ the Chariot, Death, and Temperance

**Cards of new beginnings:** all aces and twos ＊ six of cups ＊ six of wands ＊ the Fool, Death, the Tower, and the Sun

**Cards of the passage of time:** two and seven of disks ＊ the Chariot, the Wheel of Fortune, Temperance, and the Universe

**Cards of great speed:** ace, six, and Knight of swords ＊ ace, eight, and Knight of wands ＊ the Chariot and the Wheel of Fortune

**Cards of retreat:** two, four, five, eight, and Knight of swords ＊ Knight of wands ＊ the Magician, the Hermit, and the Hanged Man

**Cards of confusion:** five, seven, eight, nine, ten, and Knight of swords ＊ two and five of disks ＊ four, five, seven, Page, Queen, and Knight of cups ＊ eight and ten of wands ＊ the Devil, the Tower, and the Moon

**Cards of lack of free will:** two, five, eight, and Page of swords ＊ four and eight of cups ＊ ten of wands ＊ the Chariot, Justice, and the Hanged Man.

**Cards of nonproductive habits:** five and Knight of swords ＊ three, four, five, and Knight of cups ＊ the Magician, the Devil, and the Moon

**Cards of wasted talent:** three, eight, nine, ten, and Knight of swords ＊ five of disks ＊ five and Knight of cups ＊ five and ten of wands ＊ the Devil and the Moon

**Cards of being alone:** two, three, four, five, seven, eight, nine, ten, Queen, Knight, and King of swords ＊ five, eight, and King of cups ＊ the Hermit, the Hanged Man, Temperance, and Judgement

**Cards of depression:** two, three, four, eight, nine, ten, and Knight of swords ＊ the Devil and the Moon

**Cards of pain:** three, eight, nine, ten, Knight, Queen, and King of swords ＊ five and Page of cups ＊ Death, the Devil, and the Moon

**Cards of sorrow:** three, four, eight, nine, ten, and Queen of swords ＊ five and eight of cups ＊ the Hermit, the Hanged Man, Death, and the Devil

# Appendix B — Tarot Cards
## with Similar Meaning

**Cards of illusion:** seven, Queen, Knight, and King of cups ∗ the Magician, the Devil, the Tower, and the Moon

**Planetary cards:** the Wheel of Fortune, the Star, the Moon, the Sun, and the Universe

**Cards of the earth:** all disks, especially the two, seven, nine, Queen, and Knight ∗ the Empress, the Priestess, the Wheel of Fortune, Death, and the Universe

**Cards of legal matters:** Page, Queen, and King of swords ∗ three, seven, eight, Page, Queen, and King of disks ∗ King of cups ∗ Justice and Judgement

**Cards of reconciliation:** ace, two, and six of cups ∗ six of wands ∗ the Lovers, the Star, and the Sun

**Cards of separation or divorce:** five, nine, ten, Queen, Knight, and King of swords ∗ Page of disks ∗ five of cups ∗ five and Knight of wands ∗ Justice, the Hermit, the Hanged Man, Death, the Tower, the Moon, and Judgement

**Cards of phone calls:** ace, six, Page, and Queen of swords ∗ Page of disks ∗ six and eight of wands ∗ the Emperor

**Cards of the end of a cycle:** ten of swords ∗ Judgement and the Universe

**Cards of healing:** all sixes ∗ seven, eight, Queen, and Knight of disks ∗ Strength, Temperance, and the Sun

**Cards of criminal activity:** seven, Knight, and King of cups ∗ the Magician, Justice, the Devil, the Tower, and the Moon

**Cards of debt:** five and eight of swords ∗ ace, two, five, and seven of disks ∗ the Devil and the Moon

## APPENDIX C:
## TAROT CARDS IN PARTICULAR POSITIONS OF THE GRAND CROSS SPREAD

This section illustrates how to fine-tune the meaning of a card to fit a spread placement, and offers many examples of adjusting the definition of a card to a position in the spread layout.

The Grand Cross is fully described on pages 46-49. There you will find complete instructions for utilizing this Tarot spread in a reading.

### Swords

Ace of swords as your **Self Card** depicts you forging ahead with great determination and unification of purpose. Your mind is completely made up concerning the subject matter of the reading, and you know exactly how to proceed toward your goal or intention.

Five of swords as your **Obstacle** means that you are taking the opinions of others either too seriously or not seriously enough, depending on the nature of the reading. Try not to let people get to you mentally, and keep a clear, steady mind even when those around you are losing theirs and distracting your focused intellectual energy. At the time of the reading, you should avoid feeling defeated by any losses you have incurred, as this would block your forward progress.

Seven of swords as your **Future Environment** shows you very much doing your own thing in an attempt to take advantage of your unique destiny. In the future, you will become alienated from your social group. You will decide to break from your clique or colleagues and establish your own beliefs, thoughts, morality, general philosophy, and preferred lifestyle.

Eight of swords as your **Hope and Fear** pictures you desperately trying to free yourself from some form of self-induced bondage. You are responsible for your helpless and powerless state, about which you complain to anyone who will listen. You secretly wish to extricate yourself from the emotional prison you have created, even though certain issues may be so painful that you cannot deal with them directly at this time. It is totally up to you whether you liberate yourself in the days to come; the card that surfaces in the outcome position of the spread indicates the likelihood of you making this release from what holds you back mentally.

Nine of swords in your **Difficulty in the Past** states that you wanted something to happen very badly, but the matter did not turn out as you had hoped. Though you have suffered pain due to the unkindness of others, you have emerged from a period of anxiety and despair and are ready to put the past behind you. This time of testing will serve you in the future, as you are now hardened toward hatred, criticism, and bad treatment directed at you by unhappy people.

Queen of swords as your **Last of the Present** characterizes your headstrong quality as well as your intellectual abilities. As the Queen of swords, you communicate endlessly in an effort to push through the plan you were working on, which necessitated this particular behavior. As this card leaves your life, your cold, unemotional attitude no longer is required of you. You have said all you have to say regarding the subject matter of the reading, and your reign of severity comes to an end.

## Disks

Ace of disks as your **Self Card** shows you having a definite gift or talent that could blossom if given time, creative assistance, or even material support in the form of financial aid, an opportunity to learn, or a chance to get involved in a new field of interest where you would have great potential for success. As your self card, the ace of disks implies that you must develop any abilities that lie dormant inside you, waiting to be put to use.

Four of disks as your **Obstacle** describes how you want to know exactly what you own in order to establish some genuine permanent security for yourself. Whether or not you are content with what you have gained thus far, your need to accumulate possessions is somehow blocking your progress right now. Also, the four of disks as your obstacle would stress the trouble you are having supporting yourself financially. This card helps you get in touch with your own personal power and gives you a chance to prove yourself wherever it lands in the spread.

Six of disks as your **Hope and Dream** would reveal that you want to establish a creative or monetary partnership with another that involves a complementary exchange of assets or talents in order to get ahead in your chosen field. If this disk represents a love relationship, it describes two people who have much to give each other materially. This union will grow into a practical and workable balanced arrangement.

Eight of disks as your **Last of the Present** specifies that you have just finished a project you have worked on for a long time to produce the best possible results. You took full responsibility for completing tasks that were handed to you so you could undergo an apprenticeship and master a valuable skill or talent through your efforts.

Page of disks as your **Outcome** shows that you will eventually play the role of the serviceable, helpful, detail-oriented, and hardworking Page of disks. You may ultimately end up in a position where you have to deal with documents, literature, contracts, or getting information down in writing. You may be called upon to keep track of financial records as an assistant to a King of disks type in the world of commerce, where he will train you to handle all aspects of a certain operation.

## Cups

Four of cups as your **Present Environment** means that at the time of the reading, you are not taking action on any emotional issues. Instead, you are waiting out a period of feeling distant and distracted from the person with whom you are currently involved. You remain in an unhappy situation that can be relieved only when someone or something better comes along to give you the initiative to break the already weak tie. You are in a fog about ending the alliance and disgusted at having to continue the masquerade with a person you do not love. As the influence of the four of cups leaves your life, you will feel more stable and know exactly what sort of relationship you want next.

Six of cups as your **Present Environment** implies that you are extending your social circle in an effort to increase your personal happiness. You are trying to give more of yourself in all your encounters with others by expressing your feelings more openly and readily. You are going to great lengths to meet positive, loving people outside your usual environments and are experiencing a rebirth of emotion for those you reside with or already know through your daily activities.

Seven of cups as your **Present Environment** illustrates that you are making a choice between fantasy and reality right now. It also implies an increase in your imaginative faculties and shows you dreaming quite intensely about all the wonderful things you want to accomplish in the future. Though many of your visions will come true, some are figments of your own invention and will never be actualized.

Nine of cups as your **First of the Future** depicts how emotionally satisfied you will become shortly. This card lets you know that permanent happiness is close at hand. You should prepare yourself for all the good things to come in the days ahead that will make you more blissfully content than ever before.

Knight of cups as your **Outcome** adds a question mark to the end of the reading. It is hard to interpret exactly how this Knight will manifest himself because of his generally elusive nature. As your outcome, this card indicates that you will receive an offer you will welcome, but there will be a twist to the true value of what could come your way through the Knight of cups character. The matter the reading examines will turn out differently than you expect, and you should be extra discriminating toward the person to whom you must say yes or no.

King of cups as your **Outer Influence** refers to a male authority figure who will become prominent in the days ahead. He may represent a business deal pending between you and an equally matched intense and intriguing person. In love, this card would symbolize someone you feel terribly attracted to in a hopeless way. The person this card indicates will add spice to your existence and could become the single most important individual to you later on.

## Wands

Ace of wands as your **Difficulty in the Past** shows the trouble you have had as you attempt to start over again in your life. Somehow, through sheer willpower, you have struggled to recharge your batteries with an exhilarating surge of fresh energy. You are completely ready to develop yourself by taking creative action in the future. You are fully prepared to strike out in new directions, and this is highly beneficial to your ultimate success.

Six of wands as your **Self Card** implies that you have the capacity to achieve great things. At the time of the reading, you are waging a fight to win a particular battle. This entanglement requires an indefatigable spirit to defeat any negativity that could block you from reaching your goal. This six implies that your will is in accordance with your actions, as you strive for a passionately fulfilling life.

Eight of wands as your **Present Environment** describes you pulling together many loose ends within a short period of time concurrent with the reading. You are experiencing an urgency that makes you move as fast as you can in the areas of your life that the reading discusses. In terms of love, the eight of wands could depict you being overwhelmed by impulsive, almost obsessive feelings for one individual.

Queen of wands as your **Difficulty in the Past** reveals that you have been strong, demanding, and relentless in how you treat those around you in an effort to establish yourself creatively. Due to the control you have over the situation the reading examines, you can go forth in the future and develop your social and artistic skills. The Queen of wands can also represent another person who would have had a similar influence over you in the past and, because of that previous role, will be a support to you in the coming days.

King of wands as your **Last of the Present** indicates that a prominent individual has been a true friend to you, but is now leaving your life. Even if he remains a part of your world, his power over you is on the wane. This King can symbolize a person who has been very good to you or has done you a righteous favor. In love he could stand for someone you cared for who is fading quickly into the past. As the King of wands is crystal clear in his intentions, you were always certain of the exact nature of his feelings for you. It is best to regard him as a kindly man who you came together with to experience supportive, mutual, and perhaps platonic love.

## Trumps

The Fool as your **First of the Future** means there will soon be sudden changes and surprises in the area of your life that the reading explores. Expect the unexpected and be aware of everyone and everything in your orbit in the days to come, for these people and things will forcefully transform you. You will feel carefree and fool-ish in terms of the subject of the spread and will not take responsi-bility for your involvement with others.

The Magician as your **Outer Influence** shows that someone who is self-centered and mysterious will directly affect the forecast of things to come. He may be so secretive that you remain in the dark about his true character or intentions. The Magician can also stand for an individual you worship from afar due to his or her reputation, charisma, or public image, but whom you may not personally know. Or this trump could indicate that you are behaving like the Magician toward those around you.

The Hierophant as your **Difficulty in the Past** demonstrates that you have been through the experience of spiritual initiation, which you can now use to serve others through teaching or healing. You have remained a devoted, evolving person, no matter what the hard-ships, and are now your own judge, mentor, and guide as you make all your own decisions. Your metaphysical interests, which have met with opposition in the past, will be your strength in the days ahead.

The Chariot as your **Hope and Dream** says that you want to go on a particular trip or follow a predestined path, especially if the reading was thrown to analyze a potential journey. The twist here is that your traveling companion will be a fateful surprise to you, or you may end up taking off by yourself when you thought you were going with another or a group. Due to the exalted position of this trump in the Grand Cross Spread, you are being told that your ulti-mate dreams will come true no matter what. You are moving toward fulfilling them at precisely the correct pace for your spiritual educa-tion.

The Hermit as your **Obstacle** describes your high standards, which often lead you to seek out solitude for making the right decisions and producing perfect work. You need silence to attain total concentra-tion and master your awareness of what the reading examines. Your growing knowledge combined with your desire for independence does not make life easy right now, but eventually you will figure out how to share your wisdom with others so they can benefit from this aspect of your personality.

Strength as your **Self Card** emphasizes the unflagging courageous spirit that you have adopted in order to keep yourself healthy, strong, and prepared to take on any challenges that cross your path. This trump implies that your natural energy and talent are poised and ready to lead you to success as long as you stay clear, clean, and balanced and continue to discipline yourself to be a powerfully productive force in your environment.

The Universe as your **First of the Future** reveals just how complicated and extensive your plans will become so you can actualize the purpose of your current incarnation and follow your preordained destiny with an ever-evolving enlightenment. Your ultimate accomplishments will be much greater than you think, so be patient while in steady pursuit of your true purpose. Make yourself number one in the future, and do not let anyone or anything pull you away from the direction that your soul most desires to follow.

## ABOUT THE AUTHOR

A San Francisco Bay area resident since 1991, Nancy Shavick was born in Englewood, New Jersey, in 1957 and graduated from Ridgewood High School in Ridgewood, New Jersey, in 1974. Nancy attended Hampshire College in Amherst, Massachusetts, and received a BA in creative writing in 1979.

Nancy has worked in publishing since high school, and most notably was the assistant editor of *The New Grove Dictionary of American Music* (Macmillan Press, Ltd., 1986) and has been a college professor teaching creative writing, editing, and publishing. In 1984, she started her own publishing company, Prima Materia Books, which she ran for seven years to self-publish her first Tarot book: *The Tarot: A Guide to Reading Your Own Cards*. Nancy is listed in *Who's Who in the East* for her work with the Tarot and as an author, editor, and publisher. She is also the best-selling author of four books published by Berkley Books from 1988–1993 on reading the Tarot cards: *The Tarot, The Tarot Reader, Traveling the Royal Road: Mastering the Tarot*, and *The Tarot Guide to Love and Relationships*. Nancy's first astrology book, *Reach for the Stars: Write Your Own Horoscope*, was published by Avon Books in 1994.

Besides astrology and Tarot, her other interests include nutrition, cooking, organic gardening, natural healing, dream interpretation, ancient civilizations, rock and roll, traveling, film, poetry, and literature.

Nancy is a gifted counselor who gives highly accurate Tarot readings to an international clientele. For more information on telephone Tarot readings, workshops, and lectures, please call (415) 389-0552.

Nancy Shavick is not affiliated with any 900 number or psychic hotline nor does she have a personal e-mail address or an authorized website.